| HOUSE | |
|---|---|
| ...ITION | R... |
| AUTHOR | GREGORY 331.4(1) GRE |
| Acc DATE | 02 JUN 1999 |

D1761016

HOUSE OF COMMONS
LIBRARY

DISPOSED OF BY
AUTHORITY

# WOMEN, WORK AND INEQUALITY

*Also by Jeanne Gregory*

SEX, RACE AND THE LAW: Legislating for Equality

*Also by Rosemary Sales*

WOMEN DIVIDED: Gender, Religion and Politics in Northern Ireland

*Also by Ariane Hegewisch*

POLICY AND PRACTICE IN EUROPEAN HUMAN RESOURCE MANAGEMENT: The Price Waterhouse Cranfield Survey (*editor*)

DEVELOPMENTS IN HUMAN RESOURCE MANAGEMENT IN EUROPE (*editor*)

EUROPEAN HUMAN RESOURCE MANAGEMENT GUIDE (*editor*)

# Women, Work and Inequality

## The Challenge of Equal Pay in a Deregulated Labour Market

Edited by

### Jeanne Gregory
*Visiting Professor*
*Head of Gender Research Centre*
*Middlesex University*

### Rosemary Sales
*Principal Lecturer*
*School of Social Science*
*Middlesex University*

and

### Ariane Hegewisch
*Senior Researcher*
*Cranfield School of Management*
*Bedford*

First published in Great Britain 1999 by
**MACMILLAN PRESS LTD**
Houndmills, Basingstoke, Hampshire RG21 6XS and London
Companies and representatives throughout the world

A catalogue record for this book is available from the British Library.

ISBN 0–333–72102–0

 First published in the United States of America 1999 by
**ST. MARTIN'S PRESS, INC.,**
Scholarly and Reference Division,
175 Fifth Avenue, New York, N.Y. 10010

ISBN 0–312–22141–X

Library of Congress Cataloging-in-Publication Data
Women, work, and inequality : the challenge of equal pay in a
deregulated labour market / edited by Jeanne Gregory, Rosemary
Sales, Ariane Hegewisch.
p.   cm.
Includes bibliographical references and index.
ISBN 0–312–22141–X (cloth)
1. Pay equity.   2. Equal pay for equal work.   3. Sex
discrimination in employment.   4. Sex discrimination against women.
I. Gregory, Jeanne.   II. Sales, Rosemary, 1947–   .   III. Hegewisch,
Ariane, 1958–   .
HD6061.W636   1999
331.4'2153—dc21                                          98–50834
                                                          CIP

Selection and editorial matter © Jeanne Gregory, Rosemary Sales and Ariane Hegewisch 1999
Chapter 5 © Rosemary Sales and Jeanne Gregory 1999
Chapters 1–4, 6–14 © Macmillan Press Ltd 1999

All rights reserved. No reproduction, copy or transmission of this publication may be made without written permission.

No paragraph of this publication may be reproduced, copied or transmitted save with written permission or in accordance with the provisions of the Copyright, Designs and Patents Act 1988, or under the terms of any licence permitting limited copying issued by the Copyright Licensing Agency, 90 Tottenham Court Road, London W1P 9HE.

Any person who does any unauthorised act in relation to this publication may be liable to criminal prosecution and civil claims for damages.

The authors have asserted their rights to be identified as the authors of this work in accordance with the Copyright, Designs and Patents Act 1988.

This book is printed on paper suitable for recycling and made from fully managed and sustained forest sources.

10   9   8   7   6   5   4   3   2   1
08   07   06   05   04   03   02   01   00   99

Printed and bound in Great Britain by
Antony Rowe Ltd, Chippenham, Wiltshire

# Contents

# List of Tables

# List of Figures

# Acknowledgements

We would like to thank Middlesex University for hosting the conference which provided the inspiration for this book; all those who contributed in various ways to an informative and stimulating event; the authors of the various chapters for their patience and co-operation; and Dot Lewis for her excellent work in preparing the chapters.

# Glossary

**Advisory, Conciliation and Arbitration Service (ACAS)**

A non-governmental organization responsible for individual and collective dispute resolution in the area of employment.

**Commission for Racial Equality (CRE)**

A non-governmental organization set up to promote racial equality and to monitor the operation of the race relations legislation.

**Comparable worth**

The application of job evaluation to identify and eliminate patterns of wage discrimination within a particular company, industry or sector of the labour market

**Equal Opportunities Commission (EOC)**

A non-governmental organization set up to promote sex equality and monitor the operation of the sex equality legislation.

**Equal value**

An assessment based on a comparison of two or more jobs which, although different in content, are held to be equivalent in terms of the demands made on the jobholders.

**Industrial tribunals**

The UK system of labour courts in which a legally qualified chair usually sits with two lay members, one nominated by trade unions and one nominated by employers, to adjudicate in individual disputes between employers and employees.

**Job evaluation**

A system of comparing different jobs to provide a basis for a grading and pay structure.

**Pay equity**

The requirement to raise wages for jobs which are currently underpaid and undervalued.

# Notes on the Contributors

**Robin Allen, QC** practises in the field of discrimination, European, employment and human rights law. He is Chair of the Employment Law Bar Association and a member of the executive committee of the Discrimination Law Association. He writes and lectures frequently on discrimination law.

**Alan Arthurs** is at the University of Bath. His previous publications in this field include 'Equal Value in British Banking: the Midland Case', in E. Meehan and P. Kahn (eds) *Equal Value/Comparable Worth in Britain and the United States* (Macmillan, 1992) and 'Job Evaluation', in M. Poole and M. Warner (eds) *The IEBM Handbook of Human Resource Management* (International Thompson Press, 1998). He is an ACAS-appointed Independent Expert on Equal Pay.

**Kalwant Bhopal** is a research officer at the Thomas Coram Research Institute (Institute of Education, University of London). Her research interests include 'race'/ethnicity, gender/feminism and the use of different research methodologies. Her book *Gender, 'Race' and Patriarchy: a Study of South Asian Women* was published in 1997 by Ashgate.

**Virginia Branney** is the Deputy Head of Local Government for UNISON, the UK's largest union. She is the lead Trade Union Side Secretary of the National Council for Local Government Services. Born in New Zealand, Virginia has worked for trade unions in that country and the UK. She is well known within local government for her involvement with employee training and development, part-timers' rights and equal pay.

**Irene Bruegel** is Reader in Urban Policy Studies at South Bank University, London. She worked for many years developing equal opportunities policies at the local level with trade unions and local authorities in Britain. She is a feminist economist with a background in political economy and has published widely in the area of women and the labour market.

**Martha Coleman** is a founding member and spokesperson for the Coalition for Equal Value Equal Pay. She is joint author with Janice Burns of *Equity at Word: An Approach to Gender Neutral Job Evaluation*, published by the New Zealand Department of Labour and the States Services Commission in 1991. Formerly a trade union official and now a lawyer, Martha currently works as a Judges' Clerk at the New Zealand Court of Appeal.

**Deborah Figart** is Associate Professor of Economics at Richard Stockton College, Pomona, New Jersey. She is joint author with Peggy Kahn of *Contesting the Market: Pay Equity and the Politics of Economic Restructuring* (Wayne State University Press, 1997). She has published numerous articles on discrimination and equal opportunities in economics and social science journals. Her current research focuses on minimum wages, family wages and living wages in the twentieth century.

**Jeanne Gregory** is Visiting Professor and Head of the Gender Research Centre at Middlesex University. She is author of *Sex, Race and the Law: Legislating for Equality* (Sage, 1987) and has published articles on equal pay, sex and race discrimination, sexual harassment and women refugees. She has undertaken research for the Equal Opportunities Commission and the European Commission on the implementation of sex equality laws and is a founder member of the Pay Equity Project.

**Sue Hastings** works as a freelance specialist adviser on grading and pay structures. This involves a range of activities, from acting as technical adviser on major national projects in the public sector, such as the Clinical Grading Review for Nurses and Midwives, and the more recent Local Government Single Status Job Evaluation Scheme, to contributing to pay structure developments in small private sector organizations. She has provided technical advice and acted as expert witness in a number of equal pay and equal value claims before industrial tribunals and participated in negotiations aimed at achieving equal pay for work of equal value.

**Ariane Hegewisch** is a teaching fellow and senior researcher in European Human Resource Management at Cranfield School of Management, Cranfield University. She is co-editor and contributor to *Policy and Practice in European Human Resource Management: the Price Waterhouse Cranfield Survey* (with C. Brewster, Routledge, 1994); *Developments in Human Resource Management in Europe* (with C. Brewster, Kogan Page, 1993); *The European Resource Management Guide* (with C. Brewster, L. Holden and T. Lockhart, Academic Press, 1992) and has published many articles, book chapters and reports on topics such as flexible working practices, equal opportunities, pay policies, human resource management in the public sector and employment policy trends in Europe. She is a founder member of the Pay Equity Project.

**Catherine Hoskyns** is Professor of European Studies at Coventry University. She has written widely on the issue of EU policies relating to women and is the author of *Integrating Gender: Women, Law and Politics* *in the European Union* (Verso, 1996). She is a long-time member of the European Forum of Left Feminists.

**Marisa Howes** is women's officer of UNISON.

**Peggy Kahn** is Professor of Political Science at the University of Michigan Flint and teaches in the women's and gender studies programme. She is co-author with Deborah Figart of *Contesting the Market: Pay Equity and the Politics of Economic Restructuring* (Wayne State University Press 1997). With Elizabeth Meehan she edited *Equal Value/Comparable Worth in the UK and the USA* (Macmillan, 1992). She has recently been studying work restructuring and work–family dilemmas among low-paid women in the US and UK service sectors and the impact of new welfare policies on single mothers' work and family lives in the US.

**Patricia McDermott** teaches in the area of gender and the law in the Division of Social Science at York University, Toronto, Canada. Her specific interest is employment and pay equity legislation in Canada and other common law jurisdictions. She has published a number of articles on pay equity and is joint editor, with Judy Fudge, of *Just Wages: a Feminist Assessment of Pay Equity* (University of Toronto Press, 1991) and with Linda Briskin of *Women Challenging Unions: Feminism, Democracy and Militancy* (University of Toronto Press, 1993).

**Gay Moon** is a solicitor at Camden Community Law Centre specializing in employment and discrimination law. She is co-author of *Discrimination at Work* (Legal Action Group, 1997) and *The Cohabitation Handbook* (Pluto Press, 1981). She is solicitor for the applicants in *R v Secretary of State for Employment ex parte Seymour-Smith*.

**Ellen Mutari** is Assistant Professor of Economics at Monmouth University in West Long Branch, New Jersey. She is co-editor of *Gender and Political Economy: Incorporating Diversity into Theory and Policy* (M.E. Sharpe, 1997). Her current research is on the socioeconomics of work time in Europe and the US.

**Rosemary Sales** is principal lecturer in the School of Social Science, Middlesex University and programme leader of the MA Gender and Society. Until recently she also held the position of campus Equal Opportunities Officer. Her book *Women Divided: Gender, Religion and Politics in Northern Ireland* was published by Routledge in 1997. She has also published articles on migration, exclusion and European integration.

**Cecilia Tacoli** is a research associate at the International Institute for Environment and Development in London. Her research interests include labour markets, migration (both international and internal), households and gender. She currently co-ordinates an international research programme on rural–urban interactions conducted in collaboration with several researchers in the South.

# 1 Introduction

Jeanne Gregory, Ariane Hegewisch and
Rosemary Sales

During the last 25 years, there has been a steady increase in the participation of women in the labour markets of Western states. Much of this period has been accompanied by the development of equal opportunities legislation, including measures to achieve equal pay or comparable worth for women workers. In North America and the member states of the European Union, these policies have been governed by apparently straightforward principles regarding pay equity. Such approaches are intended to provide the tools for detailed intervention in the pay and grading structures of employers and offer potentially radical forms of intervention in the labour market and the individual employment relationship.

At the same time as such approaches are becoming more sophisticated, global economic trends are undermining their effectiveness and impeding the ability of individual welfare states to pursue independent economic policies. Technological and industrial changes have resulted in high levels of structural unemployment and a widening gap between well-paid professional workers and those in low-paid service sector jobs. We are currently witnessing a dramatic shift towards a casualized and deregulated labour market, with the widespread use of short-term contracts and part-time employment, to the point where these are becoming normal, rather than atypical working practices. Policies such as privatization, reductions in public sector budgets and relaxation of employment regulation have, on the whole, accentuated these trends. Developments in the field of industrial relations and human resource management, particularly the decentralization of pay bargaining, the undermining of collective agreements and the growth of payment systems based on individual performance, have increased the polarization between low-paid and highly paid workers, a polarization that impacts particularly severely on women workers.

The pursuit of pay equity and deregulation represent contradictory policy aims. If pay equity policy is to have any impact in bringing substantive, as opposed to merely formal, equality, it must involve an interventionist and regulatory approach to the labour market. Deregulation, on the other hand, embraces the values of neoliberalism, which sees the solution to economic problems in the 'freeing up' of the market, reducing regulation, increasing flexibility and driving down costs. Inevitably, these policies have a disproportionate effect on those already most disadvantaged within the labour market. In spite of these contradictory elements, governments have proclaimed their commitment to both policies.

It was against this background that the Gender Research Centre at Middlesex University and the Pay Equity Project, a campaigning organization based in the UK (but with an international membership), decided on a joint initiative. The plan was to provide a forum in which all those concerned with pay equity issues, including academic researchers, lawyers, trade unionists, industrial relations practitioners and policy-makers, could come together to compare experiences and discuss strategies for ensuring that the impetus towards pay equity was not lost. Originally conceived as a one-day seminar with a European focus, the strength of the response to the idea led to a much more ambitious event, spanning two days and involving some 40 speakers and over 100 participants. Several European countries were represented, as well as New Zealand, Canada and the United States. It was clear that the vexed issue of how to make progress on pay equity in an increasingly hostile economic and political climate was exercising the minds of equal pay advocates everywhere and that the opportunity to explore these issues had an international appeal.

The present volume contains a selection of the papers presented at the conference, updated and revised in the light of the discussions at the conference and subsequent events. Some of the papers not included in this volume have been published elsewhere (see, for example, Fredman, 1997; Armstrong and Cornish, 1997; Joshi, 1996; Kilpatrick, 1997; Fieldes, 1999). The purpose of this introductory chapter is to identify the major themes explored in the following chapters and to convey the spirit of the conference as a whole. The dynamic and productive mix of academic researchers and practitioners meant that there was from the outset a concern with outcomes, not only in the form of publications, but also in the practical sense of creating new networks for the exchange of information, learning new strategies and seeking to influence policy-making.

## EUROPEAN PERSPECTIVES

Although the scope of the conference expanded to include contributions and perspectives beyond Europe, the relationship between the European Union (EU) and individual member states provided an important focus and helped to highlight the tensions resulting from the pursuit of contradictory policies. The starting point for these discussions is Article 119 of the Treaty of Rome, establishing the principle of equal pay for equal work, and the three Equality Directives passed in the 1970s, elaborating this principle. As member states are required to ensure that their national legislation complies with European law, these developments have provided an essential framework for equality campaigns. Nowhere have these tensions proved greater than in the UK, where the Conservative governments in power from 1979 to 1997 embarked on a policy of labour market deregulation, while at the same time being compelled by membership of the EU to strengthen equality laws in a number of important respects. Since there has been more litigation in the UK under the sex equality laws than in any other member state, these tensions have had frequent public exposure.

Some of these issues were highlighted by Christine Crawley, Member of the European Parliament (MEP) in her opening speech to the conference. As Chair of the European Parliament Women's Committee, she has been at the forefront of attempts to strengthen and broaden EU policies on equality. She reported that three issues were giving major cause for concern. The first was the huge gap between the statements of principle enshrined in EU law and their implementation in practice, as it is left to member states to choose the method of compliance best suited to their national legal systems. The second concerned the distortions in equality policy which spring from the exclusive preoccupation with gender and with the labour market, with no legal basis from which to challenge other forms of discrimination and inequalities in other areas of society. The third arose from the failure of the UK government to sign the Social Chapter of the Treaty on European Union (the Maastricht Treaty), regarded by the other member states as an essential framework for the protection of workers in the transition to the Single European Market.

In the run-up to the Intergovernmental Conference (IGC) in June 1997, the European Parliament Women's Committee formulated three key priorities for consideration by the IGC: (1) the strengthening of Article 119 and a new legal basis in the Treaty to cover equal treatment for women and men in all realms of society; (2) a new anti-discrimination clause to cover age, 'race', religion, sexual orientation and disability in addition to sex; and (3) the inclusion of the Protocol and Agreement on Social Policy (the Social Chapter) into the Treaty to act as a counterbalance to the harsh convergence criteria for Economic and Monetary Union.

Obstacles to the third demand disappeared when the newly elected Labour government signed the Social Chapter in 1997 as one of its first actions on taking office. The inclusion of the first two demands in the Treaty of Amsterdam 1997 was indicative of successful lobbying by the Women's Committee and other groups and also reflected the growing concern of member state governments with the 'democratic deficit' which had resulted in expressions of disaffection and hostility towards the project of European integration in many countries. Although the successful incorporation of the three key demands will give greater legitimacy to the proponents of equality policies within the EU, the strength of the economic and political forces pushing member states along the road of deregulation and public spending cuts have by no means abated. If anything, the contradictions between statements of principle and the harsh realities of neoliberal policies have sharpened since the signing of the Amsterdam Treaty.

Among the various groups presenting their demands to the IGC was the German Association of Women Lawyers, whose views were conveyed to the conference by Heike Simon, a German law lecturer. Many of the points echoed those of the Women's Committee, focusing on the need for EU institutions to take stronger action to bring about *de facto* equality. They also included a demand for improved representation for women in all areas of decision-making within the EU and a widening of the EU sphere of competence to cover all forms of discrimination, including action to ensure that member states take account of gender-specific forms of persecution when dealing with applications for asylum from women from non-EU countries.

Christine Crawley's reference to the under-utilization of EU sex equality laws was taken up in a paper given by Claire Kilpatrick, in which she investigated the very low levels of litigation in France. This is ironic, both because it was France that provided the impetus for the inclusion of Article 119 in the Treaty of Rome in the first place (see Hoskyns, 1996) and also because French legislation contains many of the provisions which pay equity proponents in the UK would wish to see enshrined in UK law. French employers are required to provide trade union representatives with information for collective bargaining purposes, including a gender breakdown of jobs, pay and hours worked; those with 50 employees or more must provide an analysis of this information and record the practical steps taken (and planned in the future) to achieve equality. Trade unions and women's groups of five years' standing can bring equality cases to the French labour courts; and to labour inspectors who have wide powers of access to information and workplaces and can invoke criminal sanctions when equal pay law is breached (Kilpatrick, 1997).

Despite this multiplicity of legal options, Claire Kilpatrick reported that not only had individual litigation failed to develop in France, but neither had equal value principles been integrated into collective bargaining negotiations there. This contrasts sharply with the situation in the UK where, despite the limitations of the legal framework, there has been a much greater use of litigation. This has enabled a body of expertise to develop. Industrial tribunals have gradually improved their understanding of equal value principles; media publicity given to successful cases has increased awareness among women workers. Against the background of a growing body of case law, trade unions have often been able to implement equal value through negotiation. A similar body of expertise has simply not developed in France. Neither the labour inspectors nor the labour court judges receive any equal value training and the trade unions have shown little interest in equality issues. In the UK the two Equal Opportunities Commissions (EOCs), one for Britain and one for Northern Ireland, have provided an invaluable source of expertise for individuals, unions and employers. Together with the trade unions they have developed a successful case law strategy which has helped to overcome some of the shortcomings of UK law. In France lawyers avoid using the sex equality provisions if they can, fearing the hostility of the judiciary; in the UK the more frequent use of the provisions means that the significance of EU law is acknowledged throughout the legal system. There have been a number of references on equal pay to the European Court of Justice (ECJ) from UK courts but none from the French courts.

Equality agencies play a key role in fostering the growth of an equal value culture. They provide expertise, continuity and legitimacy to equality strategies, and this in turn increases the impetus and effectiveness of trade union initiatives in this area (Kilpatrick, 1997). All three member states where significant levels of union involvement are to be found – the UK, Ireland and the Netherlands – have equality agencies. In the first two countries the agencies are empowered to bring cases before the tribunals and courts; in the Netherlands the Equal Treatment Commission itself hears complaints and issues non-binding decisions, which in the majority of cases are accepted by both parties without the need for a court hearing. Three speakers from the Netherlands provided some interesting insights into the Dutch approach to equality. As in the UK, levels of part-time work are high, particularly among women with young children. A speaker from the FNV (Federatie Nederlandse Vakbeweging, the Dutch equivalent of the Trades Union Congress in the UK), described the FNV's long-running negotiations with employers to ensure that flexible working practices are designed with the needs of women very much to the fore. Two other speakers, one a researcher and one from AbvaKabo (which translates as the general union of civil servants and Catholic union of government employees) spoke of their involvement in redesigning job evaluation schemes to ensure that the skills used predominantly by women are adequately reflected in the most widely used schemes.

Some of the practical difficulties of ensuring that equal pay law delivers its promise to women workers were revealed by a trade unionist from Denmark, who spoke about an important equal pay case brought by her union. Known as the *Danfoss* case, it was important because it led to a finding by the European Court of Justice that if a payment system lacks transparency, the burden of proof is on the employer to show that the system is not discriminatory (*Handels-og Kontorfunctionaerernes forbund i Danmark* v *Dansk Arbejdsgiverforening (acting for Danfoss)* [1989] Industrial Relations Law Reports [IRLR] 532 ECJ). The case concerned an employer who made additional payments to individual workers within particular grades on the basis of a number of criteria which were not transparent and therefore not open to challenge. A statistical analysis revealed that the average pay of women workers was lower than that of men workers in the same grade. The wider significance of this case is that any individualized payment systems that rely on subjective assessments are open to legal challenge. The difficulty in Denmark was how to give practical effect to the ECJ decision. The point of principle had been won and from then on Danish employers sought to introduce greater clarity into their pay structures, but translating the statistical findings into pay rises for individual women proved to be an uphill struggle.

Sweden is a relatively new member of the EU, joining in January 1995 at the same time as Austria and Finland. Sweden has long been upheld by the women's movement as an example of a state committed to woman-friendly employment policies, strong trade unions and equitable pay policies. In spite of these positive features Sweden has a highly segregated labour market and women earn on average 20 per cent less than men. Eva Nikell, who works in the office of the Swedish Equal Opportunities Ombudsperson, told the conference about the work of the Ombudsperson and the renewed interest in equality issues arising from Sweden's membership of the EU. She spoke of the sharp increase in the number of complaints of wage discrimination, particularly from women involved in the caring professions. She spoke also of the mixed results of a test case strategy undertaken by the Ombudsperson with support from women's groups and some trade unions and of the need to shift the emphasis from an individual, complaint-driven strategy to a class action approach.


EQUAL PAY LAW IN THE UK

A large part of the conference was devoted to considering the state of equal pay law in the UK. As we have indicated, the coexistence of contradictory policies has been particularly acute in the UK throughout the period of Conservative government from 1979 to 1997. On the one hand, the two enforcement agencies created in the mid-1970s have accumulated a wealth of expertise on equal pay issues, while an active trade union movement has become increasingly aware of the need to pursue policies of relevance to women workers and to identify strategies for challenging low pay. On the other hand, the government was unswervingly committed to deregulation, including in 1993 the abolition of the wages councils which had set minimum wages for 2.5 million low-paid workers, 2 million of whom were women. In 1988 the government put a stop to contract compliance, a policy by which local authorities made use of their purchasing power to monitor the employment policies of contractors, and replaced it with a policy of compulsory competitive tendering (CCT), which required local authorities to put out to tender an ever-wider range of services to the private sector, with the bidding process subjected to the full rigours of the market.

In response to this unfavourable climate the British and Northern Irish EOCs, together with the trade union movement, pursued a variety of strategies. Wherever the brunt of a particular policy falls disproportionately on women, it is possible to claim that it is a form of indirect discrimination against women and is therefore illegal. In such cases it is not the intention of the policy that is at issue but its effect. In the case of the abolition of wages councils, the Trades Union Congress (TUC), closely followed by the EOC in Britain, submitted detailed documentation to the European Commission outlining the adverse impact that this policy would have on women workers. At the same time it drew attention to the cumbersome and costly procedures involved in equal pay litigation, which for many women effectively prevented access to the law (TUC, 1993; EOC, 1993). Rather than taking the preliminary steps which might lead to infringement proceedings against the UK government, the European Commission delayed its response to these documents, perhaps hoping that a change of government would enable the issues to be resolved at home.

Litigation strategies have been widely used by the equality agencies and by trade unions, with an emphasis on selecting cases which will have implications for large numbers of women workers and help to clarify important points of law. As in Sweden, this strategy is hampered by the absence of collective remedies in the legislation, so that all those wishing to benefit from an equal pay claim have to file separate tribunal applications. For many women this is a traumatic experience which can cause considerable stress, especially as the complex and cumbersome procedures mean that cases often take years to resolve. In the meantime, employees may be subjected to various forms of victimization which, although illegal, are difficult to prove. Another problem is that because it is only the jobs of the claimants and the male comparators (the men with whom the women are claiming equal pay) that are subjected to scrutiny, tribunal decisions can throw collective agreements and pay structures into disarray. These shortcomings can only be overcome by challenging the payment system itself, but this would require new legislation.

A successful judicial review case against the Secretary of State for Employment provides a glimpse of what can be achieved when discrimination is challenged at the institutional level. The EOC believed that the different qualifying periods for redundancy payments and unfair dismissal laid down in the Employment Protection (Consolidation) Act 1978 (two years for employees working 16 hours or more a week and five years for those working more than five but less than 16 hours), were a form of indirect discrimination against women not permitted under EU law. The Secretary of State disagreed, but the House of Lords found for the EOC and the legislation was changed, thereby benefiting all part-time workers, without any individual needing to file a complaint. (See *R* v *Secretary of State for Employment ex parte Equal Opportunities Commission* [1994] IRLR 176 HL.) All the other cases discussed in this volume have involved named claimants and many have taken years to resolve, particularly if they concerned the interpretation of European law. Important gains have been made but at considerable cost, in both financial and personal terms.

During the conference speakers from both the EOCs talked about their litigation strategies and their recommendations for reforming the legislation which have been presented to the government on several occasions over the years but have always fallen on deaf ears. These recommendations seek to simplify procedures, improve access to the law and move towards collective solutions to pay inequalities. It is almost three decades since the Equal Pay Act 1970 was passed and some 15 years since the Equal Pay (Amendment) Regulations 1983 widened the scope of the legislation in compliance with EU law to allow equal value comparisons between women and men employed on different work. Employers have therefore had the time and information required to eliminate gender bias from their payment structures, so that a strong case can now be made for raising the stakes. Using the Codes of Practice on Equal Pay produced by the EOC (1997) and the European Commission (1997) employers could be put under a statutory obligation to review their payment systems and make proposals for eliminating any pay inequalities revealed. This process would need to be monitored and appropriate sanctions be made available for cases of non-compliance.

## RACE DISCRIMINATION AND EQUAL PAY

If the inadequacies of equal pay law were much in evidence during the conference, it became clear that these shortcomings were compounded in relation to wage discrimination on the basis of race and ethnicity. Sandya Drew, a barrister specializing in discrimination law, referred to the term 'sex plus' discrimination to describe the experiences of black women, who were even further removed from the norm of the white male than either black men or white women. The silence of EU law on the issue of race discrimination, belatedly and only tentatively remedied in the Treaty of Amsterdam, means that developments in race equality have lagged seriously behind those in sex equality in all the member states. EU law prohibits discrimination on the basis of nationality, but this refers to nationality of a member state; the unequal treatment of third country nationals is condoned and a climate of racism, which effectively restricts the free movement of black and minority ethnic people whatever their nationality, is allowed to flourish. Sandya Drew referred to the 1990 International Labour Organization Convention on the Protection of Migrant Workers, which sets out the rights of such workers to equal treatment in their conditions of work and terms of employment regardless of their documentation status. No member state has yet complied with this convention; instead, we have a proliferation of increasingly punitive and restrictive laws for dealing with migrants, asylum-seekers and their families.

In the UK the Race Relations Act 1976 makes it unlawful to discriminate against an employee in the terms of employment offered or to segregate a person on racial grounds. Given the high level of occupational segregation along racial lines to be found within the UK labour market and the concentration of black workers in the low-paid, low-status jobs, one might have expected the Commission for Racial Equality (CRE) and the trade union movement to be more active on this issue. There have in fact been very few cases. The CRE has tended to regard pay differentials as the outcome of discrimination in recruitment and promotion, rather than due to pay and grading decisions, but clearly the two forms of discrimination are not mutually exclusive. There is a possibility that the growth of expertise in identifying gender bias in job evaluation schemes could be harnessed to improving our understanding of the ways in which such schemes also contain racial bias.

It is also clear that black workers have been disproportionately hit by the abolition of wages councils and by the introduction of CCT. The proliferation of individualized payment systems based on merit, performance or competence increases the scope for subjective appraisals derived from stereotypical views about race and ethnicity as well as gender. Sandya Drew referred to the successful challenge to London Underground's planned move towards more individual and performance-related criteria for pay and promotion just at a time when many black employees with long service became eligible for promotion under the existing policy. Similarly, the introduction of clinical grading in the nursing profession resulted in a disproportionate number of black nurses being allocated to the lowest grades; some of those who appealed were subsequently regraded. However, much of the discrimination remains hidden or is difficult to challenge using existing legislation.

## PRIORITIZING LOW PAY

Despite the best endeavours of equal pay advocates, the overwhelming body of evidence presented to the conference was that labour market inequalities were increasing rather than decreasing. For Jo Morris, senior policy officer at the TUC, this made low pay rather than equal pay the political priority for the UK. For many workers deregulation and casualization have created a cycle of low-quality employment interspersed with periods of unemployment, with little chance of gaining quality training, employment or pension rights. Women workers, particularly those working part-time, have been most affected by these changes; 2.5 million women earn below the lower earnings limit for national insurance contributions. Pay inequalities have increased across the labour market, with the average earnings of the poorest 10 per cent of part-time workers falling in real terms while those of the highest paid full-time workers have risen dramatically in recent years. These inequalities are also reflected in an increasing polarization within the female labour force. We are witnessing the feminization of poverty at one end and the emergence of an elite corps of professional and managerial women at the other. For Jo Morris the remedy lies in the introduction of a national minimum wage and also legislation which would guarantee equal treatment for part-time workers.

With a change of government in the UK in 1997 both these remedies have been brought within reach. A Bill for the introduction of a national minimum wage was published in March 1998, and in June the government accepted the Low Pay Commission's recommendation that the adult rate be set at £3.60 per hour. The introduction of a national minimum wage will have a knock-on effect for equal pay law, so that mechanisms will be required to ensure that workers do receive their full entitlement under both pieces of legislation. In relation to part-time workers, European draft directives designed to give equal rights to part-time workers were repeatedly vetoed by the UK Conservative government. By signing the

Social Chapter the Labour government becomes party to the Part-time Workers Directive adopted by the Council of Ministers in December 1997. It also seems that the worst excesses of CCT may be moderated as a result of the Labour government's 'best value' initiative, although ominously, the Green Paper *Modernising Local Government – Improving Local Services Through Best Value* makes no reference to equal opportunities (see Equal Opportunities Review no. 79 May/June 1998).

## THE WAY FORWARD: A 15-POINT STRATEGY

As far as the UK is concerned, it seems that the political climate may now be more conducive to making progress on equality issues than was the case in 1996 when the conference was held. However, the international focus of the conference served as a reminder that half-hearted reforms are invariably disappointing and that neoliberal solutions to economic problems are still very much in the driving seat almost everywhere. With this in mind, the closing session was devoted to the construction of a programme of action for everyone committed to the eradication of labour market inequalities. In our view this 15-point strategy has international and contemporary relevance and will enable pay equity advocates to identify those policy-makers who have a genuine and wholehearted commitment to equality and those who do not.

1. Campaign for more effective legislation and more effective procedures for implementation.
2. Support attempts to strengthen employment rights generally so that all workers have real access to equality rights.
3. Improve the mechanisms and commitment to challenge direct and indirect race discrimination in pay.
4. Ensure that our strategies reduce social exclusion and polarization between different groups of women.
5. Campaign in support of a minimum wage set at a level which provides a living wage.
6. Explore all avenues to improve the quality of information on earnings available to workers and equal pay advocates.
7. Develop national and international networks for sharing information and expertise.
8. Improve the flow of information to and from women workers and key potential actors (such as trade unionists, lawyers, judges, advice centre workers, labour inspectors, women's groups).
9. Support all measures to improve the quality of training for key potential actors (as in 8 above).

10. Strengthen support structures to reduce the isolation and victimization of women claiming equal pay.
11. Make full use of collective procedures and remedies wherever possible.
12. Strengthen the position of women within the trade union movement.
13. Develop a better understanding of state institutions in order to devise more effective systems for implementing equal pay (equality agencies; contract compliance).
14. Campaign on behalf of part-time workers to ensure that the value of their contribution is fully recognized.
15. Work towards the reconciliation of the needs of family life and working life, including flexibility for male workers.

Despite differences of political history and cultural context, this was a programme of action around which all the conference participants could unite. As activists from a wide range of different countries shared their knowledge and experiences a number of recurring themes emerged. These themes are reflected in the chapters that follow. The book combines in one volume recent research and theorizing by leading feminist scholars, together with accounts of the first-hand experiences of equal pay practitioners in a variety of contexts. It assesses the current position of women in the labour market and notes the increasing polarization between different groups of women. It then reassesses the strengths and limitations of equal pay legislation and explores possible solutions to current problems. The terminology varies from one country to the next: the European reference to 'equal pay for work of equal value' translates as 'comparable worth' as we move to the United States, but the underlying issues remain the same. The terms 'equal pay' and 'pay equity' are often used interchangeably. Although 'pay equity' is more often associated with Canada and New Zealand, it was chosen by the UK-based Pay Equity Project because it was seen as embracing issues of both equal pay and low pay. The term 'compensation' is used in North America to refer to remuneration accruing from work, including wages and other financial benefits. British readers will be more familiar with the idea of compensation as a remedy for unfair treatment or injury.

## LABOUR MARKET INEQUALITIES: INTERNATIONAL PERSPECTIVES

The impact of the globalization of capital on economic and political systems has been both wide-ranging and profound. As welfare policies are reshaped and labour markets restructured in a number of countries, it seems as though the same political and economic imperatives are at work, sweeping aside alternative programmes and driving all countries towards an inevitable homogenization. Only an in-depth analysis of the experiences of individual countries can correct this one-dimensional view. Although there are striking similarities in the dominant political discourse across national boundaries, policy outcomes are invariably mediated by historical and cultural influences. Particular solutions to economic problems are by no means predetermined and considerable scope for political action remains. In the first part of the book the growth of labour market inequalities and the implications of this growth are examined in relation to a number of countries. In chapter 2 Catherine Hoskyns explores these tensions in the context of EU policy on women's rights. This provided the impetus for the development of equal pay law in individual member states but has also become at times a straitjacket which has stifled national developments. Hoskyns acknowledges the role of the women's movement in both ensuring the inclusion of the principle of equal pay in the Treaty of Rome in the first place and retaining the momentum of the policy ever since, despite lukewarm responses from member state governments. She reveals how the policy on sex equality continues to be driven by contradictory pressures. On the one hand, governments recognize that they have a credibility gap and that people, especially women, have yet to be convinced that European integration is a project worthy of their support. On the other hand, the new language of 'subsidiarity', itself a form of deregulation at the European level, means that decision-making is increasingly devolved to individual member states. The accumulating body of expertise on how to achieve genuine equality between men and women in the labour market is consequently enshrined in 'soft law', such as a memorandum and a code of practice on equal pay, rather than in hard-hitting directives with the full force of law behind them.

Although the commitment to equality is both broadened and deepened by the Amsterdam Treaty, Hoskyns' main concern is the failure of the Treaty to highlight issues of class, social division and poverty, as she believes that treating gender as a separate issue will further increase the polarization between those women who benefit from equality policies and those who do not. She writes of the need for more complex coalitions of activist groups to highlight the interlocking nature of sexism, racism and poverty, the need for closer cooperation between the women's movement and the labour movement at EU level, and the need to broaden the focus beyond the labour market to tackle all forms of social disadvantage.

In chapter 3 the focus shifts to the United States, where Deborah Figart and Ellen Mutari draw attention to the similarities between the European and American responses to globalization. In particular they examine the implications of the eclipse of Keynesian economic policies and the feminization of labour markets, as employers seek to drive down wage costs at the same time as increasing workforce flexibility. The employment of women workers has served to undermine male-dominated wage bargaining strongholds and male career patterns based on the assumption of full-time permanent employment. The drive for pay equity runs counter to these developments. The authors demonstrate how the opponents of pay equity have shifted their arguments to accommodate these developments. At the same time they point to the contradictions in the conservative position, which simultaneously mourns the passing of the male breadwinner model while claiming that the introduction of pay equity would cause low-paid women workers to lose their jobs.

Figart and Mutari believe that the response of the Left has also been inadequate, with an emphasis on returning to past patterns of working which institutionalized relatively high wages for certain groups of white men while excluding many other groups of workers. However, they take heart from the new 'living wage' movement which seeks to 'de-gender' the concept of the family wage and to campaign on behalf of previously marginalized groups. This approach provides a challenge to the opponents of pay equity by making it possible to launch a sustained attack on poverty wages without prioritizing particular household structures or family forms.

The special interest of New Zealand for all those involved in equal pay lies in the policy extremes it has experienced. Formerly regarded as a pioneer of employment regulation, trade union rights and centralized bargaining, New Zealand now holds the dubious distinction of having the most deregulated labour market of all the member countries of the Organization for Economic Cooperation and Development (OECD). One of the casualties of this swing away from employment protection was the Employment Equity Act 1990 which, for the few weeks of its existence, was the envy of pay advocates everywhere. In her chapter on New Zealand Martha Coleman, one of the authors of a generic job evaluation scheme designed to give effect to the legislation, documents the impact of these policy shifts. Although traditional forms of centralized wage fixing were by no means free from gender discrimination – hence the need for equal pay legislation – they did provide minimum standards of protection. By contrast, the dismantling of the regulatory framework in 1991 with the passing of the Employment Contracts Act left workers at the mercy of market forces. The Labour government claimed that the new regime would reduce gender inequalities, but the opposite has proved to be the case.

Coleman refers to the results of New Zealand research which show that women workers in the private sector have experienced a massive decline in trade union membership and that casual workers and part-time workers, most of whom are women, have suffered a drop in pay. Echoing the comments of Jo Morris in relation to the UK, Coleman argues that at the top end of the labour market the situation of some women may have improved due to labour market restructuring, but that at the bottom end the majority of low-paid women have experienced a deterioration in pay and conditions. Current legal strategies to challenge this state of affairs include using an Equal Pay Act passed more than a quarter of a century ago (and left on the statute book when the more innovative Employment Equity Act was repealed) in conjunction with the New Zealand Bill of Rights Act 1990. This will at least ensure that pay equity issues remain in the public eye.

Irene Bruegel takes up the themes of differentiation and polarization. Her carefully researched contribution explores the contradictory impact of globalization, noting the differences as well as the similarities in the ways that governments have responded to similar economic pressures, so that deregulation has to be regarded as a policy choice rather than an inevitability. Using London as a testing ground, she examines Saskia Sassen's thesis that globalization has polarized incomes in the nodal cities of the global economy. She finds that globalization and deindustrialization have produced increased pay inequalities across the board and reaffirms Coleman's finding that part-time workers are losing out relative to full-time workers. At the bottom end of the pay structure the gender pay gap has narrowed, but this is entirely due to the relative decline in men's pay. At the top end women are closing the pay gap as their qualification levels rise, but they are still experiencing wage discrimination. Sassen's thesis is largely supported by the London data, except that Bruegel identifies a small elite group of women workers: highly educated, young, single and childless, who cannot be accommodated within Sassen's depiction of women as an undifferentiated source of cheap labour. Once they become mothers the picture changes: mothers work below-average hours, in contrast to fathers who work above the average. Only a few privileged women with access to childcare are able to continue to make progress in their careers. The overriding picture painted by Bruegel is one of widening inequalities between different groups of workers. She concludes that even if inequalities between women and men within some households have declined, inequalities between households have undoubtedly increased.

'RACE', MIGRATION AND EMPLOYMENT

In Part II the theme of inequality is further developed through an exploration of the experiences of migrant and minority ethnic women. Rosemary Sales and Jeanne Gregory show how EU policies on citizenship and immigration have created a complex stratification of civil and social rights. The hierarchies of 'race' and sex cut across the formal rights of citizenship, as in every member state white men dominate the high-status positions so that 'race', ethnicity and gender are closely related to life chances and social outcomes. Despite the increasing diversity of migration flows, the majority of migrant women originating from non-member states are to be found at the bottom of the hierarchy. Many of them arrive as dependants and domestic slaves and find themselves trapped in exploitative relationships without residence or work permits, forced to live in a twilight zone of illegal and unprotected work.

Despite a formal commitment to combating social exclusion, policymakers at both EU and national level have pursued increasingly restrictive immigration policies, leaving some 15 million people currently living within the EU but denied citizenship. In relation to the UK, Sales and Gregory show how recent policies have added to the hardships experienced by asylum-seekers and their families. The existence of insecure residents who are controlled and policed in a variety of ways helps to breed a climate of racism which affects all who are perceived as outsiders, including long-standing minority groups such as second, third and fourth generation black Europeans. Even those with full citizenship rights are disproportionately confined to low-paid, insecure areas of work or are unemployed. For migrants, refugees and asylum-seekers, the problems are compounded.

In his study of racism in 16 European countries (1996) John Wrench draws a broad distinction between northern and southern European states. In the former the major cause for concern is the high level of unemployment among migrants and visible minorities and their unjustified exclusion from job opportunities. In Southern Europe, where immigration is relatively new, newcomers experience a perverse form of 'positive discrimination'. They are recruited because they are vulnerable and cheap and then suffer 'negative discrimination' through highly exploitative and illegal working conditions. He believes that a future convergence is likely, as Northern Europe experiences an expansion in its illegal labour market and Southern countries begin to implement anti-discrimination measures for settled migrants. The chapter by Sales and Gregory indicates that some convergence has occurred already. Exploitative conditions are by no means confined to immigration in Southern Europe and although some Northern European countries, such as the Netherlands and the UK, do have long-standing race discrimination measures, these laws are in practice well beyond the reach of most migrants.

In the next chapter the focus shifts to Italy, where Cecilia Tacoli's research on Filipino migrant workers provides greater support for Wrench's categorization. Tacoli gives an account of the growing need for domestic workers as Italian women were drawn into the labour market in the context of a low level of public support services and the unwillingness of men to share the burden of domestic work. She shows how the existence of bilateral agreements between Italy and the countries of emigration created national groupings confined to specific sectors of the labour market. Although the majority of both men and women from the Philippines are employed in domestic service, gender differences persist in so far as women are more likely to live in and to have caring as well as cleaning responsibilities. Men generally prefer to live out and to work part-time for a number of employers, making them less susceptible to the development of 'false kinship' relationships, which are highly exploitative.

Tacoli demonstrates how even migrant workers who initially had full documentation can find themselves pushed into the informal sector. This arises not from the absence of regulation, but from the failure of employers to observe the regulations. In almost half the cases included in her research employers were refusing to pay national insurance on behalf of Filipino workers. As resident permits are linked to the receipt of such contributions, these workers will lose their legal status as soon as their permits are due for renewal. Employers rely on the fact that vulnerable workers are unlikely to report them for legal violations.

Kalwant Bhopal examines the situation of South Asian homeworkers living in east London. Like the Filipina women in Italy, these women also work long hours in poor conditions for very low pay. Citizenship status is not an issue here, as the 12 homeworkers interviewed by Bhopal were all born in Britain. Nor were they subjected to 'false kinship' since most were genuinely related to the employer. It is clear from their responses that they regarded themselves as fortunate in being able to 'choose' a form of employment that enables them to fulfil their roles as wives and mothers while also contributing to the family income. It is equally clear that they are being exploited and that their situation is both a response to racialized labour markets and to an extreme form of private patriarchy.

The contradictions inherent in their situation are vividly portrayed in the interviews. These women are trapped by ties of loyalty and family obligation, but they are also aware that their work is tiring, isolating and undervalued and that it has an adverse impact on their health and quality of life. It is encouraging that some of them are meeting to see how their situation might be improved and that homeworkers have been included in the national minimum wage legislation. However, Bhopal's analysis suggests that these developments are unlikely to have any long-term effect unless they are accompanied by the dismantling of patriarchal structures and a concerted attack on institutional racism.

## EVALUATING EQUAL PAY LAW

It is apparent from the wide range of analyses contained in the first two parts of the book that a number of complex factors are accentuating labour market inequalities. Pay equity advocates often find themselves swimming against the tide as a powerful combination of economic, political and institutional forces seemingly conspire to neutralize or even reverse hard won gains. A strong legislative base is undoubtedly essential if women are ever to achieve equal pay with men but it is not sufficient, as the experience of Canada demonstrates. Like the New Zealand Employment Equity Act, the Ontario Pay Equity Act 1989 was regarded by the proponents of equal pay in other countries as a piece of model legislation; unlike the New Zealand law, the Ontario legislation is still on the statute book.

Almost a decade after its enactment Patricia McDermott provides an evaluation of the Canadian law, beginning with an acknowledgment that the legislation has had very little impact on the gender pay gap. Its strength lies in its coverage of both the public and private sectors and in its 'proactive' approach which requires employers to examine their pay structures and to take steps to remove any discrimination found. Its weaknesses are due in part to the political compromises enshrined in the legislation itself and in part to the subsequent attempts at damage limitation by employers. McDermott points specifically to the widespread use of traditional job evaluation which, in combination with the prescribed procedures for comparing male and female job classes, has resulted in the creation of elaborate, confusing and often ineffective processes. The futility of this approach has been encapsulated by two American authors (Evans and Nelson, 1991) who, in a phrase borrowed from Audre Lorde, suggest that it seeks to use 'the master's tools to dismantle the master's house' (p. 236).

McDermott believes that, given the political will, it would be possible to cut through this technical quagmire and proceed directly to an analysis of wage data. Pay adjustments phased in over a number of years could be used to make steady progress towards closing the gender pay gap. In the meantime economic restructuring has ensured that any potential benefits from the legislation are beyond the reach of an increasing proportion of women workers. The author presents the case for a reconceptualization of equal pay law which, rather than assuming a traditional employment relationship based on permanent full-time work, addresses the problems faced by the most vulnerable groups of workers and ensures their access to equality.

The remaining two chapters in this part provide an evaluation of equal pay law in the UK. Unlike the Ontario legislation, the UK law is almost entirely complaint-driven, so that the courage and patience of individual women prepared to put the law to the test is crucial to its success. In the first of these two chapters Sue Hastings draws on her considerable experience as an adviser to the trade union movement in equal pay cases to identify some of the obstacles to effective implementation of the law. She highlights three main areas of difficulty, all of which can be attributed to the way in which the Equal Value (Amendment) Regulations 1983 were constructed. None of these was required under European law.

The first arises from the way in which employers have attempted to prevent comparisons across separate bargaining units; the second involves the use of job evaluation schemes to block equal value claims and the third is due to the requirement that both the applicant and her comparator(s) work for the same employer. Hastings explores each of these problems in turn, showing how they have encouraged the development of pay and grading structures antagonistic to the achievement of equal pay. She identifies some recent cases in which, with the help of European law, applicants and the trade unions supporting them have begun to fight back and then concludes by suggesting some additional legal challenges which would be worth mounting.

Alan Arthurs, who is an independent expert involved in equal value claims, also takes the Equal Value (Amendment) Regulations as his starting point. Under the original Equal Pay Act 1970, industrial tribunals were required to reach a decision on the evidence presented to them without the benefit of any additional expertise. When the law was widened in 1983 to incorporate the principle of equal pay for work of equal value, a panel of independent experts was created to undertake job comparisons on behalf of the tribunals. This procedure has been subjected to a number of criticisms, including the way the experts were initially selected, the choice and variety of methodologies they have employed in reaching a determination on the equal value question, and the length of time taken to accomplish this task.

Arthurs places these criticisms in context by providing a detailed account of the work of independent experts. He makes a clear distinction between the tasks they are required to undertake and the use of traditional job evaluation techniques. The latter are influenced by such factors as market forces, existing pay differentials and the acceptability of pay decisions to the parties involved. Independent experts are required to ignore such considerations and to focus on the demands of the jobs that claimants and comparators actually do in order to arrive at a determination free from sex discrimination. However, during the process of cross-examination at the tribunal hearing, the experts are frequently required to defend their methodologies by reference to existing norms of job evaluation. Although the objective is equality, the outcome in practice is often a compromise. Despite these difficulties, Arthurs concludes that in the absence of collective remedies which would make it possible to change entire pay structures, independent experts still have an important role to play in relation to individual claims.

THE STRATEGIC USE OF EQUAL PAY LAW

Successful strategies are founded on good quality information. The better our understanding of the factors currently shaping labour market inequalities and the better informed we are about the strengths and limitations of equal pay law, the easier it will be to think strategically about possible courses of action for improving women's pay. Different situations require different approaches, as the chapters in this section demonstrate. Although we can learn a great deal from each other's experiences, what works in one location may well not work elsewhere and timing is crucial; we have to think innovatively and be prepared to change tactics when a particular strategy is exhausted. A vivid illustration of this is contained in the chapter by Peggy Kahn and Deborah Figart who give a detailed account of recent attempts to implement equal pay for work of equal value or 'comparable worth' in one state in the United States.

In most countries the first equal pay law to be introduced is often fairly timid. This was certainly the case in New Zealand and in the UK, where the scope of the legislation was only widened some years later. In the US the federal Equal Pay Act 1963, as interpreted by the courts, restricted comparisons to jobs that were 'substantially equal' and so ruled out 'comparable worth' comparisons across different occupations. During the first half of the 1980s case law strategies involved trying to persuade the courts to interpret another anti-discrimination law, Title VII of the Civil Rights Act 1964, as including comparable worth. After some initial successes, this strategy proved increasingly ineffective and came to an abrupt halt with President Reagan's conservative appointments to the judiciary (see Gregory, 1992).

Kahn and Figart give an account of an alternative strategy which became increasingly important during the 1980s, involving public sector workers and their trade unions in alliance with Democrats in state governments. The authors chart the expansion of the pay equity movement in the US in the mid-1980s, at the same time as the new politics of deregulation were gaining the ascendancy. As a result of these contradictory pressures the pay equity movement was only partly successful in achieving its objectives. In Michigan a report from a comparable worth task force highlighted the undervaluing of women's jobs, but also accepted the relevance of market forces and budgetary constraints in determining pay levels. Consequently comparable worth was never fully implemented. Kahn and Figart argue that room for further gains in this area is limited, as in the new climate of deregulation and casualization public sector employees are generally perceived as privileged and overpaid in comparison to workers in the private sector. The authors regard this as an opportunity for pay advocates to rethink their strategies and to become more informal and decentralized in their approach. This would involve joining with trade unions in bargaining at the local level, giving priority to low-paid women and minority workers and linking up with anti-poverty and welfare rights struggles.

The history of the struggle for equal pay in the UK has followed a rather different path, mainly because the UK Equal Pay Act was widened in scope, not as a result of a government commitment but as a direct consequence of UK membership of the EU. Despite the complexity and limitations of the equal value provisions, it has proved fruitful to pursue a litigation strategy. In their chapter Robin Allen and Gay Moon describe the background to and progress of an important test case brought on behalf of two women workers. Reminiscent of the judicial review case brought by the EOC against the Secretary of State for Employment (see above), this case involved the same Secretary of State. The lawyers' target on this occasion was the law that prevents workers from lodging a complaint of unfair dismissal until they have worked for the employer for two years. They argued that this was a form of sex discrimination not permitted under European law.

Crucial to the success of the case was, first, to show that the two-year rule was a form of indirect discrimination against women, because they were more likely to have shorter periods of continuous employment than men. Second, once this was demonstrated it was necessary to refute the government's argument that jobs would be lost if the rule were to be changed and hence that the discrimination was justified. If the EOC showed courage in taking on a powerful government department (which happened also to be its paymaster!), the protagonists in this case were even more unevenly matched. The Camden Law Centre, dependent on the success of their clients' applications for legal aid to bring the case at all, elicited the services of academic statisticians and social scientists to marshall the evidence they needed and to refute the arguments put forward on behalf of the government. Allen and Moon give a graphic account of the triumphs and setbacks experienced during this long-running saga, providing tangible evidence of what can be achieved when women workers, lawyers and academics pool their expertise, resources and determination to achieve the same goal.

In the final chapter Virginia Branney, Marisa Howes and Ariane Hegewisch outline the strategies employed by the trade union UNISON on behalf of its low-paid women members. A recent amalgamation of three public sector unions, UNISON now represents more than one million workers, the majority of whom are women working in local government, the health service, higher education and the privatized utilities. The union has used a combination of campaigning, negotiation backed up by the threat of litigation, and test cases designed to limit the damage caused by deregulation. This threefold strategy is encapsulated in the call to 'educate, negotiate and litigate'.

The chapter includes an account of the *Ratcliffe* case, which constituted a major challenge to the Conservative government's policy of compulsory competitive tendering. In order to compete with the bids from outside contractors as required by the CCT legislation, North Yorkshire County Council made its school meals assistants redundant and re-employed them at lower hourly rates, thereby reneging on its own job evaluation scheme. The House of Lords upheld a claim by the women workers for equal pay with the male workers who were still receiving the rates of pay awarded under the JES. This may seem like a pyrrhic victory, with the local authority bid always being undercut by outside contractors, but once again European law has proved helpful. The Acquired Rights Directive was designed to ensure that when the ownership of a business changed the terms and conditions of the workforce would be protected. The case law on this issue is complex, but this in itself has made some potential contractors wary of setting their bids (and hence the wages offered to employees) too low. The existence of these complications has enabled UNISON to make use of the *Ratcliffe* decision in subsequent negotiations with employers.

The authors also describe the long-running campaign by the union to achieve equal pay for women workers in the highly segregated electricity supply industry. After several years of fruitless negotiation UNISON embarked on a strategy of litigation, only to find itself dealing with several separate companies due to the privatization of the industry. The absence of collective remedies in relation to equal pay meant that the success of the strategy depended on the willingness of individual women to lodge claims with industrial tribunals. Favourable reports from most of the independent experts involved in these cases across the country strengthened the union's negotiating position in generalizing the benefits of individual successes to other workers in the industry (see also Gilbert and Secker, 1995). A similar outcome was achieved in the case involving the Royal Victoria Hospital in Belfast, but only after the case had been running for 11 years.

Although traditionally trade unions have preferred to negotiate rather than litigate, there can be no doubt that UNISON's negotiating position has been strengthened by adopting a dual strategy. This has also had an educative effect within the union itself, as witnessed by the recently negotiated 'single status' agreement covering both manual and non-manual local government workers and incorporating equal value principles. At the same time UNISON is attempting to implement a policy of fair representation within the union itself, to ensure that particular groups of workers, including part timers, have a voice within the organization.

As the chapters in this book demonstrate, the factors contributing to the persistence of labour market inequalities are both complex and numerous and, for many, the goal of equal pay for work of equal value seems as far away as ever. Just as trade unions begin to acknowledge the importance of pay equity, their bargaining powers are under threat. The fragmentation of the labour market makes it increasingly difficult to retain an overview of the terms and conditions which workers are experiencing in practice. In these circumstances, it is more important than ever for the proponents of pay equity to share their knowledge and experience so that no opportunity to make progress on this issue is lost.

## REFERENCES

Armstrong, P. and Cornish, M., 'Restructuring pay equity for a restructured workforce: Canadian perspectives', *Gender, Work and Organization* vol. 4(2) (1997) 67–86.

Equal Opportunities Commission, *Request to the Commission of the European Communities by the Equal Opportunities Commission of Great Britain in Relation to the Implementation of the Principle of Equal Pay.* Manchester: EOC, 1993.

Equal Opportunities Commission, *Code of Practice on Equal Pay.* Manchester: EOC, 1997.

European Commission, *A Code of Practice on the Implementation of Equal Pay for Work of Equal Value for Men and Women.* Luxembourg: Office for Official Publications of the European Communities, 1996.

Evans, S.M. and Nelson, B.J., 'Translating wage gains into social change: international lessons from implementing pay equity in Minnesota', in J. Fudge and

P. McDermott, *Just Wages: a Feminist Assessment of Pay Equity*. Toronto: University of Toronto Press, 1991.

Fieldes, D., 'Equal Pay and Decentralization of Wage Fixing', *British Journal of Industrial Relations* (forthcoming 1999).

Fredman, S., *Women and the Law*. Oxford: Clarendon Press, 1997.

Gilbert, K. and Secker, J., 'Generating equality? Equal pay, decentralization and the electricity supply industry', *British Journal of Industrial Relations* vol. 33(2) (1995) 191–207.

Gregory, J., 'Equal value/comparable worth: national statute and case law in Britain and the USA', in P. Kahn and E. Meehan, *Equal Value/Comparable Worth in the UK and the USA*. Basingstoke: Macmillan, 1992.

Kilpatrick, C., 'Effective utilisation of equality rights: equal pay for work of equal value in France and the UK', in F. Gardiner (ed.), *Sex Equality Policy in Western Europe*. London: Routledge, 1997.

Paci, P. and Joshi, H., 'Wage differentials between men and women: evidence from cohort studies', *Employment Research Report 71*. Sheffield: Department for Education and Employment, 1996.

Trades Union Congress, *Complaint to the Commission of the European Communities for Failure to Comply with Community Law*. London: TUC, 1993.

Wrench, J., *Preventing Racism in the Workplace: a Report on 16 European Countries* for the European Foundation for the Improvement of Living and Working Conditions. Luxembourg: Office for Official Publications of the European Communities, 1996.

# Part I
# Labour Market Inequalities:
# International Perspectives

# 2 Then and Now: Equal Pay in European Union Politics
## Catherine Hoskyns

An appreciation of the content and trajectory of the European Union's policy on women's rights is crucial to an understanding of the way in which equal pay policies have been developing in EU member states. The EU policy, now in operation for 40 years, provides a framework for developments, on the one hand setting some liberal principles with which states are expected to comply, and on the other imposing often restrictive interpretations of law which inflect national practice. The EU policy itself has pursued a tortuous path, responding to a variety of irregular pressures and to a complex and changing environment. The new measures on gender equality and social policy introduced in the 1997 Amsterdam Treaty represent the latest stage in this process.[1]

The relevance of the EU policy on women's rights to the concerns of this book flows also from the fact that the starting point for the policy was the commitment in Article 119 of the Treaty of Rome to the principle of equal pay between women and men. Thus, not only does EU policy set a framework for subsequent developments, it also provides a basis from which to evaluate the significance of the equal pay principle as a springboard for the further advances in favour of women. Why, for example, after women won the vote, was equal pay the next legal right to be struggled for? Why did the negotiators of the Treaty of Rome take this up at such an early stage? What measures follow most easily from the starting point of equal pay?

This chapter will attempt to give some answer to these questions. It will also try to explain why the EU policy on women's rights developed so strongly in the past and what this suggests about the present situation and possible developments in the future.

The EU policy on women's rights is now firmly based on:

- Article 119 on equal pay (interestingly amended in the Amsterdam Treaty);
- six major directives (binding pieces of EU legislation);
- more than 12 pieces of 'soft' law (communications and resolutions);
- four action programmes on equal opportunities (setting priorities and guidelines);

- more than 80 cases on equal treatment in the European Court of Justice (ECJ).

All this is embodied in a great many words about women from which one can glean some sense of what lies behind the policy, and what is being attempted. It is interesting to note that this complexity in policy-making, and the varied forms of participation which have developed with it, have not been replicated in other areas of EU social policy. The EU women's policy remains unique, and at the same time something of a weathervane by means of which, in the social policy field at least, one can judge the force and direction of the winds from Brussels.

There is no space in this chapter to discuss the history of the EU women's policy; this has been covered in detail elsewhere (Pillinger, 1992; Hoskyns, 1996). What I will discuss here is *why* it grew in this particular way and then compare that process with the needs, pressures and resistances that make up the present policy environment.

## PAST PERFORMANCE

### Early Developments

The key period for the development of the policy was the 1970s when a particular combination of factors came together to make some progress possible. These advances rested on the fact that the Treaty already included Article 119 on equal pay, which gave competence in this field to what were then the institutions of the European Community (EC). Article 119 was included in 1957, not just for economic reasons as is usually stated, but as an indirect result of women's activism before, during and after the war (Hoskyns, 1996, pp. 52–7). It is significant for what follows that the equal pay provisions (as Article 46) were originally intended for a section of the Treaty entitled 'distortions to competition', and that they were given a strong formulation, which was seen as necessary for measures in the economic field. This formulation was carried over when the provisions were eventually transferred, now renumbered as Article 119, to the social policy Title of the final Treaty. Equal pay was already on the international agenda in the post-war period, and this seems to have been one of the reasons why the negotiators were able to contemplate including these provisions.

Article 119 was hardly mentioned in the 1960s, but its existence was crucial to policy development in the 1970s. This, I would argue, was due to the coincidence at this point of the material need to open up the market to new forms of labour and the widespread mobilization among women across Europe. This period saw demand in Europe for a larger, more flexible labour force, a 'gap' which in many cases women were well suited to fill. At the same time, in almost all EC member states, second-wave feminism was bursting into the public arena as women became aware of the extent of the mismatch between their expectations and reality (Rowbotham et al., 1979; le Doeuff, 1984).

The economic concerns of the EC, together with the specific focus of Article 119, made it likely that this ebullience would be channelled at European level into measures which focused on the employment situation of women. The activation of Article 119 led to directives expanding and clarifying the right to equal pay, and dealing in addition with employment rights more broadly and with employment-based social security. During the 1970s the policy moved on from a concern with the situation of women already in employment (primarily the question of pay) to the targeting of issues which were seen as affecting women's access to employment and the expansion of the female labour force.[2]

In this period, then, the fact that the needs of the market matched at least some of women's demands, which in turn were gaining political resonance, led to significant policy development. The process was helped by the belief of many policy-makers that they could do 'something for women' without disturbing what was seen as the core balance in industrial relations (Teague, 1989). They were able to hold this view because campaigning for women's rights at both national and European level took place for the most part outside the formal structures of the labour movement, and was in many cases opposed by trade union leaders. This was certainly true at EC level where the European Trade Union Confederation (ETUC) on a number of occasions in the 1970s bitterly opposed any separate EC policy for women workers. Only recently has there been a change in this respect (Cockburn, 1995).

This dissonance allowed the women's policy to go forward on a separate track and created a divide at European level between women-centred action and the broader labour movement, which has proved hard to bridge.

## Maintenance and Expansion

In the 1980s the policy was maintained, and to some extent expanded, partly at least by the development of an infrastructure around it. A Women's Bureau (now the Equal Opportunities Unit) with a budget line was established in the European Commission; the European Parliament was pressured into setting up its own Committee on Women's Rights; expert groups started work. Together these set a framework for lobbying and networking which began to involve more directly a wider range of women. Exceptionally, an EC policy had been initiated which had some bearing on the needs of a politically aware, grassroots constituency. The importance of equal opportunities for middle-class women gave the policy a firm political base.

The principle of equal pay in European law had by this time been expanded to include equal pay for work of equal value, and the rulings of the ECJ were beginning to bring rights for pregnant workers and for part-time workers within the remit of the policy.[3] Core employment rights were being established in a relatively strong form, although the methods of implementation at national level were often weak. As different groups of women became more involved, pressure grew to expand the scope of the policy into the private as well as the public sphere and to take up issues involving sexual politics, caring and the behaviour of men. In general, the policy was being pushed outwards from a concern with women's rights in employment to a consideration of gender relations more broadly.

The resistance to this was considerable: the Court famously stated that the directive on equal treatment 'was not designed to settle questions concerning the organisation of the family, or to alter the division of responsibility between parents'.[4] This restrictive and blunt ruling was in marked contrast the Court's usual 'generous and teleological mode of interpreting law' (Scheiwe, 1994, pp. 252–3).[5]

At a more political level, it was noticeable that by comparison with the strong directives of the 1970s, the 1986 directive on women in family businesses and in agriculture was drastically weakened during the negotiation process. Both politicians and officials were reluctant to see the rights which had been achieved by women in employment extended to women in circumstances where work and family overlapped, and the dominant thinking at governmental level was against such social regulation (Hoskyns, 1996, pp. 148–51; Prechal and Burrows, 1990, p. 293).[6]

Despite this opposition, the policy did expand in some areas, and began to raise issues about the relation between the public and private roles of women and men, most noticeably in the areas of sexual harassment, childcare and parental leave. All of these issues were handled tentatively with none of the robust legislation of the 1970s. However, the aim of reconciling work and family life (it was never quite clear whether for women or women *and men*) became an important overall objective for the policy.[7] As Luckhaus and Ward (1997) have pointed out, by this stage it was becoming clear that the principle of equality was inadequate to deal with the disadvantages faced by women with few resources and an uneven attachment to the labour market. For them, and for men in a similar position, provisions were needed which gave more value to, and associated benefits with, the caring role.

One further and significant expansion in scope was that the issue of 'women and decision-making' was taken up for the first time in the Third Action Programme (1991–5). This involved EU-funded research on the extent of women's involvement in decision-making in political, economic and social arenas, and resulted in cross-national comparisons and the identification of good practice (Leijenaar, 1997). This issue was pressed hard by the European Parliament's Women's Committee and taken up strongly by professional women's groups across Europe. It represented a shift outwards from the strict employment remit towards the sphere of public politics.

**The Women's Constituency**

Despite all this activity, it was clear by the early 1990s that women as a constituency were by no means fully engaged with the project of European integration. This was demonstrated by the opposition of women in Denmark to the adoption of the Maastricht Treaty, and in Sweden to EU membership. The reasons for this seem to be: first, the failure of the EU to provide any real space for transnational politics or participation at a popular level; and second, the lack of clarity as to what values the EU stood for in the modern world. Securing peace in Western Europe and creating the framework for economic recovery seemed no longer enough to justify the 'permissive public opinion' of earlier decades. Women were in the forefront of an increasingly wary public.

The various developments discussed above created a coalition of interests which, even if blocked in certain directions and by no means engaging all women, preserved a strong core to the women's policy. As we have seen, this resulted in expansions in some directions and defeats in others. Up to this point, the women's policy maintained its character as something unique as far as European social policy was concerned – indeed, it seemed to be running on a different track. One demonstration of this was the unusual commitment shown by many of the officials working in the Commission's Equal Opportunities Unit and by the contacts which they had with groups and people not usually seen in Brussels.

THE FOURTH ACTION PROGRAMME, 1996–2000

There have been signs since the ratification of the Maastricht Treaty in 1993 that this conjuncture is beginning to change in two apparently contradictory directions. On the one hand, there are indications that the special character of the women's policy and its particular resonance is beginning to fragment; on the other, there is a new concern being shown at EU level for the social framework within which economic activity takes place, and the need to create some kind of democratic legitimacy. The Fourth Action Programme on Equal Opportunities (AP4), and its application so far, provide some interesting evidence for both developments.

AP4 was negotiated during 1994 and 1995 and came into force in 1996.[8] It was thus devised and first implemented during a period when EU officials and member state governments were having to deal with a growth in public scepticism about European developments. This had been demonstrated by the problems experienced in the ratification of the Maastricht Treaty and was exacerbated by the tough monetary measures seen as necessary to ensure convergence in the run up to economic and monetary union and the adoption of the single currency.

In devising and implementing the programme, therefore, those who wished to push the policy further and into new directions had to contend with the determination of many in authority at both national and European level, to discourage the development of policies which would cost money and which might demonstrate in an inconvenient way (as the women's policy certainly had in the past) the supranational aspects of European regulation. At the same time, even at the top echelons there was a realization that the policy on gender had gone too far to be put back in the bottle, and that there was still considerable mobilization behind it. The emphasis was therefore on attempting to keep future developments under control rather than preventing them altogether.

The consequences of these changes in context, and the contradictions they produce, can be illustrated by examining in more detail four aspects of AP4: its general ethos, its organization, the attitude to law which it demonstrates, and the attention paid to disadvantaged women. Since AP4 is still in its early stages such an examination must be tentative. Nevertheless, some interesting trends emerge.

## Ethos and Organization

In contrast to the first three action programmes, in AP4 the Commission is cast in the role of facilitator rather than director, and the main impetus for action on women's issues is seen as coming from member states. 'Community added value' is expected to derive from comparing and evaluating national actions, and from giving them a transnational dimension. This chimes in with the emphasis on the principle of 'subsidiarity' in the

Maastricht Treaty, a principle which, in line with the concerns just discussed, has been widely used by governments to curb the powers of the Commission and to slow down the transfer of competencies to the European level.[9] At the same time, the programme puts much emphasis on the 'mainstreaming' of equal opportunities, the stated objective of which is to ensure that gender equality is incorporated into every aspect of the Community's actions.[10]

In general, the main emphasis in AP4 is on the location of action rather than its substance. In matters of substance, however, priority is given to women and decision-making, to individualization of benefits and to the reconciliation of family and working life (this time it is clear that both women and men are targeted). On employment rights, particular attention is paid to job segregation and to the continued undervaluing of women's work. The formulations and the analysis in the employment sections seem lacklustre by comparison with earlier documents, despite the extent of experience in this field.

The emphasis on mainstreaming was clearly desirable and marked a recognition of the dangers of ghettoising equal opportunities in one section of the Social Affairs Directorate-General (DG V) of the Commission. For this to be an effective policy, however, given the decentralized nature of the Commission and its complex working practices, it was assumed by many observers, and at least some of those involved, that a strengthened equal opportunities infrastructure and a larger resource base would be required. But to the surprise of many, as AP4 came into operation there seemed to be a deliberate dilution of the organizational base, with a number of important expert networks being wound up, and a new agency, ANIMA (not an acronym!) being created to run the programme. The role of the Equal Opportunities Unit (EOU), for so long the centre of the policy, has since then become somewhat anomalous. The result has been a shift of power to the hierarchy in DG V.

## Use of the Law

The women's policy in the past has rested strongly on measures in European law and on the promotion of enforceable legal rights. In the 1980s progress in this direction slowed down due to the reluctance on the part of governments to pass further equal treatment legislation with its uncertain ramifications and outcomes. The result has been a greater emphasis on so-called 'soft law' and on other ways of implementing existing principles and generating new ones.

A good example of this was the attempt by the EOU over the past five years to substantiate, clarify and make more useful the existing right to equal pay for work of equal value. A firm commitment on this was made in the Third Action Programme, and a comprehensive research document on work of equal value was produced, followed by a memorandum from the Commission, and finally a code of practice intended for use in collective bargaining and as a basis for challenging existing wage rates and grading.[11] The research and expertise upon which these documents are based is exemplary, but they have not had the impact they might have done, largely because governments have shown themselves reluctant to give publicity to the issues or encourage their implementation in the public sector. They remain a tool for activists rather than a demonstration of collective will on the part of the EU.

As a result of experiences such as these, it is not surprising that the legal route is played down in AP4, though the guaranteeing of rights in law remains a long-term objective. Paradoxically, the possibilities of developing European social policy more generally were enhanced at this time due to the need to reassure public opinion and create at least some kind of agreed social framework for continuing economic integration. The favoured way of proceeding involves the so-called 'social dialogue' between employers and trade unions, finally accepted by the UK government in 1997, and incorporated under the Social Agreement into the Amsterdam Treaty.

This is by no means a wholly negative development for women, as the recent adoption of a Directive on Parental Leave via this route demonstrates.[12] However, it seems to remove the exceptional status of 'women's law' and to leave it to be developed in a setting which is less open to mobilization. Though much of this framework may be beneficial, in the current political climate the focus on equality may well be used to legitimize and generalize the levelling down of rights, and the reduction rather than the enhancement of social protection as the case law discussed below illustrates. The intention seems to be to incorporate the legislative side of the women's policy, previously developed on a separate track, into this broad framework of social law – and perhaps by this means to keep it more closely under control.

The judgments of the European Court of Justice have in the past played a large part in developing the scope of the women's policy and giving it publicity. Since Maastricht, the ECJ appears to have moved in a more restrictive direction, at least as far as women are concerned. Three significant cases demonstrate this: *Avdel*, *Nolte* and *Kalanke*.[13] In *Avdel* the Court ruled that levelling down to achieve equality was permissible, even if women were substantially disadvantaged in the process. *Nolte* showed the Court willing to accept that 'minor' employment (less than 15 hours a week) should not be subject to equal treatment law, even if it was customarily carried out disproportionately by more women than men. In *Kalanke* the Court ruled that positive action for women in the selection process went against equality norms if it could be shown that individual men were being disadvantaged. The lack of emphasis on the needs of women and the willingness to use equality laws on behalf of men made the new ethos clear.

Since these rulings fewer cases have been coming through, suggesting perhaps that this new interpretation of equality is deterring litigation. The recent *Grant* case concerning a lesbian railway worker in the UK denied travel concessions for her partner was an exception but this also has ultimately failed. In spite of the Danish Advocate General's Opinion that to deny these concessions constitutes sex discrimination under the 1975 Equal Treatment Directive, the Court ruled against *Grant*.[14] Had the Court followed the Advocate General's view, as is the normal practice of the Court, it would have constituted a substantial endorsement of gay rights and a progressive linking of gender equality to associated forms of discrimination.

## Disadvantage

AP4 is the first action programme to make no direct mention of migrant or ethnic minority women or of other groups of disadvantaged or poor women. In explanation, one of the officials who helped draft the programme stated that these issues were either outside the competence of the EU or dealt with elsewhere in its programmes. However, the 69 projects approved for funding under AP4 in December 1996 do show more concern with disadvantaged and marginalized women – a response perhaps to the continuing vibrancy and relevance of women's grassroots activity. Without endorsement in the written text, however, such support remains patchy and uncertain.

In 1996, the year AP4 came into operation, the EU agreed to designate 1997 as its Year Against Racism, a decision which gave both money for projects and visibility to issues of racial disadvantage. There was immediate pressure for a strong gender dimension to be included in these initiatives, a move which the EOU was in a weak position to support since AP4 was silent on the race issue. The mainstreaming initiative, so strongly advocated to increase gender awareness, has not so far been seen as equally essential in the case of racism.

The *Grant* case and the Year Against Racism raise again the nature of the link between sex discrimination and other forms of disadvantage.

This issue, long debated in feminism, centres on the question of whether the gender divide, and disadvantage stemming from it, are qualitatively different from other forms of disadvantage, and thus need to be fought separately, or whether all forms of disadvantage are linked and intertwined, both as situations and as struggles. There are sound arguments in support of each position, and indeed they are not necessarily mutually exclusive. In terms of practical politics, however, if gender is treated for too long as a 'pure' issue, and if the differences between women are not addressed, it is only too easy for a policy 'for women' to become a policy for some women only, and for the women's constituency to be split.

The extent to which gender has been prioritized in EU policy, taken together with the particular formulations of AP4, means that these have become questions of great practical significance at European level. They take on a new meaning in the light of the changes embodied in the Amsterdam Treaty.

## THE AMSTERDAM TREATY AND GENDER EQUALITY

The Amsterdam Treaty, adopted in June 1997, has generally been depicted as a weak document. However, in the areas of human rights, social policy and gender equality some significant changes have been made. The detailed process by which these were adopted (and the bargains they embody) is as yet unclear and thus any comment must be tentative (Duff, 1997). It is evident that despite the continuing secrecy surrounding the negotiations, this time social and popular movements had more access to information and were able to exert some pressure. The difficulties experienced in ratifying the Maastricht Treaty also meant that politicians were more aware of the need to carry public opinion. This resulted in caution as well as boldness.[15]

In Article F, for the first time a clear statement is made that the Union itself is founded on 'the principles of liberty, democracy, respect for human rights and fundamental freedoms'; these principles were previously presumed to be guaranteed through the practice of the member states. Again for the first time, sanctions are provided at EU level against states which are in 'serious and persistent breach' of these principles (Article F.1). These provisions go some way towards answering the question 'what does the EU stand for?' although the likelihood is that they were included more as a warning to current and future applicant states than as a reassurance for existing citizens.

Social policy received a huge boost in the Treaty as a result of the lifting of the UK ban on the incorporation of the Maastricht Social

Agreement. This brings the new measures agreed by 11 states in 1991 into the Treaty of Rome, and substantially amends Articles 117 and 118. The scope of potential legislation in the social policy field is increased and for the first time the 'co-decision procedure' (Article 189b) can be applied to social policy issues. Co-decision, the process for which has been simplified in the new Treaty, gives the European Parliament a greater say in the negotiation process.[16] The relation between this procedure and the social dialogue route already described, remains unclear (Barnard, 1997).

The issue of employment is 'mainstreamed' throughout the Amsterdam Treaty, and a full chapter on employment has been inserted just after the provisions on economic and monetary policy. Overall, the Treaty facilitates the establishment of a social policy framework alongside the single market and the currency union. The content, however, remains to be determined.

The priority given to gender equality in the new Treaty is perhaps surprising. Article 2 of the Treaty of Rome has been amended to include 'equality between men and women' as one of the aims of the Union, and in Article 3, which lists its main activities, a new paragraph has been added which states that in all its activities the Community 'shall aim to eliminate inequalities, and to promote equality, between men and women'. This is mainstreaming with a vengeance. Sex is also included in the new general anti-discrimination clause (Article 6a) but the formulation here is weak. No direct rights are conveyed and new provisions can be developed only by member states acting unanimously. However, the scope is broad and covers discrimination based on: 'sex, racial or ethnic origin, religion or belief, disability, age or sexual orientation'. This enables sex discrimination to be linked to and, potentially at least, tackled alongside a wide range of other forms of disadvantage.

In addition, Article 119 has been substantially amended beyond what was agreed in 1991. First, equal pay for work of equal value is specifically included in the definition of the equal pay principle. Second, a new paragraph has been added expanding the scope of the article to cover 'equal opportunities and equal treatment of men and women in matters of employment and occupation' and allowing measures to this effect to be taken under the co-decision procedure described above.

Finally, as a partial answer to the *Kalanke* judgment, it is stated that the principle of equal treatment shall not prevent member states 'from maintaining or adopting measures providing for specific advantages in order to make it easier for *the under-represented sex* [my emphasis] to pursue a vocational activity or to prevent or compensate for disadvantages in professional careers'. At Amsterdam, the phrase 'under-represented sex' was substituted for 'women' as used in the original text of the Social Agreement.

This both puts the emphasis firmly on numbers and opens up the possibility of using positive action to benefit men as well as women. A (non-binding) declaration was included at the end of the Treaty to say that such measures should 'in the first instance, aim at improving the situation of women in working life'.

Overall, then, the Amsterdam Treaty appears to be creating a more open public space with some attention being paid to group identities, and to the need for a social framework at European level. Issues of class, social division and poverty are not highlighted, although the social dialogue retains a residual element of this concern. Social cohesion between countries is emphasized but neither the narrowing of the gap between social groups nor public expenditure on the disadvantaged seem likely outcomes of these provisions.

THE PRESENT DYNAMIC

On the issue of gender, the Amsterdam Treaty reinforces the emphases in AP4 in some respects, and contradicts them in others. Since this is the context within which we shall have to work, it is worth speculating – and at this stage it can only be speculation – why this should be so.

The Treaty emphasises mainstreaming and strengthens the hand of those who wish to take up gender issues in areas of Community activity outside the remit of DG V. It says nothing, however, about the content of those gendered policies, leaving this to be decided by political bargaining on the spot. It will be interesting to see whether this high-level endorsement of mainstreaming leads to more resources being fed into the key structures in DG V and what happens to the EOU and ANIMA in the process.

The Treaty shares with AP4 the lack of overt concern for poverty and social disadvantage and for redistribution more generally. Obviously, one cannot know in advance how the social framework is going to be developed, but the lack of attention to these issues in the texts reduces the bargaining power of those who would argue for policies which address them. The doctrine of subsidiarity which is used to justify this absence means that once again responsibility for the social consequences is removed from those who are increasingly taking the key economic and political decisions in Europe.

Where the Treaty does diverge from the trends identified in AP4 is in continuing and even strengthening the separate strand of women's law under Article 119. The inclusion of work of equal value in the text, the establishment of a clear legal base for employment initiatives beyond the issue of pay, and the possibility of taking action under the co-decision procedure are all welcome changes. However, it is still the case that the new Article 119 moves hardly at all beyond the employment/equality nexus, despite the fact that this strand of law at European level seems to have run its course, and has over the past 40 years been shown to provide an inadequate basis for challenging women's disadvantage (Luckhaus and Ward, 1997).

The one area which goes beyond this is the clarification of the right to positive action measures (para. 4). As discussed above, this has been drafted in a restrictive fashion and in a way which in the long run may be used to benefit men. However, in the recent judgment in the *Marschall*[17] case, the ECJ modified its stance in *Kalanke*. This was a similar case, also from Germany, and although the (British) Advocate General endorsed the *Kalanke* ruling, the Court modified his opinion by declaring that in cases where discretion remained some kinds of positive action were allowable under EU equality law. In making this ruling it seems likely that the judges were influenced by the new amendment even though the Treaty has not yet been ratified.

Clearly, in the revision of Article 119, a different dynamic was operating from that which produced AP4. One senses that a more legalistic perspective is being adopted, with a concern to follow the logic of the Court's jurisprudence in including equal value within the scope of this article and to create a firm legal base for equality measures which would remove the necessity of resorting to 'general' articles, such as Article 100 or 235. The political will for such measures, however, is currently at a low ebb. Despite these new formulations, it seems likely that the present policy of adopting broad framework laws in areas of interest to women (as has been done in relation to parental leave and part-time work) will continue, setting quite low minimum standards and leaving considerable discretion to governments.

Legal developments in this area remain unpredictable. The existence of new rights and procedures may encourage the formation of different coalitions and alliances to fight for particular measures – and political will can change. The use of co-decision in Article 119 and for social policy more generally may also prevent the extreme watering down of measures which has been the pattern in the recent past.

## FUTURE DIRECTIONS

As already argued, one characteristic of the 1970s which supported the use of the original version of Article 119 was the expansion of the economy and labour market. This created a material need to remove at least some of the barriers to women's employment. The situation now is very different. Women are in the labour market and the position of the majority, combining low-paid work with continuing domestic responsibilities, suits current market needs very well. Market pressure is now more likely to be directed at persuading men into insecure and risky jobs rather than at improving any further the situation of women. One exception to this is at the top end of the market where there is a perceived need for a wider variety of skills in management and for a larger pool of talent to draw on. This combination is likely to make it easier to achieve cracks in the glass ceiling than to gain advantages for women in low-paid, low-skilled jobs.

The final and crucial factor in any of these long drawn-out negotiations on women's rights is the degree of mobilization among women themselves and the pressure exerted on the process by groups of women acting through different channels and in different ways. Pressure seems to have been far better developed and targeted in the case of the Treaty than it was over the formulation of AP4. The European Women's Lobby (EWL), for example, followed the Amsterdam process in great detail, took expert advice, and came up with its own precise amendments and demands. In this it was supported by some very professional lobbying in the national capitals. The European Parliament's Committee on Women's Rights was also active in pressing for change.

The trend in much of this lobbying seems to have been towards continuing the exceptional status of the EU women's policy and combating moves to merge or control it. To a large extent this was successful as the new formulations in the Amsterdam Treaty suggest. The main tactic used to achieve this end was to define gender as a 'pure' issue and as the major divide between people. Thus separate and different treatment was demanded. The concerns of 'other' groups, particularly about racism and poverty, were supported. However this seems to have been largely from the outside, and as a quid pro quo, without much sense that these were issues which intimately affected the lives of many women.

This attitude is demonstrated in the EWL's useful commentary on the Treaty amendments, which, while welcoming the general anti-discrimination clause (Article 6a), states that it 'would have preferred a separate clause addressing one specific form of discrimination – discrimination against women'.[18] Although perhaps effective as a tactic, this insistence on treating sex discrimination on its own has the great disadvantage of ignoring the needs of many women. What may be necessary now is the formation of more complex coalitions which allow the interlocking nature of these different forms of discrimination to become visible, and encourage a sense of solidarity among different groups of women. In this context, the long-standing separation at European level between the campaigns on women's rights and those of the labour movement more generally, once entirely justified, may now be counter-productive.

The issue of equal pay remains at the heart of the EU women's policy and has been given greater resonance in the recent amendments to Article 119. However, in answer to the question posed at the start of this chapter, the logical next steps after equal pay provisions are measures which go beyond equal treatment and take account of all the ramifications of caring which affect the situations of women so profoundly. Both intellectually and in terms of practical politics, in addition to campaigns on pay equity and job evaluation, strategies are needed to combat the poverty and disadvantage which many women experience. This is a transition which EU policy-makers, in company with many of their counterparts at national level, find hard to accept.

## NOTES

1. The Draft Treaty of Amsterdam, amending the Treaty of European Union and the Treaty of Rome, was adopted in June 1997 through an intergovernmental conference of the EU member states. At the time of writing it awaits ratification by the member states.
2. The three Directives on equal treatment for women which were adopted during the 1970s still constitute the core of the EU policy. They are: the Equal Pay Directive 75/117/EEC; the Equal Treatment Directive 76/207/EEC; and the Social Security Directive 79/7/EEC.
3. See *Bilka* ECJ Case 170/84 (part-time workers) and *Dekker* ECJ Case C-177/88 (pregnant workers).
4. In *Hofmann* ECJ Case 184/83, paras 2, 4.
5. In general the role of the ECJ has been to expand the scope and effect of European law through its own jurisprudence. This was certainly the trend in its interpretation of the EC provisions on equal treatment for women, which was why the sharp and restrictive ruling in the *Hofmann* case caused such surprise.
6. Directive 86/613/EEC on 'equal treatment between men and women engaged in an activity including agriculture in a self-employed capacity ...'. The directive in its original form sought in effect to create an occupational status for women who previously had none.
7. See the emphasis on this in both the Third and Fourth Action Programmes on Equal Opportunities.
8. Fourth Medium-Term Community Action Programme on Equal Opportunities for Women and Men (1996–2000) CEC, V/231b/96.
9. Article 3b of the Maastricht Treaty invokes the principle of subsidiarity to support an assertion that action shall only be taken at Community (EU) level

when the objectives of a proposed action cannot be achieved by member states alone. This was inserted both to reduce the powers of the Commission and to satisfy Euro-sceptic public opinion that control was being maintained at nation state level.

10. For an excellent discussion of mainstreaming, see *Kokkola Report*, European Parliament Committee on Women's Rights, Document A4-0251/97, 18 July 1997.

11. See Beverley Jones, Working Document on Work of Equal Value, CEC, February 1993; Memorandum on Equal Pay for Work of Equal Value, COM (94) 06, June 1994; Code of Practice on the Implementation of Equal Pay for Work of Equal Value for Men and Women, Luxembourg, 1996.

12. Council Directive 96/34/EC of 3 June 1996 on the framework agreement on parental leave concluded by UNICE, CEEP and the ETUC.

13. *Smith* v *Avdel Systems Ltd* ECJ Case C-408/92; *Nolte* v *Landes. Hannover* ECJ Case C-317/93; and *Kalanke* v *Freie Hansestadt Bremen* ECJ Case C-450/93.

14. *Grant* v *SW Trains* ECJ Case C-249/96; Opinion of the Advocate General, 30 September 1997; Judgment, 15 February 1998.

15. See reports during this time of the European Anti Poverty Network (EAPN).

16. The co-decision procedure, introduced in the Maastricht Treaty, divides the decision-making process more equally between the EU Council of Ministers and the European Parliament. In the event of disagreement, a complex conciliation procedure is initiated; if this fails the measure falls. The Amsterdam Treaty expanded the scope of co-decision.

17. *Marschall* v *Land Nordrhein-Westfalen* ECJ Case C-409/95; Opinion of the Advocate General, 15 May 1997; Judgment 11 November 1997.

18. Position and Amendments of the European Women's Lobby on the Draft Treaty of Amsterdam, 14 July 1997, p. 4.

## REFERENCES

Barnard, C., 'The UK, the Social Chapter and the Amsterdam Treaty', *Industrial Law Journal* 26 (September 1997) 275–82.

Cockburn, C., 'Strategies for gender democracy: women and the European social dialogue', *Social Europe* Supplement 4 (1995).

Le Doeuff, M., *L'Étude et le route*. Paris: Seuil, 1989.

Duff, A. (ed.), *The Treaty of Amsterdam – Text and Commentary*. Federal Trust. London: Sweet and Maxwell, 1997.

Hoskyns, C., *Integrating Gender: Women, Law and Politics in the European Union*. London: Verso, 1996.

Leijenaar, M., *How to Create a Gender Balance in Political Decision Making*. Luxembourg: CEC, DG V, 1997.

Luckhaus, L. and Ward, S., 'Equal pension rights for men and women: a realistic perspective', *Journal of European Social Policy* 7(3) (1997) 237–53.

Pillinger, J., *Feminising the Market: Women's Pay and Employment in the European Union*. London: Macmillan, 1992.

Prechal, S. and Burrows, N., *Gender Discrimination Law of the European Community*. London: Macmillan, 1990.

Rowbotham, S., Segal, L. and Wainwright, H., *Beyond the Fragments: Feminism and the Making of Socialism*. London: Merlin Press, 1979.

Scheiwe, K., 'EC law's unequal treatment of the family: the case law of the European Court of Justice on rules prohibiting discrimination on grounds of sex and nationality', *Social and Legal Studies* 3(2) (1994) 243–65.

Teague, P., *The European Community: the Social Dimension*. London: Kogan Page, 1989.

# 3 Global Feminization and Flexible Labour Markets: Gendered Discourse in the Opposition to Pay Equity Reform

Deborah Figart and Ellen Mutari

## INTRODUCTION

Since the 1980s, Europe's relatively high unemployent rates ('Eurosclerosis') have been used by the Organization for Economic Cooperation and Development and other international agencies as a basis for positing the United States as a model of labour market flexibility (see Howell, 1992; Brodsky, 1994; Faux, 1995a,b). Measures to enable firms to adapt to changing markets is argued to be the necessary economic response to heightened international competition. Labour market flexibility has been depicted as a crucial dimension of this process (Brown, 1991; Curry, 1992).

Politically, the transition to a global economy has also been associated with the rise of conservative governments in the United States and other Western nations. Although taking different forms in different national contexts, the mission of the state has been revised to conform with *laissez-faire* assumptions about the beneficence of markets. In the United States, this has taken the form of supply-side economic policies to cut spending on social programmes, reduce taxes and deregulate business. Similarly, European governments, especially the United Kingdom,[1] have pursued deregulation and privatization to promote flexibility in external labour markets as a central policy objective, while they dismantled their welfare states (Howell, 1992; Faux, 1995a,b). As articulated in *Beware the US Model*, published by the Economic Policy Institute:

> The choice is between the hard-edged Social Darwinism of Thatcher and Reagan and a softer version represented by the neoliberalism of Clinton and Delors. Scratch the surface of either strand of the US

version of the model and you find anaemic job growth and plummeting wages for the majority of workers. (Faux, 1995a, p. xi)

The gendered basis of this flexibility imperative has received increased attention by feminist scholars. Standing (1989) introduced the concept of 'global feminization through flexible labour', presenting a unified analysis of trends in both developing and industrialized countries. On an empirical level, feminization refers to women's rising share of the labour force brought about by their increased labour force participation along with male workers' displacement from manufacturing jobs. In a cross-country study, Çağatay and Özler (1995) find that women's share of the labour force exhibits a U-shaped pattern over the course of development; the upward pattern of feminization has been intensified by contemporary macroeconomic policies and export-oriented growth.

For Standing, this global process of feminization entails three aspects: (1) direct substitution of women for men within jobs; (2) the expansion of traditionally female-intensive employment sectors; and (3) the expansion of forms of employment associated with women, such as part-time, temporary/contingent, and informal work (see also Jenson, Hagen, and Reddy, 1988; Mitter, 1986, 1994; Bakker, 1996b). Standing emphasizes that deregulation and flexible employment strategies foster 'the types of work, labor relations, income, and insecurity associated with "women's work" (Standing, 1989, p. 1077). Armstrong (1996) refers to the process of feminization as a 'harmonizing down', since men's and women's employment prospects are increasingly similar.

The concept of global feminization is sometimes criticized for presupposing a uniform trajectory to contemporary economic restructuring. Critics argue that this formulation oversimplifies the diversity of women's experiences in specific national, regional and cultural contexts (Cohen, 1994). Yet Bakker (1996a, pp. 8–9) argues that feminization indeed captures an important, though not inevitable, dimension of contemporary restructuring. She advocates viewing 'gender as an interactive category of analysis in a complete account of the transforming global order'. Thus, gender interacts with class, race, ethnicity, sexuality and nationality in specific historical contexts. Such an approach is sensitive to cultural as well as economic imperatives.

Discourse analysis can use language to illuminate cultural preoccupations while emphasizing the economic, political and social context which sustains them (see Fraser and Gordon, 1994). In this chapter, we analyse the language and arguments of the organized opposition to pay equity reform in order to understand the gendered basis of contemporary economic restructuring and the 'flexibility fetish' in the United States.

The vehemence of pay equity opponents' arguments suggests that pay equity questions fundamental status relationships in society (see also Peterson, 1990). We contend that attention to gender can facilitate a non-determinist perspective on the process of economic, political and social transformation, especially the contentious process of reconciling feminization with prevailing gender relations. Attention to these dynamics holds insights for the pay equity movement in many advanced industrialized countries.

In the following section, we demonstrate that the organized opposition to pay equity has found sustenance in the emerging political economy of liberalization and deregulation. Feminist researchers have identified the market as central to arguments against pay equity reform (see Greenwood, 1984; Steinberg, 1986; Bergmann, 1989; Peterson 1992). Our work links this pro-market discourse to contemporary discussions of labour market flexibility. The writings of pay equity opponents also reveal their unease at gender relations in transition, as discussed in a subsequent section. The formerly hegemonic ideal of the nuclear family supported by a male breadwinner wage appears under question, as conservatives wrestle with white married women's increased labour force participation and attachment. The conclusion addresses the prospects for alternative visions. Feminist, labour and other progressive movements are challenging the gendered basis of economic restructuring by linking pay equity to a redefinition of gender roles and a broad living wage movement.

**The 'Flexibility Fetish': Pay Equity Meets the Market**

Perhaps one of the most ironic aspects of the dominant response to economic change has been the resurrection of discredited economic theories rooted in nineteenth-century capitalism. According to Appelbaum (1995), globalization disrupted the 'virtuous circle' that enabled Keynesian policies to flourish in the United States during the post-war period. That is, growth in worker productivity and in employment went hand-in-hand, permitting increased consumption with stable prices. The key to this process was the domestic market for manufactured goods: if employers shared the benefits of increased productivity with workers in core industries (through wage increases or fiscal policy), the resultant increase in demand would fuel profits. Of course, this arrangement, sometimes referred to as the 'capital–labour accord' permitted only a limited group of workers, primarily white males in core sectors, to share in the prosperity of Pax Americana (Albelda and Tilly, 1994; Badgett and Williams, 1994; O'Hara, 1995).

As US economic and political hegemony diminished, so did the hegemony of Keynesian demand-oriented theory among economists and policy-makers. However, as the economic sociologist Fred Block noted, there was a shortage of competing visions among the left. Within this intellectual vacuum lay the opportunity for a rejuvenation of *laissez-faire* Social Darwinism. The market once again became the 'central category of economic discourse' (Block, 1990, p. 46; see also Faux, 1995a):

> Increasingly, public debate has come to hinge, not on what kind of society we are or want to be, but on what the needs of the economy are. Hence, a broad range of social policies are now debated almost entirely in terms of how they fit in with the imperatives of the market. (Block, 1990, p. 3)

Public policy was redirected to increase flexibility and eliminate rigidities so as to facilitate the smooth operation of markets, especially labour markets.

Popular discourse against pay equity, as expressed in the US by business lobby organizations, their funded researchers and Republican political officials, has warned of the dangers of tampering with labour markets. Reflecting the supposed consensus that an unregulated economy represents a model of flexibility, the relative success of US capitalism has been trumpeted. According to the Cato Institute, a libertarian public policy research institute in Washington, DC:

> Most proponents of comparable worth[2] argue that it is not an alternative to the market, that it is like other correctives to the market that have been instituted by government in recent years. I contend that this is false. Comparable worth … cannot be grafted onto the market. Rather, the market and comparable worth emanate from two entirely different normative assumptions about individual action. (Paul, 1989, p. 116)

Paul (1989, p. 113) further asserts that 'what has characterized capitalist economies since the Industrial Revolution is precisely the options that workers have, the fluidity of labour markets, and the ever-changing possibilities the market creates'.

Unlike European countries, the dominant US culture has regarded all forms of socialism as an anathema.[3] The writings of comparable worth opponents reflect this cultural preoccupation with a communist threat. The economist June O'Neill became a well-known opponent of pay equity during the 1980s, explicitly arguing that comparable worth could lead to a centrally planned economy (1984a,b). Her position resonated with conservative politicians and O'Neill became Director of the Congressional Budget Office following the 1994 elections, which gave Republicans a legislative majority. Her argument is echoed throughout the literature: 'this doctrine is an assault, whether intended or not, upon our free market economic system, and would result in substantial damage to the US economy'

(Bergren, 1984, pp. 209–17). A columnist in the conservative newspaper *The Washington Times* links wage regulation to central planning:

> Even though the marketplace is far from perfect, it is the best and should be the only arbiter of wages.... Just as the number crunchers in the Kremlin's economic central planning office cannot duplicate the accuracy and efficiency of the millions of economic decisions made by American businessmen and women every day, so also a comparable-worth commission cannot measure accurately and fairly the countless factors which determine wages in a free market. (Snow, 1985)

With the fall of the Berlin Wall, pay equity opponents have tempered their hyperbole without abandoning their pro-market rhetoric.

In an era when global economic competition has replaced the Cold War as a central preoccupation, opponents' arguments often centre on the importance of flexible wage-setting in maintaining economic competitiveness. Specifically, pay equity is argued to interfere with the ability of market forces to adapt and respond to changing economic conditions. Stephen Rhoads, a professor of government who writes for both academic and business audiences, sums up this position:

> Well-functioning market economies use rising wages to ameliorate shortages of labor in an occupation or at a particular location, and use static or falling wages to reduce surpluses by encouraging worker exit and discouraging entry. Comparable worth does not allow this flexibility. (Rhoads, 1993a, p. 40)

In particular, the cost of pay equity reform, depicted as a threat to profitability, is receiving increased attention (Rhoads, 1993b). In the following passage, Rhoads makes a broad comparison between the US and Australia:

> The economic costs of comparable worth are likely to be enormous. Since Australia began its centralized wage-fixing system in 1913, its per capita income has fallen from highest in the world to 13th, 30 per cent behind the United States. Many economists think Australia's inflexible wage system explains much of this deterioration, and all the major Australian political parties now favor more decentralized, market-driven wages as a way to improve efficiency and growth. (Rhoads, 1993a, p. 41)

Even in 1980, the Equal Employment Advisory Council (the Orwellian organization funded by employers to support labour market deregulation) was maintaining that pay equity is incompatible with efforts to improve economic performance:

> Turning to the broader issues, what we actually face, as a latent and so far unrecognized element in this new proposal for wage regulation, is

yet another large-scale regulatory intervention into the private sector.... In addition, it has at last begun to be recognized that the overall productivity of labor and capital has been slowing in its annual gains for over a decade, and now, ominously, has turned negative. Unless this tendency can be turned around quickly and strongly, there can be no hope for the continued broad improvements in real per capita incomes, including real wages, that we have enjoyed for so long. In the presence of this very real threat to national well-being, therefore, productivity rather than controversial notions of wage justice should dominate our attention. (Hildebrand, 1980, pp. 104–5)

In the writings of these business lobbyists, pay equity, along with other forms of employment regulation, are depicted as barriers to competitiveness and labour market flexibility.

Thus, the assault on pay equity policies can be analysed as part of a larger movement towards labour market deregulation. Rosenberg (1991) contends that the drive for labour market flexibility takes three forms: wage flexibility, employment (numerical) flexibility and functional flexibility. The first two reassert the central role of supply and demand forces in external labour markets, signalling a return to nineteenth-century notions of free market equilibrium. Greater wage flexibility is pursued through labour market deregulation (such as implicitly or explicitly lowering minimum wage standards) and through concession bargaining. Employers' increased use of part-time, temporary and contingent workers, as well as subcontractors and homeworkers are all strategies to increase employment flexibility. Functional flexibility focuses on introducing flexibility within internal labour markets. This internal flexibility reduces the traditional power of workers in unionized core sectors through flexible job descriptions and assignments. Functional flexibility may also be accompanied by a reduction in career mobility within firms (Standing, 1989; Bakker, 1991).[4]

Viewing economic restructuring through the lens of gender analysis can redirect our attention to neglected dimensions of social and institutional transformation. Each of these three forms of flexibility is gendered. Wage flexibility undermines the family wage for male workers; more and more jobs pay a 'woman's' wage. Employment flexibility is frequently accomplished by increased use of part-time and temporary workers, largely women. Internal flexibility transforms working conditions in male-dominated, core industries to resemble women's secondary employment: vague (or no) job descriptions and few prospects for promotion. While much of the postwar economic expansion was founded upon industrial sectors where traditionally male, unionized, jobs predominated, economic restructuring has placed feminized jobs at the centre of postindustrial economies. This change has made pay equity directly contradictory to contemporary accumulation strategies based on deregulation and informalization of work. However, conservative resistance to pay equity is not grounded in economic considerations alone. Gender-based wage differentials are also the basis of a specific set of gender relations, a form of social relations that appears to be in transition.

## Defending the Nuclear Family: Pay Equity Meets Feminization

While political economists have devoted substantial attention to the political and economic institutional arrangements fostering 'long waves of accumulation', the linkages between gender relations and accumulation during specific economic regimes have been under-theorized.[5] Feminist research has recently turned to this issue, noting that gender relations, although relatively rigid in the short run, may be redefined during the political, social, and cultural upheaval that accompanies economic restructuring.[6] Several researchers have noted that the postwar economic order was constructed upon a specific set of gender relations. The relative prosperity of white male workers in core industries rested on the family wage ideology and women's unpaid household labour (Williams, 1994; O'Hara, 1995; Bakker, 1996b). Economic policy was predicated upon 'a gender order of a stable working class and nuclear family supported by a male breadwinner' (Bakker, 1996a, p. 7). Of course, many working-class families, especially within black and minority ethnic communities, were excluded from this idealized family structure. The interaction of gender, race and class leads to several models of coexisting gender relations, even in times of relative stability.

Feminization, together with deindustrialization, has undermined the ideal of the male breadwinner without establishing a clear replacement. Williams (1994, pp. 57–8) argues that this transition should be viewed not as a passive outcome of economic change, but as the result of women's own agency and struggles over gender relations. Criticizing standard accounts of economic restructuring, she notes that 'rarely is the power of explanation or the power of agency granted to gender, "race" or any social relation other than class' (p. 57). Thus, the emergence of new concepts of masculinity and femininity is a contentious terrain with an indeterminate outcome.

The discourse against pay equity exemplifies the contemporary tension and confusion over gender relations in transition. On the one hand, opponents put forth the traditional argument that women choose female-dominated jobs in order to balance work and family responsibilities.

Representing a functionalist view of the gender division of labour, women's responsibilities for reproductive labour are seen as natural. Lower wages are explained by crowding in female-dominated occupations – an excess supply of workers driving down wages – and intermittent labour force participation which generates less on-the-job experience. One writer asserts that 'family commitments and a variety of feminine traits affecting job preference may always leave women somewhat less mobile in the labour market than men' (Rabkin, 1984, p. 190). Labour market discrimination is discounted: 'Regardless of one's views of these traditions, they are factors that must be considered separate from discrimination by employers. For example, women as a group, to a greater extent than men, have traditionally assumed the primary role for child-raising responsibilities' (Williams and Kessler, 1984, p. 20). From this perspective, gender-based wage differentials merely reflect women's supply-side decisions to value family over career.

However, conservatives have not taken a consistent position on women's relationship to the labour market. Opponents of pay equity schemes also argue that younger women's priorities are changing and that they are increasingly breaking down barriers to higher-paid occupations (Berger, 1984; Paul, 1989; O'Neill 1994). This dualistic analysis enables pay equity's antagonists to pit groups of women against each other. For example, some opponents claim pay equity harms traditional nuclear families:

> the income redistributed by comparable worth theory would flow mainly to single women and to families without young children.... We doubt that a convincing case could be made that such a redistribution of real income would be beneficial to the nation as a whole. (Nelson, Opton, and Wilson 1980, p. 399)

The assumptions behind this analysis are that married women do not work and that single women do not need to earn a breadwinner's wage. This language draws on conservative political rhetoric, equating feminism with the interests of upper-class, unmarried career women. In fact, Paul, echoing the common pronouncement that any social policy that increases wages would create unemployment, depicts working-class women as the losers if pay equity were implemented:

> However, to women reentering the labor market after a marriage has broken up, to women just out of high school, to newly arrived immigrants, and to those with little skill, the freedom to take the clerical, factory, and sales jobs is the difference between having a chance to

better themselves or being condemned to dependency. Comparable worth, by artificially raising the wages of such jobs, would restrict the number of such positions and make the lot of the poorest and least skilled women that much worse. (Paul, 1989, p. 124)

Another opponent adds that 'comparable worth, if enacted, would benefit in the main the type of white-collar credentialed jobs in which women predominate. In turn, it would discriminate against that large category of manual and service jobs that are the only opportunity for making a living for a substantial portion of American women and men' (Berger, 1984, p. 71). In this discourse comparable worth and, by extension, feminism, is portrayed as 'one of the more aggressively elitist visions of modern life that has surfaced in recent decades' (Berger, 1984, p. 71), rather than as a movement grounded in the realities of working women's lives.

These attempts to fragment women's interests are indicative of a broader right-wing strategy in the United States. This cultural onslaught attempts to alienate working-class women – who have benefited least from occupational integration and positive action and who therefore most need pay equity policies – from identifying with feminism. Nevertheless, by ignoring the real importance of paid employment for both married and unmarried working-class women in female-dominated occupations, conservatives have provided a vacuum that progressive social policies can fill.

**Strategic Implications for Pay Equity**

Jenson (1996, p. 92) notes that 'it is only by understanding the extent to which a new set of gendered employment relations is at the heart of the restructured economies that we can begin to comprehend the restructuring, as well as any space available with it for generating equality.' The challenge is to resist imposition of the so-called US model of flexibility without harking back to the so-called good old days of postwar gender relations and the male breadwinner ideology. Pay equity attempts to extend the concept of a family-sustaining wage to female dominated occupations just as the family wage for men is disappearing, undermined by the deindustrialization process. Unfortunately this has generated resistance to pay equity among potential allies (Figart and Kahn, 1997) and it is still a low priority on many progressive agendas. Progressive strategies need to be reformulated to embrace gender and race analysis. Furthermore, economic issues need to be central to revitalizing the feminist movement in the United States, long preoccupied with single-issue politics over reproductive freedom (see Burk and Hartmann, 1996).

Our analysis of the discourse of pay equity's conservative opponents exemplifies many of the cultural preoccupations of US society in the 1990s. The relative weakness of the left has enabled pro-market ideologues to marginalize Keynesian economics and beliefs in the welfare state. Further, a cultural confusion over gender emanates from the Right. We believe the latter represents an opportunity for feminist and other social activists. In a sense, we need to present a counter-discourse, as part of an active movement for economic security.

With the recent change in leadership of the US labour movement, the prospects for bringing marginalized workers into the heart of a new labour strategy has improved. AFL-CIO President John Sweeney had re-committed US labour to organizing new members, especially in the service sector. A recent survey conducted by the AFL-CIO's Working Women's Department found that 94 per cent of working women cited pay equity as their top concern.

The new language of the need for a living wage is evidence of emerging efforts to raise wages, including those for predominantly female and disproportionately minority jobs and occupations. There are three developments in the United States which can be construed as aspects of this living wage movement. First, in lobbying for passage of a minimum wage increase, advocates point out that the real value of the minimum wage has declined to well below the level needed to support a family (Geoghegan, 1996; Rubin et al., 1996). Since women comprise 60 per cent of minimum wage workers, maintaining the real value of the legislated wage floor is one way of addressing women's over-representation in low-paid jobs (Figart and Lapidus, 1995). Second, progressive critiques of recent welfare reform initiatives that mandate paid employment note that work paying poverty-level wages cannot substitute for public assistance; anti-poverty policies must include labour market reforms such as pay equity and increasing the minimum wage (Rutten, 1991; Figart and Lapidus, 1995; Kuttner, 1995). Finally, over 30 US municipalities have considered legislation requiring companies receiving corporate welfare (for example tax rebates and supplier contracts) to pay workers a living wage well above the federal minimum. Such initiatives have already been adopted by Baltimore (Maryland) and Santa Clara County (California) (Garza, 1996; Tyson, 1996; Uchitelle, 1996).

These efforts help to degender the concept of the family wage as a movement to ensure that all workers can support their families, embracing a diversity of family forms. In the context of changes in the economy and family structure, the new living wage movement provides a potent antidote to the opponents of pay equity.

NOTES

1.  This chapter was written before the electoral victory of New Labour in Britain in May 1997. The policies pursued by the current government have, however, been marked by continuity with those of the previous Conservative government.
2.  Comparable worth is the equivalent US term for the European 'equal value'. Comparable worth implies that women and men are paid at the same rate not merely for identical work, but for work of comparable (or equal) value which can include comparability across different occupations.
3.  A central project of progressive economists in the US has been the assertion that state planning and intervention can play a positive role in reversing declining profitability (see, for example, Bowles, Gordon, and Weisskopf, 1989; Harrison and Bluestone, 1990; and Blecker, 1994).
4.  Curry (1992) makes a similar contrast between employment flexibility in external labour markets and work flexibility within the firm and production process. Brodsky (1994) suggests a shift in emphasis from the 1980s to the 1990s, from flexibility in employment to flexibility in work.
5.  A number of frameworks have been proposed to analyse the process of economic restructuring, most prominently social structures of accumulation (SSA) and regulation theory. For summaries and comparisons of these two models, see Kotz (1998); O'Hara (1994).
6.  For an historical perspective on gender and economic restructuring, see Mutari (1996).

REFERENCES

Albelda, R. and Tilly, C., 'Towards a broader vision: race, gender, and labor market segmentation in the social structure of accumulation framework', in D.M. Kotz, T. McDonough and M. Reich (eds), *Social Structures of Accumulation: The Political Economy of Growth and Crisis*. Cambridge: Cambridge University Press, 1994.

Appelbaum, E., 'New work systems in the new world order', in L. Mishel and J. Schmitt (eds), *Beware the US Model: Jobs and Wages in a Deregulated Economy*. Washington, DC: Economic Policy Institute, 1995.

Armstrong, P., 'The feminization of the labour force: harmonizing down in a global economy', in I. Bakker (ed.), *Rethinking Restructuring: Gender and Change in Canada*. Toronto: University of Toronto Press, 1996.

Badgett, M.V. and Williams, R.M., 'The changing contours of discrimination: race, gender, and structural economic change', in M.A. Bernstein and D.E. Adler (eds), *Understanding American Economic Decline*. Cambridge: Cambridge University Press, 1994.

Bakker, I., 'Pay equity and economic restructuring: the polarization of policy?', in J. Fudge and P. McDermott (eds), *Just Wages: a Feminist Assessment of Pay Equity*. Toronto: University of Toronto Press, 1991.

Bakker, I., 'Introduction: the gendered foundations of restructuring in Canada', in I. Bakker (ed.), *Rethinking Restructuring: Gender and Change in Canada*. Toronto: University of Toronto Press, 1996a.

Bakker, I., *Rethinking Restructuring: Gender and Change in Canada*. Toronto: University of Toronto Press, 1996b.

Berger, B., 'Comparable worth at odds with American realities', in US Commission on Civil Rights (ed.), *Comparable Worth: Issue for the 80's*. Washington, DC, 1984.

Bergmann, B.R., 'What the common economic arguments against comparable worth are worth', *Journal of Social Issues* 45 (Fall 1989) 67–80.

Bergren, O.V., 'A business viewpoint on comparable worth', in P. Schlafly (ed.), *Equal Pay for Unequal Work*. Washington, DC: Eagle Forum Education & Legal Defense Fund, 1984.

Blecker, R.A., 'The new economic stagnation and the contradictions of economic policy making', in M.A. Bernstein and D.E. Adler (eds), *Understanding American Economic Decline*. Cambridge: Cambridge University Press, 1994.

Block, F., *Postindustrial Possibilities: a Critique of Economic Discourse*. Berkeley: University of California Press, 1990.

Bowles, S., Gordon, D.M. and Weisskopf, T.E., 'Business ascendancy and economic impasse: a structural retrospective on conservative economics', *Journal of Economic Perspectives* 3 (Winter 1989) 107–34.

Brodsky, M.M., 'Labor market flexibility: a changing international perspective', *Monthly Labor Review* 117 (November 1994) 53–60.

Brown, D., 'An institutionalist look at postmodernism', *Journal of Economic Issues* 25 (December 1991) 1089–104.

Burk, M. and Hartmann, H., 'Beyond the gender gap', *The Nation* 262 (10 June 1996) 18–21.

Çağatay, N. and Özler, S., 'Feminization of the labor force: the effects of long-term development and structural adjustment', *World Development* 23(11) (1995) 1883–94.

Cohen, M.G., 'The implications of economic restructuring for women: the Canadian situation', in I. Bakker (ed.), *The Strategic Silence: Gender and Economic Policy*. London: Zed Books, 1994.

Curry, J., 'The flexibility fetish: a review essay on flexible specialization', *Capital and Class* 50 (1992) 99–125.

Faux, J., Preface, in L. Mishel and J. Schmitt, *Beware the U.S. Model: Jobs and Wages in a Deregulated Economy*. Washington, DC: Economic Policy Institute, 1995a, ix–xii.

Faux, J., 'Social democracy and the global marketplace', in L. Mishel and J. Schmitt (eds), *Beware the U.S. Model: Jobs and Wages in a Deregulated Economy*. Washington, DC: Economic Policy Institute, 1995b, 3–14.

Figart, D.M. and Kahn, P., *Contesting the Market: Pay Equity and the Politics of Economic Restructuring*. Detroit: Wayne State University Press, 1997.

Figart, D.M. and Lapidus, J., 'A gender analysis of US labor market policies for the working poor', *Feminist Economics* 1(3) (1995) 60–81.

Fraser, N. and Gordon, L., 'A genealogy of *dependency*: tracing a keyword of the US welfare state', *Signs: Journal of Women in Culture and Society* 19 (Winter 1994) 309–36.

Garza, M.M., 'Wage warriors', *Chicago Tribune* (9 May 1996).

Geoghegan, T., 'The state of the worker', *New York Times* (25 January 1996).

Greenwood, D., 'The institutional inadequacy of the free market in determining comparable worth', *Journal of Economic Issues* 18 (June 1984) 457–64.

Harrison, B. and Bluestone, B., 'Wage polarisation in the US and the "flexibility" debate', *Cambridge Journal of Economics* 14 (September 1990) 351–73.

Hildebrand, G., 'The market system', in E.R. Livernash (ed.), *Comparable Worth: Issues and Alternatives.* Washington, DC: Equal Employment Advisory Council, 1980.

Howell, C., 'The dilemmas of post-Fordism: socialists, flexibility, and labor market deregulation in France', *Politics & Society* 20 (March 1992) 71–99.

Jenson, J., 'Part-time employment and women: a range of strategies', in I. Bakker (ed.) *Rethinking Restructuring: Gender and Change in Canada.* Toronto: University of Toronto Press, 1996.

Jenson, J., Hagen, E. and Reddy, C., *Feminization of the Labor Force.* Oxford: Oxford University Press, 1988.

Kotz, D.M., 'The regulation theory and the social structure of accumulation approach', in D.M. Kotz, T. McDonough and M. Reich, *Social Structures of Accumulation: the Political Economy of Growth and Crisis.* Cambridge: Cambridge University Press, 1994.

Kuttner, R., 'A decent minimum wage', *Washington Post* (29 January 1995).

Mitter, S., *Common Fate, Common Bond: Women in the Global Economy.* London: Pluto Press, 1986.

Mitter, S., 'On organising women in casualised work: a global overview', in S. Rowbotham and S. Mitter (eds), *Dignity and Daily Bread.* London: Routledge, 1994.

Mutari, E., 'Women's employment patterns during the inter-war period: a comparison of two states', *Feminist Economics* 2 (2, Summer 1996) 107–27.

Nelson, B.A., Opton, Jr, E.M. and Wilson, T.E., 'Wage discrimination and Title VII in the 1980s: the case against comparable worth', *Employee Relations Law Journal* 6(3) (1980) 380–405.

O'Hara, P.A., 'An institutionalist review of long wave theories: Schumpeterian innovation, modes of regulation, and social structures of accumulation', *Journal of Economic Issues* 28 (June 1994) 489–500.

O'Hara, P.A., 'Household labor, the family, and macroeconomic instability in the United States: 1940s–1990s', *Review of Social Economy* 53 (Spring 1995) 89–120.

O'Neill, J., 'An argument against comparable worth', in US Commission on Civil Rights (ed.), *Comparable Worth: Issues for the 80's.* Washington, DC., 1984a.

O'Neill, J., 'The "comparable worth" trap', in P. Schlafly (ed.), *Equal pay for UNequal Work.* Washington, DC: Eagle Forum Education & Legal Defense Fund, 1984b.

O'Neill, J.E., 'The shrinking pay gap', *The Wall Street Journal* (7 October 1994) A10.

Paul, E.F., *Equity and Gender: the Comparable Worth Debate*, New Brunswick: Transaction Publishers, 1989.

Peterson, J., 'The challenge of comparable worth: an institutionalist view', *Journal of Economic Issues* 24 (June 1990) 605–12.

Peterson, J., 'Public policy and the economic status of women in the United States', *Journal of Economic Issues* 26 (June 1992) 441–8.

Rabkin, J., 'Comparable worth as civil rights policy: potentials for disaster', in US Commission on Civil Rights (ed.), *Comparable Worth: Issue for the 80's.* Washington, DC, 1984.

Rhoads, S.E., 'Pay equity won't go away', *Across the Board* (July/August 1993a) 37–41.

Rhoads, S.E., 'Would decentralized comparable worth work?' the case of the United Kingdom', *Regulation: The Cato Review of Business and Government* No. 3 (1993b) 65–70.

Rosenberg, S., 'From segmentation to flexibility: a selective survey', *Review of Radical Political Economics* 23 (Spring & Summer 1991) 71–9.

Rubin, R.E., Brown, R., Reich, R.B., Stiglitz, J.E. and D'Andrea Tyson, L., 'What's a minimum wage job worth? Up to a living wage', *Wall Street Journal* (1 April 1996).

Rutten, T., 'Inner cities in need of living wage', *Los Angeles Times* (2 August 1991).

Snow, E., 'Comparable worth or pay equity?', *The Washington Times* (2 August 1985).

Standing, G., 'Global feminization through flexible labor', *World Development* 17 (July 1989) 1077–95.

Steinberg, R., 'The comparable worth debate', *New Politics* 1 (Spring 1986) 108–26.

Tyson, J.L., ' "Living wage" drive accelerates in cities', *Christian Science Monitor* (10 April 1996).

Uchitelle, L., 'Some cities pressuring employers to raise wages of working poor', *New York Times* (9 April 1996).

Williams, F., 'Social relations, welfare, and the post-Fordism debate', in R. Burrows and B. Loader (eds), *Towards a Post-Fordist Welfare State?* London: Routledge, 1994.

Williams, R.E. and Kessler, L.L., *A Closer Look at Comparable Worth,* Washington, DC: National Foundation for the Study of Employment Policy, 1984.

# 4 Pay Equity: Hard Work Down Under

Martha Coleman

## INTRODUCTION: PAY SETTLEMENT AND EQUITY

In 1893 New Zealand led the world in giving women the vote. In 1894 the Industrial Conciliation and Arbitration Act (IC&A Act) set the basis for an extensive collective system of employment regulation and centralized bargaining. Today, New Zealand is a leader of a different kind: according to the Organization for Economic Co-operation and Development it now has the most deregulated labour market of any member country (OECD, 1993, p. 9). This development is directly linked to the Employment Contracts Act 1991 (ECA), which led to a complete deregulation of industrial relations. Interestingly, given their antithetical nature, both Acts were justified, at least in part, as a means of promoting women's equality. The 1894 Act was partly inspired by the 1890 Royal Commission on sweated labour (Brosnan, Smith and Walsh, 1990, p. 27) which found that 'freedom of contract', the principle governing employment relationships at that time, had resulted in the exploitation of many workers, especially female workers (Hammond and Harbridge, 1993, p. 15).

When the government enacted the ECA almost 100 years later it argued that deregulation of contracts would lead to greater equality for women, especially in relation to pay. Far from this optimistic scenario being realized, developments since 1991 suggest instead a return to the conditions of a hundred years ago. This chapter will begin by providing an overview of the system for establishing collective awards prior to 1991. The changes brought in with the ECA and their impact on women's labour market situation will be discussed in the following section. The chapter will end by suggesting a way forward for the promotion of pay equity in New Zealand in the new deregulated climate.

## PAY SETTLEMENT BEFORE 1991

The 1894 Act, and the variations which followed it, established a system of achieving occupational and industrial collective agreements called *awards*. Usually negotiated at a national level and on a centralized basis between union and employer representatives, these awards set minimum rates of pay and conditions of employment. The agreed rates and conditions would then extend, by the operation of 'blanket coverage', to all workers in the occupation and industry as defined by the coverage clause of the award. All employers and workers in the defined industry or occupation would be as legally bound by the award as if they had been parties to the negotiations themselves, thereby reducing competition between firms over wages. In addition to award specific settlements, from time to time the Arbitration Court issued standard wage pronouncements and general orders which were designed to set universal minimum wage rates and increases across all sectors.

An extensive system of pay relativities developed between wages applying in different occupations, while the ability to seek binding arbitration of unresolved issues meant that these relativities could be maintained, even by industrially weak groups of workers. Relativities also underscored pay rises for public servants. From 1948 comparisons with the private sector to establish 'fair' relativity provided the basis for general adjustments in state pay levels.

While the effects of this relativities system were still very much in evidence by 1991, when the Employment Contracts Act was passed, the system itself was already under threat. The process of labour market deregulation completed by the ECA started under the Labour government in the mid-1980s. Private sector workers lost the right to arbitration in 1984, although it was not until the late 1980s that this started to bite as unions experienced difficulties in settling national awards without conceding worsening of conditions. The Labour government also introduced major changes in the public sector. The State Sector Act 1988 largely removed the differences between employment in the public and private sectors: wage bargaining became decentralized, with chief executives of government ministries and departments becoming the employers of their staff, and the concept of fairness relative to the private sector was no longer an institutionalized feature of public sector pay fixing. Despite these changes, however, reasonably high levels of regulation were maintained through the continued existence and operation of national bargaining.

Not only was the system of wage bargaining highly regulated but so too was the operation of trade unions, particularly in the private sector. Private sector unions were able to register and, having done so, were required to conform to certain statutory conditions relating to their management and finances. In return this gave them exclusive rights to bargain for those workers covered by the union's membership rules. These monopoly bargaining rights were protected by the law which stated that no union could seek to negotiate for workers who were already covered by the membership rule of another union. The ability to have a union member-ship clause inserted into collective agreements also meant that compulsory unionism was the norm in the private sector.

Alongside centralization, however, fragmentation of membership in the unions organized mainly on an occupational or craft basis was created. A description of its own union, contained in New Zealand Clerical Workers Association's (NZCA) submissions to a government-appointed working party (NZCA, 1988), illustrates this effect. The five nationally federated clerical unions together negotiated 22 national multi-employer awards. Each award contained a provision requiring those workers cov-ered by the award to belong to the union, giving the unions a combined membership of 35,000. The average number of members per employer was, however, very low: only 2 per cent employed more than 20 cleri-cal workers, and one third of all clerical union members worked for employers who employed fewer than five members. An analysis by work-site demonstrated even more clearly how dispersed the unions' members were. Nearly half were the sole clerical union member on site, and over 80 per cent worked with only three other union members. But while a fragmented membership based on occupational lines weakened its indus-trial strength, a membership of low-paid office workers, nearly all of whom were women, ensured the union was committed politically and – within its capabilities – industrially, to advancing the interests of women in employment.

## Pay Equity and the Award System

The opposition National Party went into the election in 1990 stating that its 'employment equity proposals will achieve pay equity' (National Party, 1990). The party argued that labour market regulation, especially as epito-mized by the award system, was bad news for women because it limited employment opportunities and consequently pay.

Historically, there is some truth in these arguments. Early awards did exclude women from certain occupations, or from certain jobs within occupations (Iversen, 1987; Nolan, 1997). The 1919 Wellington Bakers award, for example, allowed women to be employed in a bakehouse to break eggs, clean pattypans and fruit and paper cakehoops but not to man-ufacture any goods or do any hotplate work. But by 1990 such overt discrimination was long gone and awards were no longer formal barriers to the employment of women in any job.

Centralized wage fixing did, however, continue to play a contradictory role in respect of women's pay. The cost of living ruling by the Arbitration Court in 1922 was the first formal articulation of the family wage in relation to men's wages. Marriage, the Court declared, was essential if men were to lead normal well-balanced lives and attain a reasonable degree of self-development; to deny men a family wage was to violate their personal dignity (Arbitration Court, 1922). The Court adhered to the family wage until 1954, refusing to implement equal pay in awards or in its standard wage pronouncements (Woods, 1963; Nolan, 1997). While the gender differential in awards did start to close slowly (Nolan, 1997), it was left to legislation (in 1960 for the state sector and the 1972 Equal Pay Act (EPA) for the private sector) formally to require equality in pay for men and women performing the same work.

The legislation eliminated specifically female rates within awards. However, the relativities between occupations covered by different awards remained unchanged in many cases as relativities were hard to break down, especially for the industrially weak amongst whom women predominated. Thus the system still offered little real opportunity for revaluing women's work. This can be seen in the case brought by the New Zealand Clerical Workers Association in 1986 under the EPA where their submissions argued for a restoration rather than a redefinition of existing relativities (NZCA, 1986).

For many years before the Equal Pay Act male clerical workers were paid 99.38 per cent of the rate for an unindentured carpenter. During the implementation period of the Act, this same relationship to a carpenter existed for a Grade 3 clerical worker, such as an experienced typist or an accounts clerk. In turn, the rate for the carpenter had a prescribed relativity to a range of other 'male' trade rates. Over time, most male trade groups received additional increases while clerical workers did not. With arbitration no longer available the union sought a remedy by means of the EPA. Even so, the basis of the case was primarily one of relativity, not of equal work value. The case was lost, the Court holding that it lacked the jurisdiction to amend an award once it had been through the equal pay implementation process unless the employer was seeking to reintroduce expressly female rates.[1] But while the relativity system may have been something of a straitjacket, it also offered valuable protections (Hill and Du Plessis, 1993) as subsequent experience under the ECA shows.

Recognition of the gender inequalities embedded in the award system finally led to the Employment Equity Act 1990. Passed in the final weeks of the Labour government the Act provided for the implementation of pay equity and equal employment opportunities. The pay equity provisions dovetailed into the collective bargaining regime. They allowed unions or groups of 20 women, who were part of an occupational group or covered by a work or position description in a collective agreement, to request a pay equity assessment by naming two male comparators. The male comparators did not need to be in the same employment. Where practicable, however, one comparator was to come from the same industry as some or all of the women, and have broadly similar skills, effort and responsibility and work under broadly similar conditions. The other could be chosen from any industry or occupational group provided he too had similar skills, and so on. The pay equity comparison would be carried out by a Commissioner for Employment Equity and the outcome available for use in collective bargaining. Final offer arbitration was available if the parties could not agree on how this was to be incorporated into the collective agreement. A small number of claims were lodged under the 1990 Act, but since it was repealed within a few weeks of the National Government taking office no assessments were made.

## THE EMPLOYMENT CONTRACTS ACT 1991

The repeal of the Employment Equity Act represented a lost opportunity for greater equity in the labour market. In contrast, the changes brought about by the 1991 Employment Contracts Act were immediate. The whole system of regulation through national occupational and industry awards and union registration which had been in effect for nearly one hundred years was swept aside. The ECA is premised on the basis that the market, not the state, should regulate employment relationships. The stated objective of the Act is the promotion of an efficient labour market, to be achieved through three central principles: freedom of association, freedom of representation and freedom of contract. According to Jane Kelsey (1997a, p. 182), a leading critic of the restructuring of the New Zealand economy, the objective expressed in the Act is something of a euphemism for the real aims: to force down wages and break the unions.

Although the ECA gives workers the right to associate with other workers for the purpose of advancing collective employment interests, trade unions as such are not specifically mentioned. Undue influence by employers over a worker's decision to join a union (or other association) is, however, made unlawful. The Act also proscribes any attempt to give preference to any worker, either in terms of any offer of work or conditions of employment, on the basis of their membership (or non-membership) of any union.

While workers have the right to freedom of association under the ECA, there is no concomitant right to collective bargaining. The separation of these concepts is reflected in the structure of the Act, with freedom of association and bargaining provisions situated in different sections. The Act gives workers the right to appoint bargaining agents to represent them in negotiations. These bargaining agents need not be a trade union, although in practice most are. Even where workers are members of unions, they must separately authorize the union to act for them in negotiations. Employers are required to recognize authorized bargaining agents, but exactly what 'recognition' means has been the subject of ongoing litigation which has made clear that recognition does not involve an obligation to bargain.

By making the issue of whether workers will be covered by individual or collective employment contracts a matter for negotiation between employer and employee, the ECA gives an employer the right to refuse to bargain collectively. The number and mix of contracts, including whether contracts will apply to more than one employer, is also a matter for negotiation. There is a right to strike (and lock out) in support of issues in the contract which are contended between the employer and the workers concerned and, in line with the principle of freedom of contract, no formal limits have been placed on what issues can be the subject of negotiation. There are, however, limits on the right to strike. Where workers are covered by a collective contract, no strike can take place until after its expiry. Striking over personal grievances is prohibited, as are strikes over the issue of whether a collective contract will bind more than one employer.

The only other real limitation on employers' freedom is the establishment of a code of minimum conditions. In addition to access to the personal grievance provisions under the ECA and to the anti-discrimination provisions in the Human Rights Act 1993, the code provides all workers with the right, after six months' service, to five days' leave to be used in cases of sickness, bereavement or family illness or emergency. It also includes a minimum wage which in March 1997 was $7.00 per hour for workers over 20, and $4.20 per hour for 16–19 year olds. All workers are entitled to paid holidays and, for those with 12 months' service who work at least 10 hours per week, also a right to one year's unpaid parental leave.

**The ECA and the Courts**

Since the abolition of the bargaining procedures of the award system the Employment Court and Court of Appeal have played an important role in determining the scope of the Employment Contracts Act.

Initial decisions by the Employment Court in relation to the Act's bargaining provisions left employers free to undermine both union representation and collective bargaining. Within three months of the ECA taking effect, *Adams* v *Alliance Textiles (NZ) Ltd* ([1992] 1 ERNZ, p. 982) came before the Employment Court. Alliance Textiles wanted to worsen significantly existing conditions and to reduce or eliminate union presence and organization on their sites. The company used a variety of tactics to persuade individual workers to sign up to a new contract. Those who did not sign were locked out.

The case went to court with the union arguing that both the contract and the company's tactics were harsh and oppressive. It also argued that by refusing to negotiate with the union, the company was unduly influencing workers in their decision whether or not to have union representation. The Employment Court disagreed. It held that since the Act was quite specific as to what conduct was prohibited, the Court was not justified in importing into the legislation a requirement for employers to remain neutral and adopt a 'hands off' stance when their vital interests were affected.

This scope allowed to employers during contract negotiations was somewhat curtailed, however, when on appeal the President of the Court, Justice Cooke, held that going behind the back of the union did not seem consistent with recognizing its authority (*Eketone* v *Alliance Textiles (NZ) Ltd* [1993] 2 ERNZ 783, 787). Nevertheless, in more recent decisions the Court of Appeal has reverted towards the position expressed by the Employment Court in *Adams*. This shift is apparent in the decision of the majority of the Court of Appeal in *New Zealand Fire Service Commission* v *Ivamy* ([1996] 1 ERNZ 85) where an employer's freedom of expression was accorded primacy over workers' rights to union representation and collective bargaining, a decision which led Judge Thomas to conclude in his dissent that collective bargaining was now largely vitiated (ibid., pp. 124–5).

Another example of the Employment Court's passivity in the early bargaining cases under the ECA occurred over the issue of partial lockouts in *Paul* v *NZ Society for the Intellectually Handicapped (IHC)* ([1992] 1 ERNZ 65). The IHC's negotiations with its staff for a new collective employment contract had become deadlocked. The IHC wanted to reduce wage costs and sought to achieve this by cutting a range of allowances. In the case of the applicant, this meant a wage cut of $10,000 per year. When the IHC could not get agreement from the workers for this they withdrew the allowances while still requiring them to perform the work itself. The Court held that withdrawal of the allowances constituted a partial lockout and, just as workers can engage in a partial strike, so too an employer can partially lock out employees.

The impact of this decision was immediate, widespread and profound (Harbridge and Kiely, 1996, p. 451; Horn et al., 62.07). Employers wanting to eliminate allowance payments such as premium rates for working overtime or unsocial hours, would usually offer a small pay rise in return. If the workers refused, they were simply locked out, or threatened with a lockout, of the allowances but without the pay rise. Thus the employer had all the advantages of a lockout without any of the economic loss. It was not until another partial lockout case, *Witehira* v *Presbyterian Support Services* ([1994] 1 ERNZ 578), came before the Employment Court some two years later, that this tactic was proscribed.

In *Witehira* the Court said its own earlier decision in *IHC* was not good law and should not be followed. A partial lockout, the Court now held, was inconsistent with the doctrine that no contract may contain any element of servility. Goddard CJ stated:

It is untenable that employees can be required to work either for nothing, or for some amount that is entirely at their employer's whim, for then the employees are no longer free but become the serfs of the employer ....

Indeed, to uphold the defendant's position as valid would consign employees in New Zealand to a position scarcely superior to serfdom for their employer could at any time after the expiry of a collective employment contract reduce their pay and conditions to any level it saw fit under the guise of applying pressure to secure acceptance of future terms of employment or compliance with the employer's other demands made in negotiations. (ibid., pp. 601–2)

Although the initial decision in both the *Adams* and *IHC* cases were later modified, by the time this occurred the whole climate of industrial relations had already undergone irreversible change (Whatman et al., 1994). The Employment Court's early interpretation of the ECA fundamentally affected both the incidence of trade union membership and collective bargaining. In less than two years union density fell by nearly one third, from 41.5 per cent in May 1991 to 28.8 per cent in December 1992 (Harbridge, Hince and Honeybone, 1995, p. 2). The coverage of collective bargaining similarly declined. In May 1991, when the ECA came into effect, 59 per cent of employees were covered by multi-employer collective contracts. This had fallen to 8 per cent by August 1992. Over the same period the number of employees covered by individual employment contracts increased from 13 per cent to 35 per cent (Armitage and Dunbar, 1993).

THE ECA, WOMEN WORKERS AND PAY EQUITY

Some 18 months after the Act was passed, the Minister of Women's Affairs stated that the ECA had 'done more towards providing equity for working women than any other development for a long time' (Skiffington, 1996, p. 42). The evidence so far suggests the exact opposite. While generally disadvantageous for all workers, the ECA has had a disproportionately adverse affect on women (Hammond and Harbridge, 1997; Harbridge and Street, 1995; Whatman et al., 1994; Hector et al., 1993; Hill and Du Plessis, 1993).

The larger private sector unions whose membership was overwhelmingly female suffered dramatic declines in membership almost immediately after the introduction of the ECA. Unions covering cleaners and retail workers reported a 20 per cent decline, while clerical unions reportedly lost 45 per cent of members (Hill and Du Plessis, 1993). Within eight months of the Act, the New Zealand Clerical Workers Union voluntarily wound up following an assessment that the union, with its fragmented membership, was not viable in the enterprise bargaining environment created by the ECA. In doing this the union hoped that an orderly transfer of members to more industrially based unions would offer the best chance of worksites remaining unionized (Franks, 1994). But while some groups did join other unions, the majority of women in small worksites were left in the cold with no union representation (Hill and Du Plessis, 1993). The loss of the clerical union was also a real blow to the interests of employed women generally since the union had in the 1980s led the campaign for pay equity industrially, legally and politically (Cook, 1994; Hill and Du Plessis, 1993).

The longer-term decline was just as dramatic. In the four years between December 1991 and December 1995 union membership in the retail, wholesale, café, restaurant and accommodation sector declined by 73 per cent (Crawford et al., 1996). Declining rates of unionization were not limited to this sector. In May 1991, when the ECA was introduced, union density stood at 41.5 per cent. By December 1995 it had nearly halved, falling to 21.7 per cent (Crawford et al., 1996).

However, despite the massive de-unionization of women in private service sector jobs women still make up nearly half of all union members (Crawford et al., 1996). This is a result of much higher levels of unionization in the public sector. In the same four-year period union density in this sector declined by a comparatively moderate 17 per cent (Crawford et al., 1996) and over half of all women workers in the public and community services sector remain covered by collective contracts (Hammond and Harbridge, 1997). The higher levels of both unionization and coverage by collective contracts have not, however, resulted in a narrower pay gap. Women in central government earn on average only 74.3 per cent of the hourly wage of their male counterparts compared to an hourly rate pay gap of 81.6 per cent in the workforce as a whole (Statistics New Zealand, 1998a). The wider pay gap in the public sector may be explained by the cutbacks in public expenditure combined with the new managerialism which has seen the virtual elimination of across-the-board pay rises for state employees in favour of individualized performance-based pay.

In the private sector, the impact of the decline in membership of female-intensive unions was highlighted in the results of a survey of 2,000 workers conducted on behalf of the government in 1993. This showed that women were less likely than men to be represented by a union in the negotiation of a new contract, with part-time and casual workers being even less likely to be represented. Around only one third of these workers were represented by a union, as compared to half of all workers generally (Ryan, 1994). The 1993 survey also reported that part-time and casual workers were less likely to have had negotiations over a new contract or indeed be covered by a formal contract. Three-quarters of all part-time workers are women, and part-time workers make up around 20 per cent of the employed workforce (Statistics New Zealand, 1998b). The survey also showed that while a majority of male workers, permanent employees and full-time staff reported an increase in take-home pay, an even larger proportion of casual and part-time workers had suffered a decrease.

Another study, carried out in the same year by the Service Workers Union, echoed these findings (Harbridge and Street, 1995). Respondents in this survey were mainly part-time workers covered by collective employment contracts, the large majority of whom were women. Only one third of all respondents reported an increase in hourly pay rates in the first two years of the ECA, while for 10 per cent hourly pay actually decreased. A quarter reported a reduction in overtime pay rates and 30 per cent stated that their overall take-home pay had declined. Harbridge and Street speculate that this figure may underestimate the true extent of reductions experienced since the respondents may not have been representative of the union's membership. On the whole the respondents were in an older age group (60 per cent were over 40 years of age) and 85 per cent had been in their jobs for more than two years. This is significant in the light of anecdotal evidence mentioned in the report, which suggested that younger workers who had been employed for shorter periods of time were the most likely to have experienced deteriorations in employment conditions (see also NDU, undated).

An analysis of over 3,000 collective employment contracts covering around 400,000 workers also points to the gendered effects of the ECA

(Hammond and Harbridge, 1997). This shows that men are significantly more likely than women to be employed on collective employment contracts including premium rates for working overtime or at non-standard times. With the exception of the finance sector, few contracts in predominantly female sectors contain such provisions. No workers covered by collective contracts in the restaurant, café and accommodation sector receive premium rates, and neither do 86 per cent of employees in retail or 61 per cent of public employees. On the other hand, premium rates are prevalent in industrial sectors where men are over-represented.

Hammond and Harbridge also found that women have consistently received smaller wage increases than men as a result of collective bargaining. This is a product, they claim, of the decentralization of bargaining and the removal of traditional relativities. The impact of these changes is reflected in their calculation of weighted minimum 'male' and 'female' rates within contracts. These are determined by taking the lowest rate in the contract and multiplying that by the proportion of women and men covered by that contract and then averaged across all contracts. This shows that the gender pay gap of weighted minimum rates within contracts increased from $8 per week in November 1992 to nearly $19 by December 1996.

Official statistics show that the gender pay gap has remained fairly static since the introduction of the ECA, with women earning around 81 per cent of men's hourly pay and 74 per cent of men's average weekly total earnings (Statistics New Zealand, 1998a). A study commissioned by the Ministry of Women's Affairs, however, predicts that the gender pay gap will *widen* slightly, reflecting the concentration of women in industries where the gender wage gap is widening and their under-representation in sectors with above average wage growth (New Zealand Institute of Economic Research, 1997).

The ECA has not brought a reduction in the gender pay gap, nor has it resulted in increased employment opportunities. Since the Act was passed women have become even more likely to work in predominantly female sectors and to be involuntarily working part-time (New Zealand Council of Trade Unions, 1996). The equity promised through labour market deregulation was, in the words of the secretary of the New Zealand Council of Trade Unions, nothing but a cruel hoax (Skiffington, 1996).


THE WAY FORWARD

While the government claimed that the ECA would be beneficial to women's equality, its repeal of the Employment Equity Act 1990 within a few weeks of taking office sent a clear message to employers that equity issues were, at least as far as the government was concerned, off the agenda. The difficulties in bargaining under the ECA, combined with the resource constraints for trade unions caused by a drastic decline in membership, have ensured they have not yet found their way back on.

The formation of the coalition government following the 1996 election briefly gave rise to hopes of an environment more sympathetic to equity issues. These hopes were short-lived. Despite the incorporation of a concept of fairness in wage bargaining into the coalition policy document, the government has not even paid lip-service to this commitment. Instead, it is clear that its real agenda is to remove employment issues further from the judiciary, and in particular from the Employment Court (Campbell, 1997; *The Dominion*, 1997).

Kelsey (1997b) argues that this reflects a desire to bring the judiciary to heel since it has not been captured by neoliberal ideology, at least not to the same extent as the executive arm of the state. A second more concrete motive is to eradicate any suggestion that there is something special, not to mention inherently unequal, about employment relationships. On the contrary, the government wants to ensure that employment contracts are treated no differently from other commercial agreements.

As neither the ECA nor government initiatives can be seen as a means of advancing pay equity, the focus has now returned to another piece of legislation, the Equal Pay Act 1972. Despite the general perception that the Act provided only equal pay for like work, there has been since its enactment a vigorous debate about whether or not the Act actually covers equal pay for work of equal value (Coleman, 1997). This debate appeared to have been laid to rest without reaching a conclusion when the Arbitration Court held that it lacked jurisdiction in the clerical union equal pay case.

More than ten years later that decision (and others taken by the Court under the Act) is facing a challenge. Ironically, one of the bases on which it is contended that the Equal Pay Act can be used to take forward pay equity claims is that the ECA ended the awards system. Accordingly, the 1986 decision is no longer a barrier for potential claimants. Other legislation favouring a fresh approach is the New Zealand Bill of Rights Act 1990 which requires courts, wherever possible, to interpret legislation consistently with the rights contained in the Act, including the right not to be discriminated against, directly or indirectly. Moreover, this requirement applies to legislation already in existence.[2] With the abolition of the awards system, the opportunity may be provided to argue that claims, not only under like work but also for broader pay equity, may be brought under the Bill of Rights Act.

Tempering that optimism, however, are the other limitations of the law which led the Clerical Union in 1986 to fight for fresh legislation rather than appeal the Court's decision on their equal pay case (Coleman, 1997). The Equal Pay Act 1972 was designed to deal primarily with the implementation of equal pay into awards as a one-off exercise. This means that much of it is now redundant and what is still extant may provide little more than a reactive complaints procedure, albeit one that allows group claims and claims relating to rates in collective contracts.

## CONCLUSION

The statistics which suggest that the gender pay gap has neither closed nor widened hide growing differentiation between women. The passing of the ECA together with the restructuring of the public sector may have been advantageous to some women, mainly those in professional and managerial jobs working full time. Women at the lower end of the pay scale in more casual and less professional jobs, however, have seen major deteriorations in their pay and conditions. While the old system arguably had some inequalities built in, it also provided minimum standards and protection to those least able to organize themselves. This support has now disappeared, leading to greater overall inequality.

The Equal Pay Act 1972 marked a recognition that it was unacceptable to sweep women workers under the carpet and leave them to have their pay determined by market forces (Commission of Inquiry, 1971). More than 25 years later women are once more pinning their hopes on that legislation to help resurrect the idea that pay discrimination is both undesirable and unlawful. This is, however, only a first step. Radical changes are needed to the current labour market framework if women are to have a real chance of equality with men.

## NOTES

1.  *NZ Clerical Administrative etc. IAOW* v *Farmers Trading Co & Ors* [1986] ACJ 203.
2.  *Ministry of Transport* v *Noort* [1992] 3 NZLR 260, 270; *Simpson* v *Attorney-General [Baigent's case]* [1994] 3 NZLR 667, 676.

# REFERENCES

Arbitration Court, *Further pronouncement of the Court re cost of living for period October 1921–March 1922*, New Zealand Awards Under the IC&A Act [1922] XXIII (1922) 333.

Armitage, C. and Dunbar, R., 'Labour market adjustment under the ECA', *New Zealand Journal of Industrial Relations* 18, 1 (1993) 94–112.

Brosnan, P., Smith, D. and Walsh P., *The Dynamics of New Zealand Industrial Relations*. Auckland: John Wiley, 1990.

Campbell, G., 'The Max factor – the new Labour Minister wants a tougher Employment Contracts Act', *New Zealand Listener* 158, 2974 (1997) 24–6.

Coleman, M., 'Equal Pay Act 1972: back to the future?', *Victoria University of Wellington Law Review* 27, 4 (1997) 517–53.

Commission of Inquiry, *Equal Pay in New Zealand – Report of the Commission of Inquiry*. Wellington: Government Printer, 1971.

Cook, M., *Just Wages – History of the Campaign for Pay Equity 1984–1993*. Wellington: Coalition for Equal Value Equal Pay, 1994.

Crawford, A., Harbridge, R. and Hince, K., 'Unions and union membership in New Zealand: Annual Review for 1995', *New Zealand Journal of Industrial Relations* 21, 2 (1996) 188–93.

Dominion, The, *Employment Court Role Questioned*. 9 June 1997.

*Employment Reports New Zealand (ERNZ)* 1992, 1.

Franks, P., 'The Employment Contracts Act and the demise of the New Zealand Clerical Workers Union', *The New Zealand Journal of History* 28, 2 (1994) 194–210.

Hammond, S. and Harbridge, R., 'The impact of the Employment Contracts Act on women at work', *New Zealand Journal of Industrial Relations* 18, 1 (1993) 15–30.

Hammond, S. and Harbridge, R., '*The Impact of Decentralized Bargaining on Women: Lessons for Europe from the Antipodes*', Paper presented at the Fifth International Industrial Relations Association European Regional Congress, Dublin, 26–29 August 1997.

Harbridge, R., Hince, K. and Honeybone, A., *Unions and Union Membership in New Zealand: Annual Review for 1994*, Working Paper 2/95, Victoria University of Wellington Industrial Relations Centre, Wellington, 1995.

Harbridge, R. and Kiely, P., 'Activism and passivism: the role of the judiciary in New Zealand's Employment Contracts Act', *Canadian Labour and Employment Law Journal* 3, 3&4 (1996) 437–60.

Harbridge, R. and Street, M., 'Labour market adjustment and women in the service sector', *New Zealand Journal of Industrial Relations* 20, 1 (1995) 23–34.

Hector, J., Henning, J. and Hubble, M., 'Industrial relations bargaining in the retail non-food sector: 1991–1992', *New Zealand Journal of Industrial Relations* 18, 3 (1993) 326–41.

Hill, L. and Du Plessis, R., 'Tracing the similarities, identifying the differences: women and the Employment Contracts Act', *New Zealand Journal of Industrial Relations* 18, 1 (1993) 31–43.

Horn, P., Bartlett, P., Muir, P., Toogood, C. and Wilson, R., *Employment Contracts*. Wellington: Brooker & Friend (various dates).

Iversen, S., 'Why women get paid less', *Broadsheet* Auckland, New Zealand, 146 (1987) 38–40.

Kelsey, J., *The New Zealand Experiment – a World Model for Structural Adjustment?* Auckland: Auckland University Press/Bridget Williams Books, 1997a.

Kelsey, J., 'Mad Max and the future of the ECA', *Labour Notes* March 1997 (1997b) 6–7.

National Distribution Union (NDU) *Shortchanged: Retail Workers and the ECA*, Wellington, undated.

National Party, *Breaking Down the Barriers*, Election Policy Document. Wellington: National Party, 1990.

New Zealand Clerical Workers Association (NZCA), *Submissions to the Arbitration Court on Equal Pay and the Equal Pay Act 1972*. Wellington: NZCA, 1986.

New Zealand Clerical Workers Association (NZCA), *Towards Employment Equity*. Wellington: NZCA, 1988.

New Zealand Council of Trade Unions (NZCTU), *The Contracts Act – Effects on Women*, Election Backgrounder no. 12, August 1996.

New Zealand Institute of Economic Research (NZIER), *Gender Wage Gap: Scenarios of the Gender Wage Gap*. Wellington: NZIER, 1997.

Nolan, M., *Breadwinning? Women and the New Zealand State, 1890–1980* (unpublished manuscript, 1997).

Organization for Economic Co-operation and Development, *OECD Economic Surveys 1992–1993: New Zealand*. Paris: OECD, 1993.

Ryan, R., *A Survey of Labour Market Adjustments under the ECA 1991: Gender Analysis of the Employee Survey*, Report to the National Advisory Committee on the Employment of Women. Wellington: NACEW, 1994.

Skiffington, L., 'Employment Contracts Act 1991: a cruel hoax?' *Employment Law Bulletin* 3 (1996) 42–5.

Statistics New Zealand, *Quarterly Employment Survey November 1997*. Wellington: Statistics New Zealand, 1998a.

Statistics New Zealand, *Household Labour Force Survey, December 1997*. Wellington: Statistics New Zealand, 1998b.

Whatman, R., Armitage, C. and Dunbar, R., 'Labour market adjustment under the Employment Contracts Act', *New Zealand Journal of Industrial Relations* 19, 1 (1994) 53–73.

Woods, N., *Industrial Conciliation and Arbitration in New Zealand*. Wellington: Government Printer, 1963.

# 5 Globalization, Feminization and Pay Inequalities in London and the UK

Irene Bruegel[1]

Gender relations in many newly industrializing countries are being restructured by the globalization of capital (Mitter, 1986; Nash and Fernandez-Kelly, 1983). Globalization is also restructuring employment patterns in the core economies of the West, but the gender dimensions of this restructuring are much less often discussed (Kofman and Youngs, 1996). This chapter examines two aspects of globalization and gender relations in Britain: the impact of globalization on the UK *gender order*; and the specific development of male/female pay relativities in London in the context of its development as a *global city*, a central node in the global command structure.

The amalgam of labour market, welfare state and family structures operate to construct nationally distinctive gender orders which lock women into 'women's work' in different ways in different economies (Bruegel and Perrons, 1995). Despite the integration of European economies and development of EU equal opportunity policies, the division of labour between men and women and the division of income between them reflects national patterns of development. Thus even within industrialized Western economies the proportion of household income earned by women ranges from 19 per cent in Spain, 22 per cent in Ireland and 25 per cent in the Netherlands to 36 per cent in the UK and over 40 per cent in Scandinavian countries (UNDP, 1995). Many of the differences in women's status between different advanced economies arise from distinct national institutional frameworks: national wage setting systems, the scale and scope of the public sector and systems of social security as well as explicit equal opportunities policies (Blau and Kahn, 1996). The gender order is an element of that institutional framework as well as an outcome of it.

The institutional framework of the national gender order allows for wide differences in the position of women in any given economy: differences of class, ethnic background and locality. In particular the 'place' of any locality within the global economy gives rise to local employment and household structures, which in turn influence gender relations and relativities.

While much of the literature on globalization has focused on homogenizing processes, globalization is also a force for differentiation between localities and groups of people. Global cities tend to offer better employment opportunities to women. For example, women earn 40 per cent of total income from employment in London, compared with a national average of 36 per cent of earned income going to women.[2] Global cities also display particularly large income inequalities between households, reflecting greater inequalities in earnings for both men and women.

This chapter attempts to put the British experience of changing gender pay relativities and the increasing inequality of income between women, into the general context of the globalization of the British economy.


## GLOBALIZATION AND THE UK LABOUR MARKET

Globalization, like Fordism or flexibilization, is a term that at one level appears to be no more than a new way of describing trends which have been apparent for many years. It became fashionable during the 1980s but has come under more critical scrutiny recently as the all-encompassing nature of processes of globalization have been questioned (Hirst and Thompson, 1996). The concept of globalization may be useful in pointing to the fact that we live in a capitalist world, with only a limited ability to affect our own lives. It is more frequently taken to signal the end of national policy, the point at which there is nothing for the nation state to do but bow to external market forces.

States' responses to the pressures of globalization have not, however, been uniform. Economic relations are always embedded in wider social relations, institutional structures and systems of regulation. The gender order reflects these and colours responses to perceived globalization pressures. One example is the current drive for flexibilization. As analyses of international trends in part-time work have shown, forms of flexibilization still differ between countries, reflecting gendered work patterns as well as bargaining frameworks (Rodgers and Rodgers, 1989; Bruegel and Hegewisch, 1994). It is therefore important, but not always easy, to avoid using a simple cause-and-effect model and to see globalization as a context which produces an array of possible gendered outcomes.

At the national level two main effects of globalization can be seen to have impacted on gender relations in the UK. First, the decline of manufacturing capacity and with it many traditional men's jobs and sites of trade union power. Increased global competition is certainly an element in the relocation of some of this production (Wood, 1994). Technical change has also drastically affected the skill requirements of the remaining jobs, though it is in competition with Western economies that British job losses have been particularly marked (Hutton, 1997). Skills may have been 'upgraded', but the change has devalued traditional male manual skills and sometimes led to a re-evaluation of traditionally female skills, particularly those associated with communication, sales, training and personnel management (Gallie, 1996). The growth of male unemployment relative to female since the late 1970s reflects the declining significance of traditional manual skills in the context of a sharp decline in the qualifications gap between men and women. According to the Labour Force Survey (LFS) women were 46 per cent of those seeking work in the late 1970s, but by 1992 this had fallen to 33 per cent. In 1995 women accounted for 35 per cent of job seekers. Trends in the sex composition of the registered unemployed are similar, but less dramatic.

The second way in which globalization has impacted on gender inequalities has been through deregulation. Labour market deregulation can be viewed as a response to globalization, an attempt to increase competitiveness at the cost of conditions of employment. It was not, nevertheless, the only possible response, but a specific policy choice. Labour market deregulation has taken a variety of forms: reduced workers rights, increased trade union regulation, privatization and moves from national to local and individual-level pay determination. These have had a variety of effects for different groups of workers (Bruegel and Perrons, 1998). In particular, deregulation has been seen to promote part-time working, and with it an increase in women's employment. More critically, deregulation has contributed to increasing pay inequalities within each sex group, that is, between men and between women. Many of the losers have been men, with the result that patterns of gender inequality across the pay spectrum have changed quite dramatically.

Both these aspects of globalization – deindustrialization and deregulation – impact strongly on the London economy. But there are other particularities which arise from the City of London's position in the global financial system. Metropolitan centres like London can be said to have become global cities with the global concentration of capital in transnational firms (King, 1989). Even if the firms themselves decentralize and disperse operations through a range of peripheral sites, they continue to operate through a small number of nodes in the global system. The impact of globalization on London has been heightened by the deregulation of the financial markets in 1986, itself a response to global competition. As a leading sector of the London economy, finance acts to funnel global market interests across the whole London economy, its employment and wage structures.

DEINDUSTRIALIZATION, DEREGULATION AND GENDER
INEQUALITIES

The globalization of capital has fuelled a set of policy responses in the UK
which, alongside deindustrialization, have had the effect of increasing pay
inequalities across the board. These have in turn impacted on inequalities
between men and women. Overall women's occupational status has
improved, reflecting the rising qualifications of women entering the labour
market. As a result the gender pay gap has narrowed, for full-time workers
at least. As Table 5.1 shows, the weekly pay of full-time women workers
reached 72 per cent of the male median in 1995, compared to just under
65 per cent in 1981. The table shows how the weekly income of the top
10 per cent of full-time men and women increased rapidly, with the gender
pay gap narrowing from 33 to 28 per cent of the male wage, as top-earning
women increased their average pay slightly more than the highest earning
men. The gender pay gap between the poorest paid full-time men and
women narrowed even more: from 33 to 22 per cent. This was entirely due
to the fact that the pay of the lowest 10 per cent of men fell relative to the
median man (from more than 65 to 56 per cent), since the pay of the lowest paid group of women also fell relative to the male median (from 44 to
43 per cent). Throughout this period the weekly pay of those part-time
women included in the New Earnings Survey (NES) just kept pace with
the median man. This disguises a relative decline in pay for part-time
women workers as a whole, since those below the national insurance
threshold, whose pay dropped most, are not included in NES figures.

  Amongst manual workers the weekly wage of the lowest paid men
has fallen to barely half that of the median man in the economy as a
whole, putting it just above the level of the poorest paid manual women.
The best paid group of manual men did no better than the average man in
the period. As a result, for manual work as a whole, but particularly for the
lowest paid, the gender pay gap narrowed sharply (Table 5.1). Much of the
decline in male manual workers' pay reflects deindustrialization associated with globalization. In London in particular, manufacturing offered
manual men relatively high pay, which was not much lower than that of
the non-manual labour force in the sector. Deindustrialization has affected
women as well as men, but its impact on overall pay levels and on disparities in pay is much greater for men than women, not least because only
15 per cent of women worked in manufacturing by 1985. The figure was
just 10 per cent in 1995, with only 7 per cent of women in manual manufacturing jobs, compared to one third of men. In general the spread of pay
between manual and non-manual workers is less in manufacturing than in

*Table 5.1*   Trends in gender pay differentials

Weekly pay relative to the male median according to position in own sex
distribution (all male median = 100)

|  | 1981 | 1995 |
|---|---|---|
| (ft) female median | 64.82 | 72.5 |
| gender wage gap* at median full-time | (35.1) | (27.5) |
| part-time female median | 30.38 | 31.44 |
| **All employees** |  |  |
| male top 10 per cent | 167.7 | 185.9 |
| female top 10 per cent | 111.80 | 133.20 |
| *gender wage gap at top 10 per cent* | (33.0) | (28.3) |
| male bottom 10 per cent | 65.60 | 56.30 |
| female bottom 10 per cent | 44.2 | 43.64 |
| *gender wage gap at lowest 10 per cent* | (32.6) | (22.5) |
| **Manual workers** |  |  |
| male top 10 per cent | 135.97 | 135.37 |
| female top 10 per cent | 81.03 | 119.14 |
| *gender wage gap at top 10 per cent* | (40.4) | (11.9) |
| male bottom 10 per cent | 62.92 | 51.64 |
| female bottom 10 per cent | 39.29 | 48.40 |
| *gender wage gap at lowest 10 per cent* | (37.5) | (6.27) |
| **Public sector employees** |  |  |
| male top 10 per cent | 171.78 | 176.02 |
| female top 10 per cent | 125.61 | 138.77 |
| *gender wage gap at top 10 per cent* | (26.9) | (21.2) |
| male bottom 10 per cent | 70.51 | 62.62 |
| female bottom 10 per cent | 50.75 | 54.05 |
| *gender wage gap at lowest 10 per cent* | (28.0) | (13.7) |

*Difference between male and female pay as a proportion of male pay.
*Source*: New Earnings Survey 1981, 1995.

other sectors (Gregg and Machin, 1994). The decline of manufacturing employment can therefore be seen to have contributed to the widening of male pay differentials.

Squeezes on public sector finance have fuelled changing pay relativities in the public sector. The earnings of the lowest paid male public sector workers fell relative to the average for men across the economy, while the highest paid public sector men just kept pace with average male pay. While male earnings disparities in the public sector therefore widened, the gender wage gap in the public sector narrowed at both ends. The gender wage gap for the poorest paid public sector workers narrowed mainly because low-paid male wage levels failed to hold up, while low-paid women in the public sector inched their pay up relative to the male median, but by nothing like the rate of improvement achieved by high paid women.

The expansion of self-employment (from 2 million in 1980 to 3.5 million by 1990) has also served to increase inequalities in earnings. It is known that the earnings of the self-employed are highly variable (Storey, 1994), but information on earnings by gender is still sparse, making it difficult to see how the rise in self-employment has impacted on gender relativities in income.

The narrowing of the gender wage gap in Britain in recent years does not mean that wage discrimination – in the sense of women earning less pay for work requiring broadly similar responsibilities and qualifications – has fallen. As Table 5.2 shows, even in 1995 comparing men and women in similar occupations and with similar qualifications, men earned a substantially higher hourly rate than comparable women. If anything, Harkness (1996) shows that wage discrimination has tended to increase, since

*Table 5.2*    Hourly net pay by type of worker: female as a proportion of male, UK, 1995

|  | Female pay | As proportion of male |
|---|---|---|
| All female employees | £ 4.50 | 82 |
| Female full-time | £ 4.60 | 87 |
| Female part-time (all) | £ 4.38 | 83 |
| Part-time (above NI) | £ 4.78 | 86 |
| Socio-economic Group |  |  |
| Employers and managers | £ 5.55 | 78 |
| Professional | £ 6.65 | 90 |
| Intermediate non-manual | £ 5.15 | 79 |
| Junior non-manual | £ 4.11 | 84 |
| Personal service | £ 3.90 | 71 |
| Skilled manual | £ 3.50 | 81 |
| Semi-skilled | £ 3.55 | 85 |
| Unskilled | £ 3.16 | 92 |
| Highest Qualification |  |  |
| Degree | £ 6.13 | 81 |
| Above university entrance level | £ 5.64 | 89 |
| Below university entrance level | £ 4.82 | 84 |
| Other qualifications | £ 3.96 | 76 |
| No qualifications | £ 3.66 | 80 |

*Source*: Labour Force Survey, 1995: unpublished data.

women's pay has not grown as fast as the improvement in their qualifications and occupational status would warrant.

Occupational trends have nevertheless helped to narrow the gap between men and women's pay. Overall both men and women, full- and part-time, have tended to move out of manual work towards professional and managerial jobs, but the shift has been proportionately greater for women. Elias and Gregory's analysis of occupational and pay trends in the 1980s (Figure 5.1) showed that occupations that were becoming more masculine (that is, those with a decreasing female share) were those that were falling down the pay hierarchy. One example is unskilled and semi-skilled industrial plant operatives, another is secretarial work. Jobs which women were entering faster than men (or leaving less fast), fall into two groups: occupations where men's wages were high and rising relative to other men, such as health professionals and corporate managers; and jobs where men's wages were relatively low and falling, such as personal service work. The growth of women's jobs in the first group outweighs that in the second, so the overall shift of women's employment relative to men's is disproportionately concentrated at the higher end of the pay hierarchy.

This point is clearer when we look only at those occupations in which women's employment share increased faster than average between 1981 and 1991 (Table 5.3). For occupations employing very few women even in 1991, this increase is statistically unreliable. Table 5.3 therefore excludes any 'feminizing' occupations in which fewer than 45,000 women were employed in 1991. Other 'feminizing' occupations are ranked according to the scale of the shift towards female employees. At the top is accountancy, an occupation in which the proportion of women more than doubled

| | | Occupations with relative male pay | |
| | | rising 1975–91 | falling 1975–91 |
|---|---|---|---|
| Occupations with female employment share | increasing 1981–90 | Corporate managers (2) Other professionals (5) Other associate professionals (3) Health professionals (1)* | Teachers (6) Clerical (19) Personal service (20) Science and engineering professionals (8) |
| | decreasing 1981–90 | | Secretarial (13) Industrial plant operatives (15) Other skilled trades (16) |

*Figures in parenthesis are the modal rank of gross male earnings 1975–91.

*Figure 5.1*   Change in sex ratios, 1981–90, and change in relative pay, UK, 1975–91

*Table 5.3*   Feminizing occupations, 1981–91*

| Ranked by rate of feminization | Proportion female | | Employment change–index | Female pay index | PT female growth rate |
|---|---|---|---|---|---|
| | 1981 | 1991 | 1981–91 | 1981 | 1981–91 |
| **Accountants, etc.** | 10.92 | 24.38 | *1.59* | 0.95 | 3.47 |
| **Personnel managers, etc.** | 29.17 | 57.07 | *1.31* | 0.95 | 4.51 |
| **Marketing managers, etc.** | 15.90 | 31.01 | *1.69* | 0.95 | 3.00 |
| Sales representatives/agents | 14.37 | 24.99 | 0.96 | 0.48 | 1.28 |
| **Teachers in higher education** | 26.13 | 42.92 | *1.79* | 0.88 | 3.58 |
| *Office managers* | 25.44 | 41.68 | *2.07* | 0.71 | 3.92 |
| **Vocational trainers, etc.** | 27.85 | 44.55 | *1.51* | 0.88 | 1.83 |
| *All other managers* | 31.26 | 45.94 | *1.84* | 0.71 | 2.75 |
| Supervisors: clerks, civil service | 49.90 | 64.98 | 1.06 | 0.60 | 2.77 |
| **Other prof. supporting management** | 44.85 | 56.85 | *1.81* | 0.95 | 1.92 |
| Managers: wholesale/retail distribution | 27.21 | 34.28 | 1.14 | 0.71 | 1.06 |
| Laboratory/ engineering technicians/etc. | 22.46 | 28.20 | 1.13 | 0.77 | 1.42 |
| *Ambulancemen, hospital orderlies* | 76.67 | 88.48 | *2.72* | 0.51 | 3.54 |
| Total (all occupations) | 41.75 | 46.82 | 1.12 | 0.67 | 1.27 |

*Those with above-average shift to women; excludes those employing under 45,000 women, 1991 employees only.
*Source*: Census of Population, 1981 and 1991.

between 1981 and 1991; at the bottom are occupations in which the proportion of women increased by one sixth – around the national average for all occupations. Hospital orderlies and laboratory technicians are examples of such moderately feminizing occupations. Many of these feminizing occupations were highly male-dominated in 1981; only one (hospital orderlies) was highly feminized. At the same time, a substantial majority of women remained in female dominated 'women's work'; it is still only at the edges that the boundaries of women's work are breaking down.

Feminizing occupations were among the fastest growing in the country during this period. These growth occupations are marked in italics in Table 5.3. Women, therefore, rarely stepped directly into men's shoes since few were entering areas of male employment decline. The two main examples of such substitution, sales representatives and clerical supervisors, are both areas of relatively poor pay.

On the whole, strongly feminizing occupations paid relatively well (the exceptions are hospital orderlies, office supervisors and sales representatives). Examples of feminizing occupations with above-average pay for women in 1981 (marked in bold in Table 5.3) include accountancy, personnel and marketing management. The women who entered these occupations during this period not only moved into fairly highly paid jobs, they also experienced a relatively fast increase in pay over the decade to 1991. By 1991 their pay was 12 per cent above the average male earnings across the economy as a whole, whereas in 1981 it had been no more than 95 per cent of the equivalent male figure.

The tendency for women's employment to grow faster in occupations offering women better pay persisted through the 1990s. While the average pay for women was £217 a week in 1991, that in fast-expanding women's jobs (that is, where the number employed increased by over 15 per cent from 1991 to 1995) was £315 a week: 45 per cent, or nearly £100 a week, more than average pay. The scale of the shift over those few years can be seen from the fact that one women in eight was in an occupation with an average pay rate above £315 in 1991; by 1995 the comparable figure was one in six. Employment growth was also high in one traditionally female poorly paid occupation – childcare – and low in one relatively well-paid area – health professionals. The association between occupations with expanding numbers of women and occupations paying women relatively well was therefore strong, but not universal.

Rising male unemployment accompanied by deregulation began to impact on traditional gender pay relativities in the early 1990s. Individual women have long experienced a decline in relative pay when they re-enter the labour market after a period out of employment. Much of this has been associated with a move to part-time employment after having children (Joshi, 1991). Redundancy and unemployment are achieving similar results for men. Gregg and Wadsworth (1995) matched people moving into work with those already in jobs by sex, age and qualification and found that wages for new entrants were 30 per cent below those of similar

people already in work. This can be explained by a decline in the importance of collective bargaining in determining wages, but it is also associated
with the pattern of new jobs, as against existing ones. Jobs open to people
currently entering or re-entering work are geared towards smaller establishments, out of the public sector and generally towards non-unionized areas
of work. Women have long suffered from the concentration of women's
work in small establishments lacking union recognition; men starting or
returning to employment are now suffering from similar processes of
crowding at the bottom end of the labour market, particularly where they
lack formal qualifications. In this sense some men's work is coming to
resemble women's more closely, with consequences for overall pay differences between men and women.

The trend of women's entry into higher level jobs indicated in Table 5.3
is associated with the rising qualifications profile of young women identified by Crompton and Sanderson (1986). Whereas in 1974–6 at every age
group women in full-time employment were less likely than men to have a
degree, by 1990–2 women below the age of 35 who were employed full-
time were more likely to have a degree than employed men of the same
age. Figure 5.2 shows that employment growth for women between 1991
and 1995 was generally greater the higher the 'qualification score' of an
occupation. This score was arrived at by averaging the qualifications for

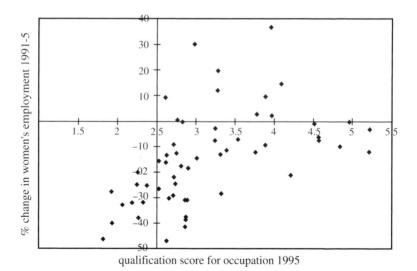

qualification score for occupation 1995

*Figure 5.2*   Occupations: relationship between female employment change, 1991–5,
and qualifications score of occupation

all people – men and women – working in that occupation, creating a range from five for academic posts to less than one for labouring jobs. There are exceptions to the association of employment growth with qualifications. Employment increased fast in childcare jobs, where the qualification score ranked low and women increasingly found jobs as general managers though its qualification score ranked only just above average. Conversely, the numbers of women employed as health professionals fell in the early 1990s, though this is a highly qualified field.

Harkness (1996) shows that in many ways women working full-time now have a better employment profile than men, in the sense that the distribution of full-time women workers across regions, industries, occupations, qualifications and life-cycle stage groups is more favourable. If economic processes were sex-blind and women were paid the same as men with similar characteristics, full-time women workers, taken as a whole, would actually earn more than men. That they do not is because they are on lower grades and pay rates within occupations and work for lower paying enterprises. The move towards individually determined pay rates, including performance-related pay, is likely to have increased the disparity between pay for similar types of work, notwithstanding the gains made through equal pay legislation (Bruegel and Perrons, 1998; Rubery, 1992). Different hours of work also contribute to disparities in weekly pay. Harkness shows that fathers have higher earnings than other men, while mothers have lower earnings than other women, even where they are working full-time. The differences are largely associated with the division of labour in the home and hence with the shorter average hours worked by mothers in full-time jobs as compared both to full-time men and to women without children. Fathers, on the other hand, tend to work longer hours than other men (Brannen et al., 1997; Dex et al., 1995).

Access to high-level jobs and high earnings tends to be greater for fathers than for other men, but motherhood still presents a hurdle for women. Table 5.4 shows the large differences in the proportions of men and women in higher level jobs who are parents. Very few women legal professionals have children, but in more traditional areas such as teaching women are as likely as men to have children. Weekly pay, however, tends to be higher in the types of work which mothers rarely enter.

## GLOBALIZATION, DEREGULATION AND PART-TIME WORK

There is a widespread view that deregulation has promoted the growth of part-time employment in Britain (TUC, 1995). However the period of fast

*Table 5.4*   Proportion of workforce who are parents by
occupation and sex, 1995

| | Parents amongst (%) | | Ratio female % = 100 |
| | Male employees | Female employees | |
|---|---|---|---|
| Legal services | 46.07 | 20.78 | 221.70 |
| Marketing managers | 43.00 | 20.40 | 210.78 |
| Personnel managers | 47.10 | 25.40 | 185.43 |
| Authors | 27.90 | 15.40 | 181.17 |
| Other finance managers | 40.70 | 23.40 | 173.93 |
| Banking | 42.80 | 25.80 | 165.89 |
| Scientists | 42.34 | 26.80 | 157.97 |
| Engineers | 37.43 | 27.03 | 138.48 |
| Doctors | 50.70 | 37.50 | 135.20 |
| Accountants/economists | 39.93 | 30.22 | 132.14 |
| Civil servants | 44.40 | 36.20 | 122.65 |
| Plant operatives | 49.70 | 40.60 | 122.41 |
| General managers | 38.30 | 32.00 | 119.69 |
| Primary teachers | 46.50 | 42.20 | 110.19 |
| Nurses | 40.70 | 43.00 | 94.65 |
| Lecturers | 39.86 | 44.40 | 89.79 |
| Secondary teachers | 42.70 | 51.60 | 82.75 |
| All occupations | 48.80 | 44.20 | 110.41 |

*Source*: Calculated from unpublished LFS data, 1995.

growth in part-time employment for women was the 1960s rather than the
1970s or 1980s. The proportion, but not the number, of British women
working part time, has been relatively static since 1975. The share
increased by only 2 percentage points between 1975 and 1991, compared
to a 10–11 percentage point increase in Germany, France and Ireland, 20
points in Belgium and 40 points in the Netherlands. It is also worth noting
that part-time work for women is by no means confined to non-unionized
areas of work; a high proportion remains in the public sector.

Analysis of the Labour Force Survey suggests that the pattern of growth
in part-time employment for women since 1981 was broadly similar to
that for full-time women workers, discussed above, namely in occupations
that were relatively well paid. While the LFS may underestimate the
extent and growth of off-the-books part-time work, the indications are that
the overall improvement in the qualifications of women entering the
labour market has had a positive effect even amongst part-timers.
Table 5.3 (column 4) shows the growth of part-time work to have been
particularly strong between 1981 and 1991 in relatively well-paid areas of

work like personnel management, the law, office supervision and higher grades of the Civil Service, though in most cases this was from a very low base. Part-time work in Britain in particular, however, is still highly concentrated in low-paid jobs. In 1991 less than 2 per cent of part-time women workers were employed in the well-paid jobs listed in Table 5.3. Moreover, the hourly wages of part-time women continued to fall relative to full-time female and male earnings. In 1977 hourly rates for female part-timers[3] reached 67 per cent of average hourly earnings for all men but declined to 63 per cent in 1993, while hourly rates for full-time women climbed steadily from 70 per cent of male average hourly earnings to 77 per cent in 1993 (Harkness, 1996).

There is little doubt that the precipitate growth of male part-time work (by 88 per cent from 1984 to 1995) is associated with deindustrialization and deregulation (Fevre, 1993). Although increasing numbers are students, part-time male workers are particularly likely to be reluctant part-timers and to work where there are no unions. Labour Force Survey data for 1994 show that only 27 per cent of male part-timers worked in a unionized place of work, compared to 45 per cent of male full-time workers and 41 per cent of female part-timers. They remain a small unrepresentative group of men since 82 per cent of part-time workers in Britain are female.

The conditions of employment for part-time workers as a whole have deteriorated, even if part-time work is now found higher up the occupational ladder. This is a result of the growth of short time part-time working – that is, where the hours fall below the national insurance threshold (Huws and Hurstfield, 1989) for which there are no benefits and until recently rights were poorer. It also reflects a decline in the coverage of part-time workers by collective agreements. There is some evidence that women's pay and conditions have proved particularly vulnerable to a range of deregulation and privatization measures that have accompanied the opening up of the UK market to wider global competition (Humphries and Rubery, 1992; Escott and Whitfeld, 1995), but set against structural changes reflected in rising qualifications of women, the net effect has been favourable to women, particularly those in full-time employment.

Deindustrialization and deregulation, by reducing the pay of the lowest paid group of men, have created a degree of downward gender pay equalization amongst lower-paid workers. Moreover, the overall improvement in the position of the average woman relative to the average man masks the widening of overall inequalities. Thus lower-paid women may now earn a higher proportion of a relatively smaller household income. Inequalities of pay between partners in a household may have declined at the same time as inequalities between households have increased. These shifts, evident at a national scale, have been particularly acute in London, in many ways reflecting its position as a 'global city'.

## GLOBAL CITY EFFECTS

In general the London labour market offers women in employment some distinct advantages. Jobs are somewhat less segregated by sex than in the economy as a whole, with women more often working in traditionally male jobs and less often in typically female jobs (Table 5.5). Moreover women who lived in inner London in 1991 experienced higher rates of social mobility between 1971 and 1991 than women living in other regions, with migrants to London having particularly high rates of upward mobility (Fielding and Halford, 1993). Women's representation in higher-level jobs is greater and their pay higher relative to men, though differences between London and the rest of the country tended to diminish after 1991.

London women are also more likely to be found in poorly paid occupations. Ranking all occupations included in the New Earnings Survey by average pay for women in the UK as a whole and comparing the numbers of London women employed in the lowest paid occupations with the national figure, shows that 13 per cent of London women workers were employed in the lowest paid occupations, compared to 10 per cent of the

*Table 5.5*   Female proportion of workforce, selected occupations

|  | 1991 | | 1995 | |
| --- | --- | --- | --- | --- |
|  | UK<br>% | London<br>% | UK<br>% | London<br>% |
| Managers | 32.04 | 36.00 | 34.22 | 35.42 |
| Professionals | 38.76 | 40.96 | 40.49 | 43.56 |
| Associate profs | 49.70 | 49.22 | 51.00 | 48.74 |
| Clerical | 78.40 | 74.87 | 77.17 | 76.07 |
| Craft | 10.70 | 8.47 | 10.74 | 11.39 |
| Personnel | 62.57 | 53.84 | 67.96 | 55.73 |
| Sales | 64.52 | 57.16 | 66.59 | 61.72 |
| Plant | 21.89 | 16.70 | 21.62 | 17.54 |
| Other | 50.97 | 45.09 | 53.79 | 48.56 |
| Total | 44.04 | 43.68 | 46.67 | 46.86 |

*Source*: LFS, 1991 and 1995.

female workforce nationally. The difference was even greater for the best-paid occupations. Something over 15 per cent of London women worked in those occupations, compared to 10 per cent of all women workers in the country as a whole. Inequalities between women as well as between men have increased somewhat faster in London than in the UK as a whole (Table 5.6), reflecting occupational changes associated with globalization.

Saskia Sassen argues that globalization has produced two types of international migration flows focused on global cities: one of high-level executives and a second of economic migrants destined for the poorest paid jobs in these cities (Sassen, 1991, 1996). London attracts highly paid, often short-duration, international migration as well as migrants of both sexes from poorer countries who are constrained by legal restrictions and low expectations to accept low-paid and insecure work. Table 5.7 shows that long-standing and recent overseas migrant workers more often settle in London.

Sassen stresses the complementarity between the two streams of migrants and between the growth of highly paid work and low-paid work in such cities. The juxtaposition of these polar opposite types of migrant labour: top executives and vulnerable impoverished migrant workers arises from two main processes associated with 'global cities'. The first operates through the land market. Globalization of financial capital squeezes mainstream manufacturing activities, and many middle-income workers from global cities through high-class office development and attendant

*Table 5.6*   Earnings inequalities by sex, 1983 and 1994, Greater London and Great Britain: difference between earnings of top 10 per cent and bottom 10 per cent 1983 and 1994, (pence per hour in 1990 constant prices)

|  | Inter-decile range 1983 (£s) | Inter-decile range 1994 (£s) | % change 1983–4 in interdecile range |
|---|---|---|---|
| Greater London |  |  |  |
| female full-time | 464.01 | 857.52 | 84.81 |
| male full-time | 834.07 | 1357.96 | 62.81 |
| female full-time |  |  |  |
| and part-time | 428.58 | 796.44 | 85.83 |
| Great Britain |  |  |  |
| female full-time | 421.09 | 697.45 | 65.63 |
| male full-time | 610.62 | 934.92 | 53.11 |
| female full-time |  |  |  |
| and part-time | 362.93 | 606.23 | 67.04 |

*Source*: Calculated from New Earning Survey 1983 and 1994.

rises in land values. Labour-intensive processes necessary to the city's functioning are therefore driven to cut labour costs and manufacturing becomes 'downgraded' from factory to sweatshop organization. This often means drawing on a disadvantaged labour force, predominantly of women. Sassen suggests that migrant women, often employed in ethnic minority enterprises, provide just such a labour force in global cities.

The second process, Sassen argues, is related to the highly labour-intensive consumption style of elites within global cities. They rely on luxury, handcrafted services in restaurants, fashionwear and laundry services and employ live-in servants and nannies. In all of these services they draw particularly on migrant workers. This is highlighted in media accounts of the resurgence of domestic service in Britain, although the existing evidence suggests that domestic servants and live-in nannies are concentrated in outer London and the south east rather than in London itself (Gregson and Lowe, 1993).

Through these processes, global inequalities in living standards between rich and poor countries are filtered down to produce inequalities at the urban level in the West. Sassen emphasizes class inequalities in consumption between women, pointing to the wives of elite men as enjoying access to luxury services. However, when considering the labour market, Sassen tends to treat women as a rather undifferentiated source of cheap labour. The London example shows however that global cities attract young well-educated men and women from other parts of the country into high-status jobs. Global cities have a disproportionate population of single and divorced people; women who settle for a traditional nuclear family household tend to move outwards, even when they are employed.

Highly educated women then are found to a disproportionate degree in the core cities of Western countries; it is in such places that women are most likely to enter elite jobs. Even here, they often have to fit in with the expectations of their male colleagues and few stay the course once they have children (Wacjman, 1996). Elite women workers in cities like New York and London are disproportionately young, single and childless. Like men they tend to buy in domestic services and work long hours, relying on late-night shops, restaurants and bars, dry cleaning services and taxis. In part, then, their freedom from domestic chores relies on the provision of cheap services, often by women from other racial or ethnic minority groups. Such services also enable them to achieve a reasonable standard of living without becoming financially dependent on a man.

The London example shows that ethnic minority men are drawn into servicing jobs to a disproportionate extent (Table 5.7). Only a relatively low proportion (41 per cent) of personal service jobs in London such as

*Table 5.7*   Composition of workforce: by sex and place of origin,
UK and London, 1995

| Proportion who were | All jobs | | Managerial jobs | | Personal service jobs | |
|---|---|---|---|---|---|---|
| | UK | London | UK | London | UK | London |
| Male | | | | | | |
| UK-born | 49.67 | 40.83 | 60.34 | 47.41 | 28.35 | 28.29 |
| Born outside UK | | | | | | |
| and Ireland | 3.14 | 10.88 | 4.78 | 15.39 | 3.17 | 14.29 |
| (of whom recent | | | | | | |
| migrants*) | 1.1 | 4.63 | 1.35 | 5.6 | 3.36 | 10.8 |
| Female | | | | | | |
| UK-born | 43.39 | 34.88 | 32.07 | 28.77 | 63.60 | 41.28 |
| Born outside UK | | | | | | |
| and Ireland | 2.70 | 10.16 | 1.81 | 6.03 | 3.31 | 11.59 |
| (of whom recent | | | | | | |
| migrants) | 1.19 | 5.02 | 1.98 | 4.5 | 1.3 | 6.8 |
| Total excluding | | | | | | |
| Irish-born | 98.90 | 96.75 | 99.00 | 97.60 | 98.42 | 95.45 |

*In the last five years.
*Source*:  Calculated from Labour Force Survey unpublished data.

cleaning, catering, hairdressing and childcare are held by UK-born women as against 64 per cent in the rest of the UK. This is due at least as much to the employment of migrant men (14 per cent of the personal service workforce) as to migrant women (12 per cent). The lower concentration in London of UK-born women in these types of poorly paid 'women's work' can be related to inequalities between migrant men and other men. Less than 5 per cent of London's workforce were recent male migrants, yet nearly 11 per cent of London's personal service workers were men who had come into the country in the last five years. Indeed recent female migrants are rather less concentrated in such jobs, at least as far as those included in the Labour Force Survey are concerned. At the other end of the scale, Table 5.7 shows the importance of international migration of managerial men to London with migrant men disproportionately concentrated in managerial jobs. This is not the case for migrant women, who account for over 10 per cent of the London labour force but only 6 per cent of managers. That proportion is not negligible, however, when compared to the proportion for UK-born women living in London. Some of these migrant women managers may be company women, drawn to London as part of a high-profile career; others may be well-qualified wives of men coming or returning to London from abroad; but the majority are likely to be long-settled ethnic minority women working in very small and precarious enterprises, managers in name but not in status or pay. Whichever group they belong to, it is clear that they are far more likely than almost any other group of women to be found in London. Both at the bottom and the top end of the labour market, then, international migration patterns associated with London's status as a global city appear to have important effects on the overall pattern of gender inequality in employment.

CONCLUSION

Globalization, which has increased inequalities within and between states, has paradoxically been accompanied by a narrowing of gender differentials in the UK. As in South and East Asia, global capital has sought to employ women rather than men in a number of roles. While this often takes the form of exploiting women's historical disadvantages and stereotypical characteristics, it also undermines the traditional power base of lower-class men. Amongst the least well-paid groups of full-time workers, the result has been a movement towards gender pay equality, albeit one based on levelling down and rising pay inequality amongst men. The opening up of higher-level jobs in the City to young, childless women may represent empowerment for these individuals, but it may equally reflect a growing instability, even in junior managerial and professional jobs. Flexibilization and the move away from company careers has crept further and further up the job hierarchy. Women, who were once regarded as a liability because they were not expected to stay and slog it up a career ladder, may now be welcomed for their supposedly more flexible approach to the idea of a job for life.

Wage inequalities have risen amongst women, too, with part-time women workers trailing further behind well-paid full-time female employees. The treatment of women as a specific, undifferentiated type of worker was never the whole story but it is becoming ever less realistic.

Differentiation between women operates across a set of dimensions which interrelate, both positively and negatively. Domestic responsibilities remain important in structuring differences between the occupation and pay positions of women and these differences are increasing. Access to higher-paid and higher-grade work has given some women more choices about when and whether to 'set up home' with a male partner and when and whether to have children, since with paid help they can overcome some of the constraints of being a mother. This is the most obvious way in which inequalities between women have enabled some to gain something approaching equal opportunities with men.

At the other end of the spectrum, while part-time workers are the group most tied to women's work at women's pay, this group is becoming less homogeneous. The range of pay and conditions amongst part-time workers reflects the diversity of their circumstances and the choices open to them. Differences in class background, education and qualifications are widening differences between part-time workers. In the past it was a long-term state which once entered was rarely left, partly because part-time workers were treated as a homogeneous group with few qualifications and skills. Qualifications and experience can now raise women out of the ghetto of low-paid, part-time work. Again differences between women by ethnic group are complex, reflecting differences within and between the various communities rather than any simple ethnic minority/ethnic majority divide.

In spite of the overall increase in job instability and insecurity and the deterioration in conditions of employment accompanying globalization, the effect has been far from homogeneous for different groups of men and women. The broader shift from a social democratic welfare state regime towards a US-style liberal model has had its impact on patterns of gender inequality. Gender inequality is still rife, for example, in pay between women and men with similar years of further education, but the widening distribution of men and women's pay means that there is a greater overlap. Many more women earn at least as much, or more, than the top 20 per cent of men; and conversely many more men earn less than the bottom 20 per cent of women than was the case 20 years ago. These earning patterns impact on household relationships and have opened up some choices to some women. To some degree, however, improvements in gender equality have been gained at the expense of wider inequalities of income between households, and therefore in many ways at the cost of women living with low-paid men; as a consequence their struggle to make ends meet has become more difficult over these last 20 years.

## NOTES

1.    Research for this chapter was undertaken as part of an ESRC research grant R000221691 Life Cycles, Life Chances and Migration in London, 1971–93. I am very grateful to Joanna Brown for all her work on the data.

2.    Calculated from Labour Force Survey data on gross weekly earnings cover-
      ing all employees, 1995.
3.    These figures are taken from Harkness (1996) who used the Family
      Expenditure Survey. In principle this covers all part timers and not just
      those above the national insurance threshold.

## REFERENCES

Blau, F. and Kahn, L., 'Wage structure and gender earnings differentials: an inter-
    national comparison', *Economica* 63 (1996) S29–S62.
Brannen, J., Moss, P., Owen, C. and Wale, C., 'Working fathers', *Labour Market
    Trends* (July 1997) 259–66.
Bruegel, I. and Hegewisch, A., 'Flexibilisation and part time labour in Europe', in
    R. Crompton and P. Brown (eds), *The New Europe? Economic Restructuring
    and Social Exclusion*. London: UCL Press, 1994.
Bruegel, I. and Perrons, D., 'Where do the costs of unequal employment fall?',
    *Gender, Work and Organisation* vol. 2 (1995) 113–24.
Bruegel, I. and Perrons, D., 'Diverse trends in women's employment in a deregu-
    lated labour market', *Feminist Economics* 4(1) (1998) 103–25.
Central Statistical Office, *New Earnings Survey* various years. London: HMSO.
Central Statistical Office, *Labour Force Survey* various years. London: HMSO.
Central Statistical Office, *Census of Population* various years. London: HMSO.
Crompton, R. and Sanderson, K., 'Credentials and careers: some implications of
    the increase in professional qualifications among women', *Sociology* 20(1)
    (1986) 25–42.
Dex, S., Clark, A. and Taylor, M., *Household Labour Supply*. Sheffield:
    Employment Department, 1995.
Elias, P. and Gregory, M., *The Changing Structure of Occupations and Earnings
    in Great Britain, 1975–1990*. London: Employment Department Group, 1994.
Escott, K. and Whitfield, D., *The Gender Impact of Compulsory Competitive
    Tendering in Local Government*, EOC Research Discussion Series no. 12.
    Manchester: EOC, 1995.
Fevre, R., 'Informal practices, flexible firms and private labour markets',
    *Sociology* 23(1) (1989) 91–109.
Fielding, A. and Halford, S., 'Geographies of opportunity: a regional analysis of
    gender specific social and spatial mobilities in England and Wales 1971–81',
    *Environment and Planning* A vol. 25(1) (1993) 421–40.
Gallie, D., 'Skill, gender and the quality of employment', in R. Crompton,
    D. Gallie and K. Purcell (eds), *Changing Forms of Employment: Organisation,
    Skills and Gender*. London: Routledge, 1996.
Gregg, P. and Wadsworth, J., 'A short history of labour turnover, job security and
    job tenure, 1975–1993', *Oxford Review of Economic Policy* 11(1) (1995) 73–90.
Gregg, P. and Machin, S., 'Is the UK rise in inequality different?', in R. Barrell,
    *The UK Labour Market: Comparative Aspects and Institutional Developments*.
    Cambridge: Cambridge University Press, 1994.
Gregson, N. and Lowe, M., *Servicing the Middle Class: Gender and Domestic
    Labour in Contemporary Britain*. London: Routledge, 1993.

Harkness, S., 'The gender earnings gap: evidence from the UK', *Fiscal Studies* 7(2) (1996) 1–36.

Hirst, P. and Thompson, G., *Globalisation in Question: the International Economy and the Possibilities of Governance*. Cambridge: Polity Press, 1996.

Humphries, J. and Rubery, J., 'The legacy for women's employment: integration, differentiation and polarisation', in J. Michie (ed.), *The Economic Legacy 1979–1992*. London: Academic Press, 1992.

Hutton, W., *The State to Come*. London: Jonathan Cape, 1997.

Huws, U. and Hurstfield, J., *What Price Flexibility?* London: Low Pay Unit, 1989.

Joshi, H., 'Sex and motherhood as handicaps in the labour market', in M. Maclean and D. Groves, *Women's Issues in Social Policy*. London: Routledge, 1991.

King, A., *Global Cities: Post-imperialism and the Internationalisation of London*. London: Routledge, 1989.

Kofman, E. and Youngs, G., *Globalization: Theory and Practice*. London: Pinter, 1996.

Mitter, S., *Common Fate, Common Bond*. London: Pluto, 1986.

Nash, J. and Fernandez-Kelly, P., *Women and Men in the International Division of Labour*. Albany: SUNY Press, 1983.

Rodgers, G. and Rodgers, J., *Precarious Work in Western Europe: the State of the Debate*. Geneva: ILO, 1989.

Rubery, J., *The Economics of Equal Value*, Research Discussion Series No. 3. Manchester: EOC, 1992.

Sassen, S., *Global City: New York, London, Tokyo*. Princeton: Princeton University Press, 1991.

Sassen, S., *Losing Control? Sovereignty in an Age of Globalisation*. New York: Columbia University Press, 1996.

Storey, D., *Understanding the Small Business Sector*. London: Routledge, 1994.

TUC, *Has Deregulation Delivered the Jobs?* London: Trade Union Congress, 1995.

UNDP, *Human Development Report United Nations Development Programme*. Oxford: Oxford University Press, 1995.

Wajcman, J., 'Women and men managers', in R. Crompton, D. Gallie and K. Purcell (eds), *Changing Forms of Employment: Organisation, Skills and Gender*. London: Routledge, 1996.

# Part II
# Race, Migration and Employment

# 6 Immigration, Ethnicity and Exclusion: Implications of European Integration
## Rosemary Sales and Jeanne Gregory

Contemporary processes of European integration have significant and complex implications for the citizenship rights of people resident within the European Union (EU). Two distinct sets of formal rights are developing. There have been moves towards establishing a common framework of rights for EU citizens, particularly in the area of employment. Under the Single European Act 1986, which provided the legal framework for the Single European Market (SEM), they have freedom to work anywhere within the EU, while employment and welfare rights are being harmonized through the gradual implementation of the Social Chapter.[1] At the same time, mobility within the EU of legally resident third country nationals[2] is increasingly restricted and conditional on employment, while the conditions under which they are able to enter and to reside and work in Europe have become more stringent, thus also affecting their access to broader social, political and civil rights.

An exclusive focus on the distinction between EU citizens and non-citizens masks, however, a complex hierarchy of rights associated with different forms of residence status. Non-citizens, for example, include legal permanent residents, or 'denizens' (Wrench, 1990), temporary labour migrants, refugees and asylum-seekers, and a growing number of undocumented migrants and those whose residence status is insecure. Each status is accompanied by a different set of civil and social rights (Morris, 1997) which has different implications for men and women since women migrants, whatever their actual economic role, are often dependent on men for their residence status and access to social and civic rights (Kofman and Sales, 1998).

Furthermore, although EU citizens are entitled to the same set of formal rights, the substantive rights they are able to claim are dependent on their economic and social status which is shaped by class, gender and ethnicity. The strategy of economic and monetary union (EMU) has been based on a broad consensus around market-oriented policies which have curtailed social spending, undermining established social rights and increasing inequalities. The subordinate economic and social position of black and ethnic minority citizens renders them less able to benefit from the possibilities of mobility within the EU, while their labour tends to be concentrated in sectors most likely to suffer from the competitive pressures resulting from the single market (see, for example, Wrench, 1993). Deregulation, casualization and the development of flexible work practices disproportionately affect women and black and ethnic minority workers. Restrictive migration policies have also had implications for minority ethnic citizens by fostering a climate of control and suspicion in which xenophobia and racism flourish.

European equality law has had limited power to reverse these growing inequalities. It gives little protection to workers who are outside the formal labour market, either the unemployed or those working in the 'informal sector'. Most vulnerable are migrants from non-member states, including the growing number of asylum-seekers, without secure rights of residence.

In this chapter we discuss the implications of these developments for migrant and ethnic minority women in Britain. We begin by examining the social and economic policies underlying European integration, and migration policy at European and British[3] levels. We then discuss the implications of these processes for women's access to, and status within, the market.

There are limitations to the available data. Figures for labour migrants and asylum-seekers, for example, are not broken down by gender (Home Office, 1997). The assumption that the man is 'head of household' is, however, likely to be reflected in the gender composition of applicants for visas and asylum. Data on ethnicity are uneven, and in discussions of labour market inequalities there has been a tendency to conflate ethnic minority citizens with migrants (see, for example, Bhavnani, 1997). The categories used in the Census, the most comprehensive source of information, are inadequate in relation to recent migration flows. There is no category available, for example, for Turkish/Kurdish people who form a substantial proportion of recent refugees and who are likely to be among the most disadvantaged in the labour market, but are generally categorized as 'white' or 'other'. Other racialized groups such as the Irish are not generally included as a distinct category in ethnic monitoring although recent research suggests that they continue to be systematically disadvantaged within the labour market.[4]

## ECONOMIC AND SOCIAL IMPLICATIONS OF EUROPEAN INTEGRATION

Although the EU[5] was conceived primarily as a structure for the development of economic cooperation and the promotion of free trade, from the outset it had a significant social policy dimension. The latter was seen as necessary to the achievement of the goals of fair competition and free movement of labour, goods, capital and services, but it also provided a wider legitimacy to the process of integration. Commitment to improved living and working conditions throughout the EU was intended to demonstrate that ordinary people would share the benefits of membership. This marked a recognition that markets are social institutions requiring active policy to promote their efficient functioning.

The postwar consensus around Keynesian demand management and welfare policies, together with the high levels of growth and employment, allowed some degree of correspondence between economic and social goals up to the 1970s. The tensions between them intensified during the 1980s with the exhaustion of the economic boom which had underpinned social democratic policies in Europe. As global economic competition undermined the ability of individual states to carry out independent economic policy, all EU states embraced with varying degrees of enthusiasm neoliberal policies during the 1980s, with welfare regimes subordinated to promoting profitability. The goal of economic and monetary union and the move towards a common currency necessitates the harmonization of economic conditions between member states. The convergence conditions agreed with the Maastricht Treaty of 1993 are based not on harmonization of real economic indicators but on financial targets which require states to keep rigid control over spending.[6] These policies have produced deflationary pressures, increasing unemployment and exacerbating inequalities (Bennington and Taylor, 1993, p. 126).

As the completion of the Single European Market extends the free movement of capital, commodities and labour within the EU, the European Commission has pressed for a wider development of the social dimension in order to mitigate the worst ravages of competition unleashed by the SEM (social dumping).[7] These developments have remained limited and fragmented (Bailey, 1992; Leibfried, 1993) and have been obstructed by member governments, particularly the British Conservative government, which succeeded in diluting and blocking many proposals for new social legislation. Its opt-out from the Social Chapter of the Maastricht Treaty established the precedent for individual countries to opt-out of unpalatable provisions, a precedent which may appeal to some states currently seeking membership. There has been a shift of emphasis from 'harmonization' to 'mutual recognition of difference' and a growing acceptance of the idea of a 'two-speed' Europe. The British Labour government elected in May 1997 has now signed the Chapter, and adopted a more positive stance toward the European Union, although it has retained much of the previous government's social policy agenda.

EU social policy has been confined mainly to attempts to define common goals rather than to create common institutions. The Social Chapter proposed certain minimum standards, many of which are existing practice in some member states. Its key principles are the promotion of employment, improvement of living and working conditions and adequate social protection through financial benefits for those unable to work. This excludes groups outside the formal labour process, such as the elderly and workers in 'informal' employment such as home workers, workers in unregulated establishments (sweatshops), casual labourers and domestic workers. These categories are growing in numbers and diversity and are disproportionately made up of women and of migrants, particularly those with insecure residence status.

The most vigorous element of EU social policy has been the development of equal opportunities policies (see Hoskyns, this volume) but this has been confined largely to promoting equal treatment between men and women based on Article 119 of the Treaty of Rome. While a substantial body of policy initiatives have been developed in this area, in practice the proportion of women workers able to make use of their rights under EU laws is declining. These laws are based on individual or groups of workers making complaints, and are confined to the formal labour contract. In the absence of a high general standard of employment protection, the existence of such laws tends to accentuate the hierarchy of employment. Only those people with secure, permanent jobs and the protection of a strong trade union may be in a position to insist on their rights. Those who are most vulnerable and, therefore, most in need of legal protection are precisely the groups with least access to the law. The progressive deregulation of the labour market is leading to a greater polarization, with an increasing proportion of people finding themselves in a twilight zone of temporary, casualized, unregulated work.

By its very existence, sex equality law recognizes the need to interfere with the operation of 'free' market forces. But while legal protection is available within the EU to address the unequal treatment of women workers, parallel provisions are not available for racial and ethnic minority groups. Discrimination on grounds of nationality is illegal under EU law, but this protection is restricted to full citizens of member states who exercise their right to move within the EU. By accepting the official definitions of nationality and citizenship in use within member states, EU law condones and reinforces exclusionary practices in the labour market.

Although laws against racial discrimination do exist in some member states, they are generally weak and ineffective and there is no obligation under EU law to take action in this area (Forbes and Mead, 1992).

Ironically Britain, which has been reluctant to promote equal opportunities measures within the EU, has the strongest legislation against racism. This legislation too is rooted in the individual labour contract, while its general standards of employment protection are among the weakest in the EU, rendering the measures 'practically irrelevant to large sections of its ethnic minority workforce' (Wrench, 1996, p. 168).

The European Parliament and Commission have produced a number of reports on racism which have recommended European legislation on the issue. Member states, however, have consistently opposed such moves. The Amsterdam Treaty of 1997 refers to opposition to racial discrimination in Article 6(a) (see Hoskyns, this volume). Any action under this heading would, however, require the unanimous agreement of all member states.

## EUROPEAN UNION POLICY ON MIGRATION

European Union policy on migration is beset by a number of contradictory tendencies. On the one hand, member states have proclaimed the end of labour migration and imposed increasingly draconian controls on those deemed unacceptable for entry to the EU. On the other hand, there has been a growing concern with the issue of social exclusion, much of which has focused on migrant and ethnic minority groups (Samers, 1998). These apparently incompatible positions reflect the repercussions of the extension of market forces which have undermined collective rights and provision and created growing insecurity. The publicly stated goal of zero immigration also belies the continuing reliance by European economies on immigrant labour. Labour migration has not been halted, but EU states have become more selective in the forms and origins of migrant labour, and have introduced stricter conditions in order to divest themselves of the social costs of this labour (Fekete, 1997).

These contradictory elements also indicate differences between the European Commission and the European Parliament on the one hand, and individual member states on the other, over the extent and character of harmonization of migration policy. This reflects a more general conflict between the integrationist and interventionist project of the European Commission and the reluctance of member states to cede national authority. The latter have preferred to operate through intergovernmental groupings, in which national states remain decision-makers, rather than through the institutions of the European Union.

As well as differences over who should take the initiative in relation to policy on migration, there have been serious disagreements over the content of policy. The European Commission and Parliament have pursued some limited measures to extend the rights of migrants resident within the EU, albeit within a general policy of closure. On the other hand, the agenda pursued by intergovernmental bodies has been narrowly restrictive, and has produced policies reflecting the least liberal interpretation of international obligations. Much of this conflict has centred on refugees and undocumented migrants, with individual governments adopting an increasingly strident populist response to asylum-seekers, often pursuing even more restrictive policies than those agreed by intergovernmental bodies (Fernhout, 1993).

Most EU governments had placed restrictions on primary migration during the 1970s as the postwar boom which had brought demands for migrant labour slowed down. The pace of these developments, however was uneven. While Northern Europe attracted large-scale labour migration during the early 1950s[8] Southern European states such as Spain and Italy became 'new countries of immigration' as their industrial development boomed in the 1970s. The increase in asylum-seeking in the late 1980s brought pressure from other European states for these countries to place restrictions on entry. Southern Europe was seen as 'soft' on migration, and it was claimed that once migrants were able to enter, the removal of internal border controls would allow them to reach Northern Europe.

The Schengen Convention was signed in 1985 by six European Union states (including Germany and the Benelux countries) in anticipation of the SEM. It provided for freedom of movement for citizens within the Schengen area and strengthened external borders. The main policy initiatives include the development of uniform visas, issuable by one signatory state but valid for the entire territory of signatories, for nationals of external states. A common list of countries whose citizens require visas has been drawn up and includes states whose nationals had not needed visas to enter individual states. Other initiatives include fines on airlines and ferries found to have carried aliens without valid travel documents (carrier's liability); the 'one chance rule' by which asylum-seekers refused in one country may not make further applications; and data sharing on travellers, targeting criminal activity and asylum-seekers.

Schengen now includes nine EU states. The UK remains outside since the government has been unwilling to cede responsibility for maintaining border controls to European institutions. Similar policies, however, have been pursued through both official EU legislation under the Maastricht Treaty and ad hoc intergovernment agreements including all member states. Agreements reached by these bodies, whether ratified or not by individual parliaments, have brought restrictions on migrants, and a decline in the number of asylum-seekers granted refugee status. In Britain, refusals were 20–5 per cent of decisions in the 1980s, increasing to more than 80 per cent in 1997 (Home Office Statistical Bulletin, 1997).

While there has been increasing coordination of immigration policy at European level, substantial differences in state responses to immigration, or 'incorporation regimes' (Soysal, 1994) remain within the EU. The history of the formation of the nation state, colonial relations and patterns of immigration have created different traditions of citizenship, institutional systems of rights and forms of acquisition of citizenship. As European integration has brought common policies towards the admission of refugees, resettlement policy remains largely under the control of individual states and reflects individual notions of nationhood and citizenship (Duke, Sales and Gregory, 1998). Most EU states provide at least the minimum levels set out in the Geneva Convention 1951 to those to whom they grant full refugee status ('convention status'), but there has been only limited development towards harmonization of policy in this area.

## BRITISH MIGRATION POLICY

As increasingly stringent controls on migration are developed at European Union level, individual governments have implemented their own restrictions. Recent legislation in Britain which is aimed specifically at asylum-seekers is more overtly repressive than previous measures, but is not outside the tradition of British immigration policy. This has been based – even in the heyday of the 'liberal' 1960s – on the assumption that its primary purpose is to keep people out, that immigrants are a problem, to be allowed in only on sufferance (Spencer, 1994).

In contrast to this negative official position on migration, Britain's economy has relied heavily on migrant labour. Migration from Ireland has been prominent for over a century, with Irish workers filling specific niches such as construction, nursing and domestic work. During the period of postwar reconstruction new forms of migration developed. Nationals of former colonies (the Commonwealth) acquired citizenship rights in Britain as part of the process of decolonization. The state tended to be passive in recruitment since potential migrants could not be prevented from obtaining the formal benefits of citizenship (including rights of residence and welfare). Commonwealth citizens were, however, encouraged to take up work in areas of labour shortage, especially the health service which recruited large numbers of women. Citizenship rights allowed families to enter as of right. Many women entered through family reunion, but in many groups (notably the Irish and Caribbeans) single women made up a large proportion of labour migrants. These populations therefore tended to have a fairly even gender balance.

The Commonwealth Immigration Act 1962, the first of a series of increasingly restrictive measures, introduced the requirement for an employment voucher for Commonwealth subjects. The Immigration Act 1968 included a new concept of 'patriality' which gave the right to claim British citizenship to people with a grandparent who was a British citizen. This clearly favoured those from Australia and Canada above those from the predominantly black 'New Commonwealth'. The Immigration Act 1981 extended the link between citizenship status and ethnicity by removing the automatic right to citizenship of those born in Britain, and of spouses of British citizens. The latter had to demonstrate that the 'primary purpose' of the marriage was not immigration – a rule which was used to deny access to potential spouses, particularly from the Indian subcontinent even where the legality or genuineness of the marriage was not in question (JCWI, 1997).[9]

The Asylum and Immigration Act 1993 introduced new powers to curb the rights of asylum-seekers to welfare services and to appeal against negative decisions. These restrictions were extended in the Asylum and Immigration Act 1996 which made it a criminal offence to employ a person with 'no immigration entitlement to work', thus requiring employers 'to act as de facto immigration officials' (Refugee Council, 1995, p. 5). The Act also withdrew welfare benefits for the majority of asylum-seekers (that is, all in-country asylum applications and those taking their case to appeal) leading to an increase in homelessness and poverty (Carter, 1996). There has been a growing tendency for welfare and other services to be used for surveillance, with access conditional on proof of immigration status (Owers, 1994). As public services are increasingly regulated by financial targets, it has become easier to exclude those deemed not to qualify on account of immigration status since health services, for example, are unable to claim from the health authority for the cost of treating them.

There are, therefore, diverse citizenship rights amongst British residents, in both *de jure* and *de facto* terms. Britain now has a substantial black and ethnic minority population with full citizenship rights. These racialized[10] groups occupy a generally subordinate position within the labour market, although their experiences are extremely diverse. Irish citizens have had full citizenship rights in Britain since the partition of Ireland and now participate as EU citizens in freedom of movement. Patterns of Irish migration to Britain have become more diversified in recent decades (McLaughlin, 1994) but continue to reflect relations of inequality (Hickman and Walter, 1997). There are increasing numbers of residents with limited or insecure rights of residence and access to social rights. This diversity of status has different implications for men and women, since women's residence is often dependent on men. At the extreme end are the 'undocumented' who have no legal right to remain because they entered clandestinely, 'overstayed' a temporary visa (for example a student visa or work permit) or their application for asylum has been refused.

## GENDER, RACE AND EMPLOYMENT

In tightening the conditions under which they may reside, work and gain access to social rights in Britain, non-citizens have become more vulnerable and open to exploitation within the labour market. The social and economic agenda of European integration, in particular the deregulation of the labour market, has exacerbated inequalities between workers and has tended to affect those sectors in which black and ethnic minority women are concentrated. Although second- and third-generation migrants, and those born outside Britain who have acquired British citizenship, have the same formal employment rights as local workers these groups have been disproportionately affected by these policies. In the following sections, we examine the implications of these processes for women with different citizenship and migration status.

### Black and Ethnic Minority Citizens

The past two decades have seen a general shift to the service sector, and a casualization of women's work (Morokvasic, 1993). Their concentration in occupations classified as 'unskilled' or 'semi-skilled' has made women particularly vulnerable in the processes of restructuring which have accompanied the development of the single market (Mason, 1994). These problems have been exacerbated in Britain, where labour market deregulation has been part of a strategy of competing with other European countries through cheapening labour. Wages councils, which used to set minimum wages for workers in low-paid sectors such as hotels and catering, were abolished in 1993. A quarter of all black and Asian employees work in these occupations (Wrench, 1993). According to Bhavnani (1994) black women are over-represented in occupations in decline; where they are to be found in areas of growth, the jobs are being offered on less advantageous terms than formerly. Private contractors are relying increasingly on a black labour force, including refugee labour, in areas such as cleaning and catering. On the other hand, the expansion of white-collar service sector jobs such as financial services and retailing has benefited mainly white women (Bhavnani, 1997).

These trends have brought differential levels of unemployment for black and ethnic minority workers. In 1995 unemployment for young blacks was more than twice as high as that for white workers (TUC, 1996). The differential is also apparent in youth unemployment:[11] in 1997, this was 15 per cent for all ethnic groups, but for young black people it was as high as 36 per cent, 31 per cent for Pakistanis and Bangladeshis, and 26 per cent for Indians (Social Trends, 1998).

Official statistics are misleading in that they exclude women working in an unpaid capacity in family businesses and as undocumented domestic workers and homeworkers, both groups in which black and ethnic minority women are likely to be over-represented. A recent report for the Equal Opportunities Commission (Owen, 1994) showed that ethnic minority women face disproportionately higher unemployment, and earn lower incomes in spite of higher than average skills. European welfare states were constructed on the assumption of a 'family wage' and women's dependence (Williams, 1989). In Britain the benefit system creates a disincentive for wives of unemployed men to enter the labour force, since the men incur loss of benefits if their wives earn. Women are now more likely to be out of the labour force if their husbands are unemployed than if they are in work (McWilliams, 1991). There is, therefore, a disproportionately large number of ethnic minority families in which neither partner is in work. The system creates a particular disincentive for women whose partners are unemployed to work part-time. Bruegel's (1989) study of sex and race in the labour market showed that part-time work is not merely 'women's work' but primarily 'white women's work' since their partners are more likely to be in employment. Subordination of women is thus compounded by racism. The changes in tax and benefit structure introduced in the 1998 Budget in order to promote 'welfare to work' may change this picture, since it aims to establish minimum levels for family income. Critics have pointed out, however, that in the absence of spending to boost employment, unemployed people are likely to find themselves forced into low-paid, casualized employment.

Unemployment has led to high levels of self-employment in some communities, particularly Asian communities (Owen, 1994, p. 95). Women also often work in family businesses, or engage in homeworking (see Bhopal, this volume). While this may be seen as a particularly exploitative form of control over women's labour, it can also be a response to exclusion from the formal labour market (Brah, 1993).

For those in formal employment, the rewards for black and ethnic minority workers tends to be lower. A study by the Trades Union Congress based on the Labour Force Survey found that in 1995, the gross hourly earnings of black employees[12] was on average 5 per cent lower than that of white workers (TUC, 1996, p. 4) and the differentials were greatest at the highest and lowest earnings bands (ibid., p. 7). According to this report, the difference was almost entirely in the male rate, with black women earning almost as much as men. As Bruegel (1989) shows, however, it may be misleading to compare national earnings levels, since black and ethnic minority women are disproportionately concentrated in cities (particularly London) where earnings are higher. She shows that if black and white women's earnings are compared for London, the differentials are much greater.

## Labour Migrants

Labour migrants without permanent right of settlement face increasingly stringent conditions on their residence and access to social rights. These developments apply to professional workers as well as to those in low-status employment. Work permits have become more difficult to obtain for Commonwealth citizens (Fekete, 1997, p. 3) and the conditions attached to them more stringent. Rights to other social rights such as welfare benefits have been restricted, with child benefit removed from those holding work permits in 1997.

Freedom of movement legislation has brought moves to replace non-EU citizens with those from the EU. This has been most apparent in the National Health Service, which has relied heavily on black and ethnic minority labour since its establishment, and had been exempt from the provisions of the Immigration Acts of the 1960s in order to preserve the flow of new workers (Bhavnani, 1997, p. 26). Attempts to reduce the reliance on immigration from outside the EU were called for in a report by the government's Chief Medical Officer (Calman, 1993). This has led to an extension of recruitment of doctors and nurses from within the EU (most significantly from Ireland). The shift to employing doctors from the EU has already become noticeable (*NHS Annual Report*, 1997) while medical schools are planning to expand the number of medical training places available within Britain in order to replace migrants.[13] Harmonization of employment conditions includes the mutual recognition of qualifications within Europe, which will further differentiate EU from non-EU citizens.

These changes might be expected to provide increased opportunities for black and ethnic minority citizens, for whom the NHS remains a major employer. The racism and xenophobia associated with the restrictions on migration, however, is not a positive climate in which to promote equal opportunities. A study in 1995 for the Policy Studies Institute found continued discrimination in the health service (Bhavnani, 1997, p. 27). Ethnic minority women tend to occupy the lower rungs of the professions, for example, being predominantly state enrolled nurses rather than the higher status state registered nurses (ibid., p. 26).

The majority of women migrants in Europe now work in domestic services (Anderson, 1997) and many of them are undocumented with limited rights (see Tacoli, this volume). Domestic workers are permitted to enter Britain under a special arrangement which prevents them from changing their employer for four years. They are dependent on that employer for legal residence, and have no recourse to the law if ill-treated, risking deportation if they leave. Anderson (1993) estimates that there are 4,500 abused domestic workers in Britain in the 1990s. The British government is now considering introducing new regulations for this type of labour.

There has been a growing diversity in the employment, residence and social rights of non-citizens working in the EU. Those with permanent residence status have gained some of the social rights associated with citizenship (Soysal, 1994), while increasing numbers of new migrants are being denied these rights. The logic of European integration however is to sharpen the divisions between EU citizens and non-citizens, giving renewed importance to formal citizenship status (Kofman and Sales, 1998). Non-citizens, for example, cannot take advantage of the freedom of movement legislation within Europe, and while mobility is encouraged within the EU *their* residence status becomes more tightly confined to a single state.

**Dependants**

Family reunion is now the main source of legal migration into Britain (Kofman and Sales, 1997). Although the majority entering in this way are women, men are increasingly joining wives resident in Britain. In the first half of 1997, 3,590 men were admitted in this way, and 4,390 women (Home Office, 1997). Dependants have no immediate residence status in their own right. In Britain the 'one-year rule' means that a wife who leaves her husband or is widowed or deserted within a year of entry risks deportation. Under a rule established in 1985, dependants must have 'no recourse to public funds': this means that they are not eligible for benefits, and unless they find employment are unable to support themselves independently.

Women who enter Britain as dependants through family reunion or with a man who has a work permit are often economically active, although this may not be in the formal labour market. They are currently allowed to work but are not able to apply for work permits in their own right if offered permanent employment.[14] This means that a woman's residence status continues to be dependent on her husband's employment, even if she is able to support herself.

An EU convention in late 1997 proposed to remove the right to work for family dependants (*Statewatch*, 1998). If implemented, these restrictions would lead to an expansion of informal and exploitative forms of work.

## Refugees

Refugees granted full convention status or given Exceptional Leave to Remain (ELR)[15] are entitled to work, but asylum-seekers must wait six months before they can apply for permission to work and are not allowed to register as unemployed. They must pay full overseas student fees for education and training, thus deterring them from gaining skills, language proficiency and experience relevant to the labour market.

Refugees, even when granted full refugee status, find it extremely difficult to gain employment. A research project on refugee settlement conducted for the Home Office (Carey-Wood et al., 1995) was based on interviews with 263 refugees from a range of communities. Most came from urban areas with good educational backgrounds (one third with a degree or professional qualification) and 66 per cent had been employed in their home country (ibid., p. 115). Only just over a quarter (27 per cent) of the sample was in employment at the time of the survey, and less than a quarter of the women (ibid., p. 116). Many of those in employment felt that their jobs were well below the level for which they were qualified (ibid., p. ix).

Although employment is recognized as the key to successful resettlement (Field, 1985; Phillips, 1987; Clark 1992; Carey-Wood et al., 1995; Duke and Marshall, 1995), Britain has no permanent programme for the resettlement of refugees, and support for refugees wishing to enter the labour market is patchy. Potential employers tend to see refugees as temporary residents and are reluctant to take people on, and the requirement to check immigration status reduces the willingness of employers to take on anyone whose status might be insecure. The standard Home Office letter which confirms entitlement to work is unlikely to be encouraging to nervous employers:

> You should however, fully understand that if … you take part in activities involving the support or encouragement of violence or conspiracy to cause violence … the (Home Secretary) may curtail your stay or deport you. (quoted in Refugee Council, undated)

A number of studies have pointed to the specific problems faced by refugees in gaining employment (Marshall, 1989; Carey-Wood et al., 1995). A major problem is the lack of experience in employment in Britain. Furthermore, it is unlikely that refugees will have access to references or proof of their own qualifications. While many face obstacles to gaining skills, others are overqualified for the work they do. The problem will be exacerbated as the Single Market promotes transferability of qualifications between EU states, while excluding qualifications gained outside.

Women face particular difficulties in gaining employment as a result of the scarcity of childcare and their separation from social support networks. Many women refugees are single parents, often having lost their husbands in conflict. They also face specific discrimination from employers since very often 'the only jobs that are available to refugee women involve low pay and are of a temporary or part-time nature' (Refugee Council, undated).

Refugees and migrants tend to rely heavily on social networks in their established ethnic communities to search for employment (Fraser, 1988; Smith et al., 1991; Carey-Wood et al., 1995; Duke and Marshall, 1995). This may allow them to avoid discrimination in the formal labour market, but it can also facilitate exploitation (Smith et al., 1991). Women are particularly likely to be involved in informal work, including homeworking or small, family-run businesses unprotected by trade unions or health and safety and employment legislation. A survey in Hackney, East London, estimated that 5,000 people from Turkish, Kurdish and African refugee communities, about half of them women, work in local sweatshops. Conditions are intolerable, with workers crammed into small, ill-lit rooms using old, hazardous machinery. Many more Turkish and Kurdish women take in work at home, and can expect to earn less than £1 an hour.[16] Newer refugee communities, such as Somalis, lack these networks and unemployment rates are extremely high (Sales and Gregory, 1996).

## CONCLUSION

Our analysis suggests a fundamental contradiction at the heart of EU social policy. On the one hand, the governments of most member states are committed to combating social exclusion and seeking to develop an increasingly sophisticated body of social and economic rights. On the other hand, no practical steps have been taken to ensure that the most vulnerable groups have access to these rights. These developments are producing an ever-widening gulf between formal and substantive equality, between theoretical access to the labour market and the reality of continuing discrimination, and between those with high-status, well-paid and relatively secure jobs and those who are either excluded from the labour market altogether or exist at its margins in various kinds of precarious employment. At the same time, the increasingly draconian policies on migration and asylum are leaving many more people with insecure residence status and limited access to basic social rights. In the context of high levels of unemployment and increasing casualization, it is the most recently arrived groups of migrants and refugees, particularly women, who experience social exclusion in its most acute form.

If social exclusion is to be combated seriously, a dramatic reversal of current political and economic strategies is required. This should include a determined opposition by governments of member states to all forms of individual and institutional discrimination; a recognition of the positive contribution that migrants and refugees can make to the social and economic life of Europe, given a positive and supportive framework; and a radical reformulation of the concept of citizenship, based on an acceptance of the civil, political and social rights of all EU residents regardless of national origin.

## NOTES

1. The European Social Charter of Workers' Rights, agreed in 1989, listed a number of Fundamental Social Rights which were to be introduced through a series of directives from the European Commission. A revised, and weaker, version was introduced as the 'Social Chapter' of the Maastricht Treaty of 1992, but because the British government insisted on opting out of this area, it was attached to the Treaty as the 'Social Agreement' and was not binding on all signatories to the Treaty.
2. Third country national is the EU term for nationals of non-member states.
3. We refer below to 'Britain' rather than 'United Kingdom'. While the government is formally of the United Kingdom of Britain and Northern Ireland, Northern Ireland's social and labour market structures are so different from those of Britain that it is not included in the current discussion. Although Northern Ireland has had legislation to combat discrimination on grounds of religion since 1976, the Race Relations Act was introduced there only in 1997.
4. The Commission for Racial Equality, which commissioned research on the position of the Irish in Britain (Hickman and Walter, 1997), is calling for the Irish to be recognized as an ethnic category in future monitoring such as the Census.

5.  Formerly known as the European Economic Community and later the European Community. Since the signing of the Treaty of European Union (the Maastricht Treaty, 1992) the term European Union has been commonly used.
6.  Harmonization based on real economic indicators might include policies to equalize income per head, employment levels and spending on public services. The Maastricht Agreement proposes convergence around monetary indicators including the level of inflation and the size of the public sector deficit.
7.  'Social dumping' refers to the potential for the erosion of national provision as a result of the increased competition unleashed by the SEM and the drive to cut costs. This is particularly problematic in view of the wide regional disparities within the EU – increased with recent additions to membership – and differences in social provision.
8.  This refers to postwar patterns of migration. Migration had been important in many economies before the war, most notably in Britain.
9.  The Labour government elected in May 1997 has formally abolished this rule, but it is not yet clear what impact abolition will have on this group of applicants.
10. The term 'racialized' has been used to refer to groups who have been subject to racism. In this view 'race' is a social construct, and racism involves justifying the denial to a group of equal access to resources or political rights on the grounds of supposed inherent characteristics (biological or cultural) (see Miles and Phizacklea, 1980, p. 22). The Irish are a group which have been 'racialized' in this way in Britain.
11. Unemployment of 16–24 year olds as a percentage of economically active, based on ILO definitions.
12. The report used the term 'black' to refer to all those defined as ethnic minority in the Labour Force Survey.
13. Reported in *The Times Higher Education Supplement*, 24 April 1998.
14. The Home Office has had the discretion since the 1981 Immigration Act to prevent women from changing their status, and started to enforce this rule strictly during the 1990s.
15. ELR is granted on humanitarian grounds to those who are not deemed to meet the criteria for Convention Status. It is granted initially for one year but may be extended. Those with ELR enjoy many of the same social rights as Convention refugees. A major difference is that they have no right to family reunion: they can apply only after they have been in the country for four years, and must meet the same conditions as other migrants.
16. Information supplied by Hackney Trade Union Support Group.

## REFERENCES

Anderson, B., *Britain's Secret Slaves*. London: Anti-Slavery International/ Kalayaan, 1993.
Anderson, B., 'Servants and slaves: Europe's domestic workers', *Race and Class* 39(1) (1997) 37–49.
Bailey, J. (ed.), *Social Europe*. Harlow: Longman, 1992.

Bennington, J. and Taylor M., 'Changes and challenges facing the UK welfare state in the Europe of the 1990s', *Policy and Politics* vol. 21 no. 2 (1993).

Bhavnani, R., *Black Women in the Labour Market: a Research Review.* Manchester: Equal Opportunities Commission, 1994.

Bhavnani, R., *Black and Minority Ethnic Women in the Labour Market in London: First Major Review.* London: Fair Play, 1997.

Brah, A., '"Race" and "culture" in the gendering of labour markets: South Asian young Muslim women and the labour market', *New Community* 19(3) (1993) 441–58.

Calman, K., *Hospital Doctors: Training for the Future*, Great Britain Working Group on Specialist Medical Training. London: Department of Health, 1993.

Carey-Wood, J., Duke, K., Karn, V. and Marshall, T., *The Settlement of Refugees in Britain.* London: HMSO, 1995.

Clark, G., *Refugees and the Greenwich Labour Market.* London: Local Economic Policy Unit, South Bank Polytechnic, 1992.

Carter, M., *Poverty and Prejudice: a Preliminary Report on the Withdrawal of Benefit Entitlement and the Impact of the Asylum and Immigration Bill.* London: Refugee Council, 1996.

Duke, K. and Marshall, T., *Vietnamese Refugees since 1982.* London: HMSO, 1995.

Duke, K., Sales, R. and Gregory, J., 'Refugee resettlement in Europe', in A. Bloch and C. Levy (eds), *Social Policy in Britain and Europe.* London: Macmillan (1999).

Fekete, L., 'Blackening the economy: the path to convergence', *Race and Class* 39(1) (1997) 1–17.

Fernhout, R., ' "Europe 1993" and its refugees', *New Community* 16(3) (1993) 495.

Field, S., *Resettling Refugees: the Lessons of Research.* London: HMSO, 1985.

Forbes, I. and Mead, G., *Measure for Measure.* London: Department of Employment, 1992.

Fraser, L., *Research into the Employment, Training and Educational Needs of Refugees from Vietnam in Leeds and Bradford.* London: Refugee Action, 1988.

Hickman, M.J. and Walter, B., *Discrimination and the Irish Community in Britain.* London: Commission for Racial Equality, 1997.

Home Office, 'Control of immigration: statistics United Kingdom, first half 1997', *Home Office Statistical Bulletin* 26/97. London: Home Office, 1997.

Joint Council for the Welfare of Immigrants (JCWI), *Immigration, Nationality and Refugee Law Handbook: a User's Guide.* London: JCWI, 1997.

Kofman, E. and Sales, R., 'Gender differences in entry to Europe – implications for refugees', in *Refuge*, journal of the Centre for Refugee Studies, York University, Canada (1997) 26–30.

Kofman, E. and Sales, R., 'Migrant women and exclusion in Europe', *European Journal of Women's Studies* (1998).

Leibfried, S., 'Conceptualising European social policy; the EC as social actor', in L. Hantrais and S. Mangen (eds), *The Policy Making Process and the Social Actors,* Loughborough: Cross-National Research Papers, vol. 3 no. 1 (August 1993).

Marshall, T., *Cultural Aspects of Job Hunting.* London: Refugee Council, 1989.

Mason, D., 'Employment and the labour market', *New Community* 20(2) (1994) 301–8.

McLaughlin, J., *Ireland: the Emigrant Nursery and the World Economy.* Cork: Cork University Press, 1994.

McWilliams, M., 'Women in Northern Ireland: an overview', in E. Hughes (ed.), *Culture and Politics in Northern Ireland.* Milton Keynes: Open University Press, 1991.

Miles, R. and Phizacklea, A., *Labour and Racism.* London: Routledge & Kegan Paul, 1980.

Morokvasic, M., ' "In and out" of the labour market: immigrant and minority women in Europe', *New Community* 19(3) (1993) 459–83.

Morris, L., 'A cluster of contradictions: the politics of migration in the European Union', *Sociology* 31(2) (1997) 241–59.

National Health Service (NHS), *Annual Report.* London: HMSO, 1997.

Owen, D., *Ethnic Minority Women and the Labour Market: an Analysis of the 1991 Census.* Manchester: Equal Opportunities Commission, 1994.

Owers, A., 'The age of internal controls?', in S. Spencer (ed.), *Strangers and Citizens: a Positive Approach to Migrants and Refugees.* London: Rivers Oram Press, 1994.

Phillips, A., 'Employment as a key to settlement', in D. Joly and R. Cohen (eds), *Reluctant Hosts: Europe and its Refugees.* Aldershot: Gower, 1987.

Refugee Council, *Briefing for MPs on Second Reading of Asylum and Immigration Bill.* London: Refugee Council, 1995.

Refugee Council, *Refugee Employment and Training: a Positive Policy for the 1990s.* London: Refugee Council, undated.

Sales, R. and Gregory, J., 'Employment, Citizenship and European Integration: the Implications for Migrant and Refugee Women', *Social Politics* vol. 3 nos 2/3 (1996) 331–50.

Samers, M., 'Immigration, "ethnic minorities" and "social exclusion" in the European Union: a critical perspective', *Geoforum,* special issue on Exclusion (1998).

Smith, M.P., Tarallo, B. and Kagiwada, G., 'Coloring California: new Asian immigrant households, social networks and the local state', *International Journal of Urban and Regional Research,* 15(2) (1991) 250–68.

*Social Trends* Office of National Statistics, London (1998) 28.

Soysal, Y.N., *Limits of Citizenship: Migrants and Postnational Membership in Europe.* Chicago: University of Chicago Press, 1994.

Spencer, S. (ed.), *Strangers and Citizens: a Positive Approach to Migrants and Refugees.* London: Rivers Oram Press, 1994.

Statewatch, 'Schengen and EU agree to extend Fortress Europe', *Statewatch* vol. 8(1) 1 (1998) London.

*The Times Higher Education Supplement,* London, 24 April 1998.

Trades Union Congress (TUC), 'The wages of discrimination: black workers and low pay', in *1995 TUC.* London: TUC Economic and Social Affairs Department, 1996.

Williams, F., *Social Policy: a Critical Introduction, Issues of Race, Gender and Class.* Cambridge: Polity, 1989.

Wrench, J., 'Employment and the labour market', *New Community* 16(4) (1990) 575–83.

Wrench, J., 'Employment and the labour market', *New Community* 19(4) (1993) 669–74.

Wrench, J., *Preventing Racism at the Workplace.* Dublin: European Foundation for the Improvement of Living and Working Conditions, 1996.

# 7 Just Like One of the Family? Gender, Ethnicity and Migrant Status among Filipino Domestic Workers in Rome

Cecilia Tacoli

This chapter examines the causes and mechanisms of Filipino workers' concentration in Rome's domestic service sector. The underlying argument is that while ethnicity and migrant status are crucial in determining access to, and segregation into, this specific segment of the labour market, the latter is also cross-cut by gender. Thus, although both Filipino men and women are primarily employed in domestic service, there are significant differences in work arrangements, duties and conditions which reflect normative gender roles on both demand and supply sides. The discussion draws on doctoral research conducted in Rome in 1994–5, involving structured interviews with 154 Filipino migrant workers (123 women and 31 men), indepth interviews with a subsample of 38 respondents and semi-structured interviews with ten Italian employers.[1]

## IMMIGRATION FROM THE PHILLIPINES TO ITALY

International labour migration to Southern Europe is a relatively recent phenomenon which coincided with the introduction of restrictive policies in the more traditional Western European destinations such as Germany and France in the early 1970s. While ease of entry is often identified as an important factor in encouraging movement to this region (King and Rybaczuk, 1993), the 'new countries of immigration' of southern Europe (Italy, Greece and Spain) also reflect more visibly the global tendencies in contemporary international labour movement (Castles and Miller, 1993). Acceleration, or the steady increase in the number of people moving, and globalization, or the increase in the scope of the movement, translate into the region attracting proportionally more people from 'third world' countries than from other nations in the European Union. The 'feminization' of international migration is also more visible, with women accounting for almost half of the total number of registered migrants. This reflects major changes in the world economy during the last two decades. In the postwar period, the bulk of the migrants to the core economies were semi-skilled males who found employment in the industrial sector. However, since the 1980s the relocation of manufacturing industries to 'third world' nations has shifted demand for migrant labour to low-paid, unskilled and mainly female service sector jobs (Sassen-Koob, 1984).

Filipino migration to Italy started in the 1970s and was initially made up almost entirely of women who worked as domestic helpers. In 1993, government data showed that out of 21,400 registered Filipino citizens in Rome, 70 per cent were women and 90 per cent of these were employed in the domestic service sector (Caritas, 1993). Similar patterns are seen in migration from Cape Verde and some Latin American countries. These figures contrast with the other main national groups in Italy: migrants from North African countries such as Morocco, Tunisia and Egypt, and from sub-Saharan Africa are almost exclusively male and tend to be concentrated in agriculture, construction and mainstream services (restaurants, hotels, and so on). The overall picture of international labour migration to Italy is thus one in which the various nationality groups have an extremely skewed sex composition and find employment in different occupational niches (Carchedi and Ranuzzi, 1987; Macioti and Pugliese, 1991). The interrelation between gender and ethnicity is therefore fundamental to an understanding of how labour markets function (McIlwaine, 1995).

These differences in employment opportunities are consistent with the segmentation of the labour market along gender lines, and it has been noted in other contexts that domestic service is often the main if not the only work available for female migrants (Chant, 1992). However, the fact that the growing numbers of Filipino men in Italy also work predominantly in this sector suggests that other factors, such as state policies, gender and ethnic stereotyping on the demand side and the role of social networks in providing access to specific occupational niches, should be taken into account (Tacoli, 1995).

## DOMESTIC SERVICE IN ITALY

Until the end of the Second World War, domestic service in Italy provided employment for young women who could not be supported by their families in the countryside. Although salaries were extremely low, workers could help support their families or save up to get married while working in a 'respectable' environment in their middle-class employers' home. Most domestic service was on a full-time, live-in basis, and this made it morally acceptable for young, single women to move to the cities. The nature of the labour supply was however transformed by extensive internal migration linked to the Italian 'economic miracle' of the 1960s.[2] Whole family units moved from the still predominantly agricultural areas of central and southern Italy to the cities, where the men found work in the industrial and construction sectors. Domestic service provided the main employment opportunity for their wives, given their lack of training in non-agricultural jobs and the shrinking of handicraft activities and textile industries which in the past had been traditional employers of female labour (Sassoon, 1986). These women were not, however, prepared to reside with their employers but preferred to work on a part-time basis, combining paid housework and unpaid domestic activities in their own households. The passage from mainly full-time, live-in to predominantly part-time, live-out organization had a significant impact on waged household work, and domestic helpers' status shifted from 'one of the family' to waged worker, with legally sanctioned rights and obligations.

Moreover, in the 1970s domestic service became increasingly unattractive for younger women who, having grown up in the cities and having gained better educational qualifications than their mothers, had higher employment expectations. According to trade union officials working in this sector, few Italian domestic helpers are under the age of 55, as younger women prefer to work in conditions perceived as more dignified, such as cleaning cooperatives and other non-personal service jobs (Carchedi and Ranuzzi, 1987). The domestic service sector thus has one of the largest proportions of migrant workers: in 1991, they made up 39.23 per cent of domestics holding a regular work contract in the Latium region[3] (Caritas, 1994).

One reason for this development is that demand for domestic help has remained high. This is due to three interrelated factors: the increase in women's paid employment; the insufficiency of public social services such as childcare and care for the elderly; and men's limited participation in reproductive activities within the home. Italian women's employment rate increased from 31.5 per cent in 1980 to 34.5 per cent in 1990 (Altieri, 1993) and although this figure is relatively low compared to other EU countries, it shows a tendency towards the reduction of differentials in labour force participation by sex. That said, occupational sex segregation and the growth of female unemployment play a major role in the Italian labour market. Women are concentrated in services, which employ over 60 per cent of all female workers but only 43 per cent of males. In addition, 25.6 per cent of women work less than 36 hours per week, against 8 per cent of men[4] (Altieri, 1993). Italian women are also more likely than men to be officially unemployed: in 1992, their unemployment rate was 17.3 per cent, compared to 8.1 per cent for men (UNDP, 1995). In short, Italian women's place in the labour market is still not equal to men's, although the last two decades have seen steady improvements in their access to paid employment.

Insufficiency of public care of children and the elderly plays an important role in keeping demand for private domestic service high. Public care for the elderly is particularly inadequate in Italy, although 16 per cent of the population is aged 65 and above (UNDP, 1995). Very few local health authorities grant long-term assistance at home since it is often assumed that the larger family unit will take care of elderly relatives. As the private hiring of trained nurses is extremely expensive, migrant domestic helpers are often the only viable alternative, and care for the elderly (*assistenza agli anziani*) is an important sector of personal service. The third factor affecting the demand side is the sexual division of labour within the household. Recent research on time use has shown that, as in most countries in the world, Italian working women are still primarily responsible for household reproductive activities (Sabbadini and Palomba, 1994). For those who can afford it, hiring household help is often a better option than risking familial conflict by challenging deeply ingrained gender roles and demanding a more equitable distribution of domestic chores.

While the imbalance between a dwindling supply of national labour prepared to work in domestic service and growing demand for this type of worker plays a major role in attracting large numbers of migrant domestic helpers, institutional factors, in particular major changes in labour legislation governing domestic service contracts, also need to be taken into account. The national contract for domestic helpers established in 1974 is applicable irrespective of the worker's nationality, and defines working conditions, salaries and benefits and obligations of both employers and employees (ILO, 1991). Employers and workers alike must pay national insurance contributions to INPS (*Istituto Nazionale della Previdenza Sociale*), covering health insurance and pension funds. The amounts due are regularly updated by INPS, and average one-third of wages for employers and just over 5 per cent for employees. In addition, every year employers must pay three extra months' salaries: one for the thirteenth month (*tredicesima*),[5] one as paid holiday, and one as separation pay (INCA-CGIL, 1990). It has been suggested that this relatively strict regulation has been important in increasing demand for migrant household workers by employers unwilling to comply with labour legislation (Carchedi and Ranuzzi, 1987; Macioti and Pugliese, 1991). Immigration regulations have also been crucial in determining migrant workers' access to the Italian labour market.

## Immigration Policies and the Labour Market

Until the mid-1980s, when it became evident that Italy was becoming a country of immigration, migrant labour was dealt with only as part of wider measures relating to public order and policing (Calavita, 1994). Following calls for comprehensive national legislation from opposition parties, trade unions and welfare institutions, in 1986 Parliament passed Act No. 943, which sought to comply with the ILO Convention on the Protection of Migrant Workers by establishing the principle of equal treatment and equal opportunities for Italian and foreign workers. The Act included the regularization of migrants in dependent employment on the basis of their own or their employer's declaration. The latter would then have to pay all back taxes and national insurance contributions. However, the inherent contradiction of asking employers to increase their labour costs, or workers to risk their jobs by denouncing their employers, proved a major obstacle, and few immigrants benefited from the exercise.

Migration to Italy is currently regulated by Act 943/1986 for labour matters and Act 39/1990, which deals with political asylum, entry and residence of non-European Union immigrants. While attempting to reduce the entry of undocumented migrants, Act 39/1990 also entailed a regularization programme for foreigners who had entered the country before the end of 1989.[6] Thereafter, legal entry to Italy has been granted only for family reunification purposes and to migrant workers directly hired by Italian employers from their country of origin upon certification by the Italian authorities of the unavailability of Italian workers for the same job. Temporary residence permits are renewed only if the migrant worker can prove that s/he has a legal work contract. Alternatively, migrants must declare themselves informally employed and state the name of their employer, thus again risking the loss of their job. However, these increasingly restrictive policies do not appear to have deterred the arrival of undocumented migrants.[7]

In addition to the two Immigration Acts, bilateral agreements between Italy and migrants' countries of origin play a major role. The most relevant to labour market conditions are those regulating reciprocity and the liberal professions, and those dealing with welfare and social security. The first type allows migrant workers to be self-employed or to own businesses in Italy. The second provides for the payment of an international pension equal at least to the Italian minimum to workers who have paid national insurance contributions for a number of years. Both agreements are pending between the Philippine and Italian governments: as a consequence, Filipino migrants cannot set up businesses unless they have an Italian partner who is legally responsible for the activity. Given the current reorganization of the Italian welfare system, it is unlikely that pension transferability will be ratified in the near future. Hence, the payment of national insurance contributions is often perceived merely as a means towards the renewal of temporary residence permits, and Filipino workers are thus more willing to accept partial payments of their contributions for this purpose only. Bilateral agreements therefore appear to contradict the stated purpose of the Immigration Acts, which is to guarantee equal opportunities for Italian and foreign workers, by confining one national group to a specific labour market segment and making it potentially a cheaper labour force.

**Employers' Compliance with Legislation**

Several employers have been reluctant to pay national insurance contributions to INPS. The fact that these are only payable for registered migrants makes the hiring of undocumented workers more attractive. Almost half of the respondents in the survey had no payments made on their behalf by employers, reflecting the significant proportion of unregistered Filipino workers in Rome. This also applied however to over 15 per cent of documented respondents. Since renewal of temporary residence permits is based on the receipt of INPS contributions, it is possible that a number of previously documented migrants will be forced into irregular status once their first permit expires.

Entitlement to separation pay, thirteenth month pay and paid holiday is part of the domestic helpers' national collective contract, and, unlike national insurance payments, is not affected by migrant workers' legal status. In practice, however, both legal status and employment arrangements appear to have a significant impact on employers' willingness to comply. Thus, live-in workers (whose salaries are generally lower than those of part-timers') are more likely to be paid all three months. However, while this was the case for over 90 per cent of documented live-in household helpers in the study, it applied to only three-quarters of unregistered live-in workers. This difference was even more pronounced among part-time workers, where only 45 per cent of unregistered migrants were paid these allowances, compared with over 86 per cent of documented respondents.

Documented migrants who do not receive extra salaries explain it as a consequence of competition from unregistered, and thus cheaper, workers. In other words, as supply of domestic service labour is high, they fear that by asking their employers to respect the national contract they may risk losing their jobs. Migrant status is thus crucial in determining Filipino workers' unequal position in the Italian labour market. In order to understand how this interrelates with gender and ethnicity in structuring workers' experiences, the following sections examine the social relations which underpin domestic service employment.

## Employment of Filipino Migrants in Rome: the Importance of Gender

There are significant variations in the ways in which waged household work is structured. The main distinction is between full-time, live-in employment, and part-time, live-out employment which involves independent accommodation and hourly paid work, usually for several employers. Other differences relate to the nature of the tasks involved. For analytical purposes, these can be divided between cleaning the employers' home and caring for children and elderly members of the household. The research revealed that the range of tasks performed by domestic workers was closely related to employment arrangements: live-in, full-time domestics in the study were three times more likely than live-out, part-time counterparts to combine both categories of activity. The overwhelming majority of the latter were employed exclusively as cleaners and few respondents were required only to look after young children or elderly persons. A minority (22 per cent) of male respondents worked as live-in domestic helpers and only one combined cleaning and caring. By contrast, 58 per cent of female respondents were employed on a live-in basis, and the proportion of women combining cleaning with caring was much higher than among men (see Table 7.1).

There also appears to be a distinction between childcare and care for the elderly. The latter is perceived as a more 'male' job, since it may involve physical effort if the elder is disabled. It is also seen as more akin to nursing than domestic service, and involving a higher degree of professionalism, although previous nursing experience is not normally required by employers. As a consequence, cleaning is not part of these workers' responsibilities. Childcare, by contrast, is almost exclusively performed by women and is usually combined with cleaning duties. Thus, while both male and female domestic workers perform similar tasks, there are major differences in the ways these are organized which reflect prevailing

*Table 7.1*  Tasks undertaken by domestic service workers, by sex

| Task | Women (%) | Men (%) | Total (%) |
|---|---|---|---|
| Cleaning only | 72.6 (82) | 78.3 (18) | 73.5 (100) |
| Cleaning and caring | 22.1 (25) | 4.3 (1) | 19.2 (26) |
| Caring only | 5.3 (6) | 17.4 (4) | 7.3 (10) |
| Total | 100 (113) | 100 (23) | 100 (136) |

*Source*: Author's survey. Figures in brackets indicate number of respondents. The total number does not include those who were unemployed at the time of the interview (eleven, of which eight women and three men) and those employed in non-personal service jobs (seven, of which two women and five men).

ideologies of domestic labour as 'women's work'. Women's responsibilities more frequently encompass the whole range of reproductive activities and men's duties cover only part.

## The Social Relations of Domestic Service Employment

Aside from the small number who had previously been employed as domestics in the Middle East and South East Asia, the majority of respondents had held white-collar jobs in the Philippines and some had themselves been employers of domestic helpers. Adapting to the new environment and to their position as migrant household workers inevitably takes time, and the first few months in Rome could be very hard. In this context, relationships with employers were seen by most respondents as crucial. An essential feature of domestic service is that it takes place in employers' 'private' spaces, and involves activities which are usually expected to be undertaken by women within their own families as part of their 'natural' role. The social relations of domestic service are thus shaped by the intersection of wage labour and 'false kinship' relations. Being 'just like one of the family' often involves deeply asymmetrical relationships where employers may entrust workers with their children and their homes, but are also ready to evade labour legislation and to accuse them of stealing personal property (see also Colen, 1989; Gregson and Lowe, 1994).

Migrant workers with no relatives in Rome who spend the majority of their time alone in their employers' homes, often on a live-in basis, are particularly vulnerable in these 'false kinship' relations. One widowed respondent with four children had been working for the same family since 1979 and followed them from the Philippines to Italy. Now that her own children had grown up, she had the opportunity to remarry and return home. However, she felt that she could not leave her employers who had become her 'real family'. Another respondent, also relatively isolated in Rome, was prepared to accept below-average wages and to forfeit INPS contribution payments from her employer because the latter treated her 'like a daughter'.

Employers' perceptions, by contrast, reflected gender and ethnic stereotyping as well as a general desire to 'keep a distance' between themselves and their employees. All the employers of Filipino domestic workers interviewed had hired other household helpers in the past. Filipinos appear to rank high in the ethnic hierarchy, and are considered the most 'integrated' migrant workers in Italy (see also Eurisko, 1989). However, this concept of 'integration' is extremely contradictory, since employers expressed it in terms of Filipinos 'keeping to themselves', 'not forcing you to get to know their life circumstances and their own culture', unlike for example their African counterparts. Employers thus seemed to have a clear perception of what a domestic's place in the house is, and it is obviously not one which involves a personal relationship between employer and employee beyond the bare essentials. Indeed, the preference for migrant workers seemed to stem also from the fact that this distance is more difficult to keep with Italian workers, where class contradictions can express themselves more openly, albeit often within a patron–client type of relationship.

This model of relationship emphasizing the distance between employee and employer is also shaped by gender. Filipino male domestic workers are seen as professionals, reflecting gender roles in which women 'naturally' engage in reproductive activities but men do it as a 'real job'. Female workers may however be preferred for different reasons: as another employer put it, 'now that I have a baby I prefer to have a woman cleaning the house, as she is more aware of the hygiene needs of children than men are'. Men's 'expertise' cannot compete with women's 'natural' knowledge of household work. This, combined with the fact that women are more likely to be employed on a live-in basis, tends to make them more vulnerable to 'false kinship' relations with their employers.

## Recruitment Practices and Occupational Mobility

Since 1990, Italian employers have had two options for legally recruiting immigrant workers. The first is to employ a worker who already has a temporary residence permit, and hence is allowed to work in the country. The second is through direct hire in the worker's country of origin, which is also the only way for migrant workers to enter Italy legally.

The latter involves a compulsory two year live-in employment contract. Employers are not readily prepared to hire a person they have never seen before, and usually require guarantees of the good character of the prospective worker. These are often provided by a previous worker or one employed by persons known to the employer, and the result is that direct hire depends largely on the prospective migrant's existing social network in Rome.

The Catholic Church plays an important intermediary role in the recruitment of workers already in Rome. Indeed, there is a strong correlation between religious affiliation and employment in domestic service, with a prevalence of migrants from predominantly Catholic areas, such as the Philippines, Cape Verde and Latin America, as well as Catholic minorities from India and Sri Lanka (Macioti and Pugliese, 1991, pp. 57–8). However, while in the mid-1970s the Church was the primary source of work contacts for Filipino migrants, the development of social networks has reduced its importance, and the majority of respondents were helped by relatives, friends within Rome and sometimes by previous employers.

Possibly as a consequence of recruitment practices centred on informal networks rather than more structured channels, occupational mobility appears to be limited to different types of domestic service rather than to changes in sector. Only seven respondents were employed in non-personal service activities at the time of the interview, and all had previously worked as domestics. Other respondents who combined domestic service with a secondary activity, such as selling household products on credit, did so within the Filipino community. This extended to clerical jobs which were limited to Filipino businesses such as remittance agencies. The reasons can be traced to the restrictions imposed by the lack of a bilateral agreement between the Philippine and the Italian governments regulating self-employment, and to the lack of recognition of Philippine qualifications by the Italian authorities. All six respondents who had worked upon arrival in non-personal service activities such as nursing were either unemployed or working as domestics at the time of the interview. Here again, immigration policies have an important impact on employment opportunities: between 1991 and June 1994, the Italian government authorized the hiring of foreign-registered nurses. However, most were on short-term contracts, and when these expired they were forced to turn to personal service employment.

There is relatively high horizontal mobility within the personal service sector, both in terms of change of employers and of type of arrangement. Over 80 per cent of respondents had changed employers since arriving in Rome and over three-quarters had been with their present employers for less than three years, while one quarter had taken up their present job within the 12 months preceding the interview. This relatively fast turnover suggests that mobility may be one of the strategies available to workers to escape uneasy relations with employers. Part-time workers also tend to keep one or two 'core' employers, who guarantee payment of national insurance contributions, and have other, less stable jobs which they may take up in periods of increased financial necessity.

The second type of horizontal mobility is from live-in to part-time employment. Live-in domestic service is often preferred initially because it allows newly-arrived migrants to become familiar with employers' lifestyle and demands. A regular monthly salary and limited living expenses are also important at a time when most migrants have to reimburse debts incurred for their travel. Another advantage is that it does not involve moving around an unknown city, and for women it often provides a sense of protection. Part-time employment, by contrast, allows more personal freedom and independence, but it also involves food and accommodation expenses which can be relatively high. Moving to this arrangement often entails a reduction of remittances. Indeed, one reason for the higher proportion of women employed on a live-in basis is that their commitments and obligations towards their households in their home areas are usually stronger than men's, reflecting normative gender roles. For women, migration is usually motivated by the desire to 'look after the family' and for several respondents in the survey the decision to move was made by relatives rather than the migrants themselves. Men, in particular younger ones, are more likely to move as a result of a wish to 'see the world'. As a consequence, women tend to send higher remittances, both in absolute terms and as a percentage of their salaries (Tacoli, 1996). 'Supply'-side factors therefore play an important role in structuring migrants' employment arrangements preferences along gender lines.

## CONCLUSION

Demand for waged household work in Italy is grounded in the fundamentally unequal division of labour within households, where women still bear the main responsibility for reproductive activities despite increasing access to paid employment. Hiring domestic workers in a sense reinforces the ideology of domestic labour as 'women's work', since it allows employers to avoid conflict over the allocation of household chores between household members. The concentration of Filipino men, as well as women, in Rome's domestic service sector only apparently contradicts this. Indeed, while the combination of employers' ethnic stereotyping, Italian immigration policies and recruitment practices is pivotal in structuring Filipino migrants' segregation in this occupational niche, a closer analysis of workers' duties and employment arrangements suggests that normative gender roles underpin substantial differences between men's and women's experiences. Women are much more likely than men to combine caring and cleaning duties, and tend to be employed on a live-in basis, that is, to be perceived as 'just like one of the family' performing women's 'natural work'. Supply factors may be equally important in reinforcing gender-based differences. In particular, women's stronger commitments and obligations towards their households at home can play a major role in structuring their employment preferences. Gender differences thus appear to persist even within a sector of activity which is usually seen as typically feminized. Both female and male migrant workers share a fundamental insecurity with respect to working conditions. Since residence status depends on employment status, the fact that a significant proportion of employers do not comply with labour legislation has a double effect on migrant workers. On the one hand, they are unable to avail themselves of the benefits provided by law to workers; on the other hand, without the proof of employment issued by INPS upon receipt of employers' national insurance contribution payments, they cannot obtain or renew their temporary residence permits. They may, therefore, be forced to remain or return to the status of undocumented migrant, which involves both legal and financial vulnerability. As a result, notwithstanding efforts in the mid-1970s to regulate it, domestic service in Italy seems to be slipping increasingly into the informal sector, where this is defined as 'unregulated by the institutions of society, in a legal and social environment in which similar activities are regulated' (Castells and Portes, 1989, p. 12). In order to understand these labour market dynamics, this paper has argued that it is necessary to consider migrant status, ethnicity and gender as an integrated whole, rather than as separate categories.

NOTES

1.    I would like to thank Dr Sylvia Chant and Dr Diane Perrons, London School of Economics, and Dr Cathy McIlwaine, Queen Mary and Westfield College, University of London, for useful comments on earlier versions of this chapter. I am also grateful to Francesco Carchedi (Parsec),

Peppe Mancini (Filcams/CGIL) and Romana Sansa (INCA/CGIL) for guiding me through the intricacies of Italian immigration and labour legislation.

2. Between 1950 and 1963, the Italian economy grew at such an unprecedented rate that this period became known as 'the economic miracle'. While its essential characteristics, namely the growth of the manufacturing sector, integration into the international economy and rapid urbanization were general features of industrialized countries in those years, the territorial dualism of the Italian economy, with a modern industrial sector in the north and an almost exclusively agricultural south, also entailed massive internal migration. Economic growth during this period relied on the competitiveness of Italian exports, which in turn was based on a low-wage economy due largely to the existence of a cheap supply of labour in the south (Sassoon, 1986).

3. By the end of 1991 there were 33,079 registered domestic workers (that is, those for whom national insurance contributions were paid) in the Latium region, of whom 12,977 were not Italian citizens (Caritas, 1994).

4. Compared to other industrial countries, part-time employment is not very common in Italy. In 1989 it represented just over 5 per cent of total employment and under 11 per cent of female employment. One-third of women working part-time do so because they cannot find a full-time occupation, and thus should rather be categorized as underemployed (Altieri, 1993).

5. '*Tredicesima*', or payment of a 'thirteenth month's' salary is common in Italy for dependent workers whose category of employment is covered by a national collective contract negotiated by trade unions. Some categories with greater bargaining power, such as bank employees, can get additional extra salaries (*quattordicesima, quindicesima* and so on).

6. Another amnesty took place in March 1996. Despite calls for more restrictive policies by right-wing political parties and other European Union national governments, legislative reform had not yet been approved by the time of the fieldwork (1994–5). See also Hoskyns and Orsini-Jones (1995) for a discussion of the linkages between Italian and European legislation.

7. Undocumented migration has been the subject of much debate in Italy since the 1980s. As is usually the case, estimates of numbers vary widely, partly because of temporary or seasonal movement, especially from geographically closer areas such as North and sub-Saharan Africa. Among the respondents interviewed for the present research, 41.6 per cent declared themselves unregistered.

## REFERENCES

Altieri, G., 'L'Occupazione femminile', in M. Paci (ed.), *Le Dimensioni della Disuguaglianza*. Il Bologna: Mulino, 1993.

Calavita, K., 'Italy and the new immigration', in W.A. Cornelius, L.M. Martin and J.T. Hollifield (eds), *Controlling Immigration: a Global Perspective*. Stanford, California: Stanford University Press, 1994.

Carchedi, F. and Ranuzzi, G.B., 'Tra collocazione nel mercato del lavoro secondario ed esclusione dal sistema della cittadinanza', in N. Sergi (ed.), *L'Immigrazione straniera in Italia*. Rome: Edizioni Lavoro, 1987.

Caritas, R., *Immigrazione – dossier statistico 1993.* Rome: Sinnos, 1993.

Caritas, R., *Immigrazione – dossier statistico 1994.* Rome: Anterem, 1994.

Castells, M. and Portes, A., 'World underneath: the origins, dynamics and effects of the informal economy,' in A. Portes, M. Castells and L. Benton (eds), *The Informal Economy: Studies in Advanced and Less Developed Countries.* London and Baltimore: Johns Hopkins University Press, 1989.

Castles, S. and Miller, M., *The Age of Migration.* London: Macmillan, 1993.

Chant, S. (ed.), *Gender and Migration in Developing Countries.* London: Belhaven, 1992.

Colen, S., ' "Just a little respect": West Indian domestic workers in New York City', in E.M. Chaney and M.G. Castro (eds), *Muchachas No More: Household Workers in Latin America and the Caribbean.* Philadelphia: Temple University Press, 1989.

Eurisko, *Gli Italiani e l'Immagine dell'Immigrato.* Mimeo: Milan, 1989.

Gregson, N. and Lowe, M., *Servicing the Middle Classes: Class, Gender and Waged Domestic Labour in Contemporary Britain.* London: Routledge, 1994.

Hoskyns, C. and Orsini-Jones, M., 'Immigrant women in Italy: perspectives from Brussels and Bologna', *The European Journal of Women's Studies* vol. 2 (1995) 51–76.

INCA-CGIL, *Da diversi paesi per uguali diritti.* Rome: Ediesse, 1990.

International Labour Office (ILO), 'Filipino migrant women in domestic work in Italy', *World Employment Programme Working Paper* MIG WP53. Geneva: ILO, 1991.

King, R. and Rybaczuk K., 'Southern Europe and the international division of labour: from emigration to immigration', in R. King (ed.), *The New Geography of European Migrations.* London: Belhaven, 1993.

Macioti, M.I. and Pugliese, E., *Gli immigrati in Italia.* Laterza: Bari, 1991.

McIlwaine, C., 'Gender, race and ethnicity: concepts, realities and policy implications', *Third World Planning Review* 17:2 (1995) 237–43.

Sabbadini, L.L. and Palomba, R., *Tempi Diversi: L'Uso del tempo di uomini e donne nell'Italia di oggi.* Rome: Presidenza del Consiglio dei Ministri, 1994.

Sassen-Koob, S., 'Notes on the incorporation of third world women into wage labour through immigration and off-shore production', *International Migration Review* XVIII:4 (1984) 1144–67.

Sassoon, D., *Contemporary Italy: Politics, Economy and Society since 1945.* London: Longman, 1986.

Tacoli, C., 'Gender and international survival strategies: a research agenda with reference to Filipina labour migrants in Italy', Third World Planning Review 17:2 (1995) 199–212.

Tacoli, C., 'Migrating "for the sake of the family"? Gender, life course and intra-household relations among Filipino migrants in Rome', *Philippine Sociological Review* special issue on 'Filipinos as Transnational Migrants' 44:1–4 (1996) 12–32.

United Nations Development Programme (UNDP), *Human Development Report 1995.* New York: United Nations, 1995.

# 8 South Asian Women Homeworkers in East London

### Kalwant Bhopal

## INTRODUCTION

This chapter examines the interaction of gender and ethnicity in the experiences of South Asian homeworkers in east London.[1] It draws on the author's small-scale qualitative study to address questions such as why women become homeworkers, the conditions under which they work and women's feelings about the choices available to them. Since the mid-1970s the phenomenon of homeworking has received considerable attention as a result of concerns to improve the pay and working conditions of women workers (Allen and Wolkowitz, 1987). Early research on homework attempted to document the persistence of a large, low-paid labour force (Bolton, 1975; Jordan, 1978). These studies challenged the prevailing image of homeworkers as women supported by their husbands who did homeworking in their spare time. They showed that women were forced by economic necessity to undertake long hours of work for low wages (Allen and Wolkowitz, 1987). Mendels (1972) examined the historical contribution of this form of work to capital accumulation and industrial expansion in Western Europe and its relevance to economic development in the third world. Homework has come increasingly to be recognized as a vital element in the capitalist labour process rather than a marginal activity (Rose, 1983).

Many people work at or from home for payment of some kind, and home-based work is characterized by a diversity of labour market positions, employment conditions and pay levels (Hakim, 1985; Scase and Goffee, 1983). During the 1980s, some researchers argued that the expansion of home-based work, as well as self- and part-time employment, was beginning to change the nature of work in advanced capitalist societies and offered advantages, to employees as well as employers, over full-time work outside the home (Atkinson, 1984; Toffler, 1983). Early research on homeworking, however, revealed severe exploitation and poor working conditions, and challenged the assumption that homework is a function of the needs and preferences of its workforce (Bolton, 1975; Jordan, 1978).

It is therefore important to specify the relationships between those performing home-based work and those supplying it, and to differentiate homeworking from other forms of home-based work.

For the purposes of this study, homeworkers were defined as individuals working at or from their home with no contract of employment and no supervision by a manager. Employees are treated as temporary workers to whom the employer owes no legal obligations. They do not enjoy the rights to which full-time permanent workers are entitled such as job security, or benefits such as overtime rates, holiday pay, sick pay or maternity leave. Homeworkers are usually paid by piecework, although in rare cases employers may pay a flat rate on the basis of a particular worker's speed. Most homeworkers pay their own overhead costs such as heating, electricity and lighting.

Allen and Wolkowitz (1987) show that homework offers little security, with any reduction in the supplier's own orders being felt in less work and lower earnings for homeworkers. The intensity of work is controlled through the incentive of piecework rates, the threat that no more work will be offered if the homeworker fails to complete orders or to get others to do so, and through the spacing of the delivery and collection of work. For employers, the labour of women in their own homes creates considerable savings in fixed costs, overheads, management and labour costs. The flexible use of labour is a major element in profitability (Phizacklea and Wolkowitz, 1995).

Immigrant communities tend to engage in this type of production both as suppliers of work and as workers, the latter often being female kin (Anthias, 1983; Mitter, 1986a). Research focusing on the ethnic identity of those who supply the homework (Shah, 1975) stresses a combination of factors such as high male unemployment rates and the low setting up costs involved in employing homeworkers. These may lead members of minority groups to establish themselves as subcontractors, employing homeworkers from their own communities. Asian women workers are heavily over-represented in the clothing industry (Owen, 1994; Rai and Sheikh, 1989) and Phizacklea (1994) shows how the financial pressures on Asian families impact on women, forcing them to undertake long hours of work within the home. Homework is thus a response to racialized labour markets, which restrict employment opportunities for both men and women (Phizacklea and Wolkowitz, 1995; West and Pilgrim, 1995). Phizacklea and Wolkowitz found that only a small minority of women in their study preferred to work at home or mentioned any advantages to being a homeworker. They argue that their findings contradict cultural stereotypes of Asian women homeworkers, which assume they work at home because of pressure from their husbands. They stress the necessity of taking into account the heterogeneity of the homeworking labour force and the opportunities and constraints that different positions in ethnic and class relations bring to a sexually segregated labour market.

Walby (1990) argues that there has been a transformation in gender relations in Britain during the twentieth century from private to a more public form of patriarchy. She also suggests (Walby, 1992) that the explanation for women's position in the labour market cannot be found solely within the family or in capitalist relations but also in patriarchal structures within employment. Homeworkers work within patriarchal relations of production inside the home and a central element of that experience is the lack of separation of work and family relations.

## HOMEWORKING IN EAST LONDON

The research discussed below is part of a larger study of South Asian women in Britain investigating the dynamics of gender relations within households in relation to arranged marriages, dowries, domestic labour, domestic finance, education, employment and religion. Sixty in-depth interviews were carried out of women living in East London. All were born in Britain, but traced their ancestry to the Indian subcontinent: India, Pakistan or Bangladesh. Their ages ranged from 25 to 30. Respondents were selected through snowball sampling, personal recommendation and advertisements placed at the local university and in the local student paper (Bhopal, 1997).

### The Findings

A total of 20 per cent of respondents were homeworkers (12 out of 60). All of them had had arranged marriages and had young children. They stayed at home because of their children, while the low incomes of their husbands compelled them to do paid work. They were not short-term homeworkers, but had all been working since they became mothers and in some cases since they were first married.

The income they earned from home working was extremely low. When the research was carried out in 1993, respondents reported that the going rate for skirts varied between 80 and 95 pence. Less skilled homeworkers sew coat and jacket linings which are returned to the employer to be stitched inside the main garment by more experienced homeworkers. Linings are at the bottom of the market for machinists, rating between 30 and 40 pence per piece.

**Feelings about Being a Homeworker**

Respondents were asked to define what being a homeworker meant for them. Many spoke of the advantages of not having to leave the house to go to work which they said was good for them, their husband and most importantly their children:

> Being a homeworker, or a machinist as we call it, means that I stay at home and get paid for the work I do at home. I don't have to leave the house and just work at home .... When my children come home from school at four o'clock, I don't have to come rushing home to look after them, I am here for them and that's important.
>
> *Nasreen, two children*

> I don't have to leave my house to go to work, everything I want is all here and so that makes life easier for me and it makes my husband very happy; he knows where I am.
>
> *Harjit, two children*

For these women, being able to combine the roles of paid worker (which usually takes place outside the home) and unpaid worker (which takes place inside the home), seemed to give them 'the best of both worlds'.

> People don't understand how easy it is for us .... Our husbands want us to be happy, they don't want us to travel long distances to work in the cold and so they let us stay at home and have what we want .... We don't have to do the things white women do, they have to travel far to go to work, we just stay at home and work, it's much easier for us than it is for them .... That way, we have the best of both worlds ... we are working and we are looking after our family.
>
> *Meena, one baby*

Some of the women, therefore, did not feel disadvantaged: rather they felt that women who went out to work were disadvantaged. Being a home-worker enabled them to perform their two roles efficiently and at the same time, they felt this caused less friction and upset with their husbands. They were able to earn money as well as to be good mothers and wives. They felt it was wrong to leave their children alone and go out to work, since when they were at home the children could not be neglected.

> If my children need me, then that's fine because I am here for them .... What would happen if I went out far to work and they needed me? I would have to come home and lose a day's pay .... This way I can see

what they want, if they want food, then I can feed them and then get back to work.

*Parminder, one baby*

Some of the women did not see homework as offering a career or a source of social identity or independence. Many wanted to earn a living, but on the other hand felt it was important for them to be at home to look after their children. Some of them handed their wage packets directly to their husbands and thus gained no control over their earned income. These respondents indicated that their husbands managed the money since they did not want their wives to worry about finance in the home. As Meena put it:

When I get paid, I just give the money to my husband and it makes him happy. He looks after it and he knows what to do with it. I don't mind giving it to my husband, he doesn't want me to have to worry about the money and I don't need to organize the paying of all the bills. I leave it to him and he can do it, he knows what to do.

However, in spite of its clear advantages for many women, being a homeworker also involved feelings of isolation and extreme loneliness. This often led to depression and anxiety, as well as health problems such as backache and eye strain.

When I first got married, because my husband's uncle has a business it was the right thing for me to just sew at home and that's the way it's always been for me. I do like working at home, but sometimes I get very lonely and there are very many days when I don't really see anyone, the only people I may see are my children and my husband and he's always out. But I think that's me being selfish, I should be happy with what I have. I have a job and a family.

*Danwant, four children*

The money I make helps and comes in handy. I did use to go out to work in the factory but when I got pregnant that just got harder and so we got a sewing machine and it's been easier for me to be at home.

*Harjit*

Homeworkers are unable to make the distinction between the home and the workplace and have no real leisure time. These women were unable to relax, since they were always either sewing, cooking, cleaning or caring for their children. Men, however, were able to separate the home and work spheres and enjoyed time away from the work place, relaxing in the home. The women's lives were very stressful, they felt every spare minute of their time should be devoted to sewing. Their homes were cluttered with materials and equipment, often making it difficult for them to have a sense of order and organization in their lives.

As well as suffering feelings of guilt, many felt extremely insecure. With very few exceptions the women worked illegally. They were paid 'cash in hand', avoiding tax and claiming social security benefits. They were afraid they might be 'found out' by the council or the DHSS, perhaps if their neighbours complained about the noise from industrial sewing machines. Their homeworking remained a secret, which they wanted only their own families to know about. This secretive element contributed to the isolation and loneliness they experienced.

> If we didn't need the money, then he [husband] wouldn't ask me to do it …. When we first got married I didn't do anything for about six months and then I had to do something because the money is important and then we had our children and so you need more money when you have children … every bit helps.
>
> *Narinder*

Not all the women however felt isolated and lonely. Five of the women in the sample regularly met other homeworkers. They also attended meetings which aimed to bring homeworkers together to talk about problems and offer mutual support. These women wanted to see changes in the way homeworkers are viewed in society, as well as improving their position as paid workers. The social support they received from such meetings gave the women a sense of solidarity and enabled them to organize for change.

> It's very important for me to go and meet other women, we can share our experiences and we also want to try and change things. We want to be recognized as people who work hard and who should have proper wages and mostly we want to be taken seriously.
>
> *Shaheen, two children*

> When we go to these meetings, we find out about the things that we should be entitled to and the things we should have. If we didn't go, we would never know and think we have to put up with the horrible conditions we work with.
>
> *Surjit, one child*

**Women's Work?**

Homeworking involves an intense form of the gendered division of labour. All the homeworkers referred to it as a female activity, and saw men's work roles as very different:

> You don't find men machinists at home, they would never do it. ... it's all very different for them, they want to go *outside* [respondent's emphasis] the house so they can do other things as well, like meet people and go out with their friends.
>
> *Nasreen*

Women's identification was with a role based *inside* the home, while men's identification with their role of primary breadwinner was based *outside* the home. For women, it was considered natural to stay inside the home and participate in paid and unpaid labour. Men's work in the industry means being a presser or cutter in the factory. These male-dominated jobs require much skill and accuracy, and are recognized as skilled by being the best paid in the industry. The jobs done by homeworkers are the worst paid. Machinists, for example, also require skill and precision, but because the tasks are performed by women inside the home they are considered to require less skill. They are often regarded as something women do in their spare time rather than real work. This distinction reflects the way men's and women's work is socially constructed and the gendered way in which tasks are deemed 'skilled'.

For eight of the 12 women the firm they worked for was a 'kin firm'. In some cases their husband owned the factory, in others it was their husband's brother or uncle. This also affected the way in which they viewed their work.

> For us it's all done like a family thing ... we like to keep it all in the family .... My husband owns the business and he works with his brothers, and so my sewing all goes back to the family ... that's why he doesn't have to give me much money.
>
> *Gurinder, four children*

Family firms play an important part in maintaining the employment of homeworkers. The South Asian clothing industry in the East End of London is characterized by the delegation of work to homeworkers. Very few women control these businesses, yet many work to enable such firms to survive. They are the backbone of the industry, yet they remain invisible. The relationships between family members enable businesses to survive and women are crucial in providing cheap labour. Through family ties, a network of loyal, trustworthy and reliable female employees is formed.

The family firm is based upon a unique solidarity and on patterns of mutual obligation which depend on a highly unequal gendered division of labour.

CONCLUSION

This research supports the findings of other studies which have demon-strated the importance of homeworking to immigrant communities both as suppliers of homework and as workers (Anthias, 1983; Mitter, 1986a). Homeworking cannot be understood without reference to women's ethnic identity. It is important to examine the diversity of women's experiences as well as examining the shared constraints and difficulties women face as homeworkers. In the case of the South Asian women, the unequal gender division of labour is exacerbated by the existence of 'kin firms' which rely heavily on the employment of female homeworkers.

This sexual division of labour is based on women's role being defined as economically dependent housewives while men's role as breadwinners frees them from the role of homemaker. Although homeworkers combine paid work with the role of homemaker, because it takes place within the home, this work is not socially valued and the level of pay they receive is pitifully low. Men's paid work, which takes place outside the home, is viewed as 'real work' and is more likely to be considered skilled employment.

For the women in this study, the primary motive for undertaking home-working was the need to make paid employment fit in with looking after husbands as well as children. The decision to remain at home was influ-enced by the husband's preference regarding childcare arrangements. The fact that the homeworker has to consider her husband's needs as well as her children's serves as a useful reminder that the family responsibili-ties which limit women's work options are not confined to the care of young children. The research suggests that patriarchal relations within the household are central to an understanding of women's experience of homeworking.

Many of the women felt ambivalent about their role as homeworkers. On the one hand, they felt they were getting the 'best of both worlds', because it allowed them to earn money while still being at home with their children. On the other hand, homework is generally tedious and tiring and many of the women complained of its impact on their health. The work is also isolated, providing little scope for social interchange or collective action.

Some women, however, have come together to seek to change the situa-tion for homeworkers, meeting regularly for support and social contact and information on their rights as homeworkers. At both national and international levels, campaigning for better conditions for homeworking – including pay, benefits and job security – has been vigorous (Mitter, 1986b; Rowbotham and Mitter, 1994). Such grassroots movements have provided a means of enabling homeworkers to meet for mutual support, organize and campaign for the recognition of homeworker's rights as employees. However, as Mitter (1986b) has argued, stronger alliances must be forged between labour market and women's organized groups to ensure the success of these campaigns and their adoption by government.

The invisibility of homeworking and its precarious legal status mean that homework has remained beyond the reach of employment and health and safety or equal pay legislation. Trade unions, with some exceptions at local level, have generally been reluctant to become involved in supporting homeworkers, where the practical difficulties of organizing are enormous. As Britain moves towards adopting a national minimum wage, it is reassuring to see that vulnerable groups of women such as homeworkers are to be included in its provisions. The findings of this and other similar research, however, indicate that effective enforcement of even this straightforward measure will be fraught with difficulties.

## NOTE

1.     I would like to thank Sylvia Walby for reading earlier drafts of this chapter and providing very useful comments.

## REFERENCES

Allen, S. and Wolkowitz, C., *Homeworking: Myths and Realities.* London: Macmillan, 1987.

Anthias, F., 'Sexual divisions and ethnic adaption: the case of Greek-Cypriot women', in A. Phizacklea (ed.), *One-way Ticket: Migration and Female Labour.* London: Routledge and Kegan Paul, 1983.

Atkinson, J., *Flexibility, Uncertainty and Manpower Management.* Sussex: Institute of Manpower Studies, 1984.

Bhopal, K., *Gender, 'Race' and Patriarchy: a Study of South Asian Women.* Aldershot: Ashgate, 1997.

Bolton, B., *An End to Homeworking?* London: Fabian Society 436, 1975.

Brah, A. and Shaw, S., *Working Choices: South Asian Young Muslim women and the Labour Market.* London: Department of Employment Research Paper no. 91, 1992.

Hakim, C., *Employers' Use of Outwork: a Study using the 1980 Workplace Industrial Relations Survey and the 1981 National Survey of Homeworking.* London: Department of Employment, Research Paper no. 44, 1985.

*Homeworkers Charter.* The London Industrial Strategy. London: Greater London Council, 1985.

Jordan, D., *The Wages of Fear: A 1978 Report on Homeworking.* London: Low Pay Unit 20, 1978.

Mendels, F., 'Protoindustrialisation: the first phase of the industrialisation process', *Journal of Economic History* XXXVI (1972) 241–61.

Mitter, S., 'Industrial restructuring and manufacturing homework: immigrant women in the clothing industry', *Capital and Class* 27 (1986a) 37–80.

Mitter, S., *Common Fate Common Bond: Women and the Global Economy.* London: Pluto Press, 1986b.

Owen, D., *Ethnic Minority Women and the Labour Market: an Analysis of the 1991 Census.* Manchester: Equal Opportunities Commission, 1994.

Phizacklea, A., 'A single or a segregated market? Gendered and racialised divisions', in H. Afshar and M. Maynard (eds), *The Dynamics of 'Race' and Gender: Some Feminist Interventions.* London: Taylor and Francis, 1994.

Phizacklea, A. and Wolkowitz, C., *Homeworking Women: Gender, Racism and Class at Work.* London: Sage, 1995.

Rai, K. and Sheikh, N., *Homeworking.* Birmingham: National Unit on Homeworking, 1989.

Rose, R., *Getting by in Three Economies.* Strathclyde: University of Strathclyde Centre for the Study of Public Policy, 1983.

Rowbotham, S. and Mitter, S., *Dignity and Daily Bread: New Forms of Organising among Poor Women in the Third World and the First.* London: Routledge, 1994.

Scase, R. and Goffee, R., 'Business ownership and women's subordination: a preliminary study of female proprietors', *The Sociological Review* XXXI 4 (1983).

Shah, S., *Immigrants and Employment in the Clothing Industry: the Rag Trade in London's East End.* London: The Runnymede Trust, 1975.

Toffler, A., *The Third Wave.* London: Pan Books, 1983.

Walby, S., *Theorising Patriarchy.* Cambridge: Polity Press, 1990.

Walby, S., 'Post-post modernism? Theorising social complexity', in M. Barrett, and A. Phillips, *A Destabilising Theory.* Cambridge: Polity Press, 1992.

West, J. and Pilgrim, S., 'South Asian women in employment: the impact of migration, ethnic origin and the local economy', *New Community* 21, 3 (1995) 357–78.

# Part III
# Evaluating Equal Pay Law

# 9 Pay Equity Lessons from Ontario, Canada

## Patricia McDermott

Since its passage in 1989, the Ontario Pay Equity Act has remained arguably the most extensive equal pay legislation in the world and is in many ways unique. It must be noted straightaway that nearly ten years of implementation of this law has not significantly reduced a still relatively large wage gap.[1] However, the Ontario experience with this statute offers some insights into the strengths and weaknesses of such initiatives, which could help those in other jurisdictions, particularly in member states of the European Union, to shape more effective pay equity processes.

After focusing on Ontario's experience, this chapter will examine some approaches to legislated pay equity programmes that may be more useful in times of downsizing and restructuring, particularly data-driven exercises that do not rely exclusively on the lengthy and often costly methodology of job evaluation as Ontario, and indeed much of North America, have done. As well as exploring different ways of implementing pay equity schemes, advocates must also address the goal of pay equity. Is the goal to increase wage costs or redistribute wages? If success of a process can be measured in equalization, will this mean that the wage expectations of those doing work traditionally performed by men will be reduced for a period, until those doing 'women's work' 'catch up'? Feminist advocates for pay equity will have to decide if this formulation of the goal is acceptable.

The two features that together make the Ontario Pay Equity Act unique in the area of wage discrimination law are: first, its rare commitment to redressing gender-based pay inequity in both the public and private sectors; and second, the move from an individual 'complaint-driven' to a 'proactive' model, in which employers carry the onus of demonstrating that they are not engaged in discriminatory compensation practices. These combined features contain the potential for pay inequities to be removed.

## THE SCOPE OF THE LEGISLATION

The coverage of both the private and the public sectors is indeed unique for proactive, legislated pay equity initiatives. Throughout the United States and in the six other Canadian provinces, proactive legislation has been introduced only in the public sector, and usually only in the 'narrow' public sector involving direct state employees. In Ontario, the Pay Equity Act applies to both the narrow and broad public sectors as well as to the entire private sector of the economy.[2] This important commitment to addressing pay inequity is critical when governmental organizations are restructuring, particularly when this involves the privatization of state services. If public sector labour costs are raised by increasing wages for those doing 'women's work', state employers may, if collective agreements permit, have the option of contracting out the work to the private sector if that remains unaffected by pay equity requirements. Clearly any proactive scheme must cover both public and private sector employers to be effective.

As Figart and Khan (1997) have noted, in the US from the mid-1980s, just when the pay equity movement was in a period of growth, business was increasing its use of relatively inexpensive women's labour to succeed in competitive markets. At this time, government workers tended to be characterized as 'a drain on the market economy', while deregulation and the dismantling of the welfare state by more conservative governments combined not only to slow the expansion of pay equity in the public sector, but also virtually to halt any potential for inroads into the private sector as well. Arguments that pay equity represented a 'destructive interference with the market mechanisms and that it introduces wage rigidities and inefficiencies' gained considerable ground (Figart and Khan, 1997, p. 19; see also Figart and Khan this volume). Indeed, throughout the industrialized world pay equity is being proposed in a hostile political and economic climate and innovative strategies which acknowledge this reality must be developed. These strategies will need to cover the issue of implementation as well as the wider question of whether the goal of pay equity needs to be reassessed. In other words, will pay equity be an exercise in increased labour costs or will it have a more redistributive purpose?

## PROACTIVITY

The second feature of the Ontario Act which makes it unique is the shift away from traditional complaint-driven schemes to a proactive model whereby all employers essentially carry the liability to demonstrate that they are not engaged in discriminatory pay practices. The onus is on the employer to undertake a pay equity exercise which is set out in the Act and then redress any gender-related inequities revealed by the process. This means it is no longer necessary for employees or their unions to launch individual complaints about unequal pay for work of equal value.[3]

It must be noted, however, that although employers are required to initiate a review of their pay practices, complaints can still be launched by individuals or their unions about the implementation process of pay equity. These actions are typically about problems for an entire workplace or a job group, not just an individual. For example, cases have centred on whether the employer was defined appropriately or has challenged the lack of gender neutrality of a particular job evaluation methodology.

New employment relationships which tend to be temporary and part-time need new solutions, probably involving state regulation. If employees' relationships with their employers are increasingly casual, it is more important than ever that rights for equal pay need not be pursued by individuals, but that employers themselves must be forced to live up to a standard of pay practices free of gender bias. Pay equity advocates must accept, however, that in present conditions their proposals for state involvement in employers' wage practices will not be favourably received. A great deal of thought must go into how fair wages for women can be made more attractive to employers, politicians and probably unions as well, by ensuring that the process is not cumbersome, costly, time-consuming or potentially disruptive to an employer's operation.

It is important to stress that in Ontario in the past nine years, with a few exceptions, every significant dispute that has reached the Pay Equity Tribunal has been taken up by a trade union. This is not surprising, and it means that labour organizations will need to continue to play as central a role in proactive pay equity initiatives as they have in individual complaint-driven models. The commitment to pay equity on the part of the union leadership, however, is not necessarily a given. Feminist activists within the union will need to take an active role in getting pay equality on the bargaining table. The question of whether the goal is increased wages overall or an exercise in redistribution will also be critical in deciding how receptive the union leadership is to this.

Experience in Ontario has demonstrated that most employers are quite used to state regulation and tend to comply if they feel a mandatory process is not seriously disruptive to their competitive position. Leaving aside the issue of the implementation costs of the process itself, the key question about whether employers' overall wage costs will go up more than normally expected should be answered before decisions are made about the design of a process. If the answer is that pay equity is a gradual equalization of standard wage levels, most employers will undoubtedly be more receptive. If the goal is ultimately to make employers increase their wage costs overall, the challenge will be much greater.

The Ontario Act is silent precisely on this issue. However, equalization rather than increased wage costs is well within the mandate of the legislation.

For example, the Act requires that employers direct 1 per cent of their total annual wage costs to completing pay equity adjustments. The Act has no provision concerning whether or not the wage level in a workplace must increase, only that 1 per cent must be directed to pay equity adjustments. While adjustments to female job classes may be made over a number of years, wages in the male 'comparator' job classes could remain somewhat stable until the female job classes 'caught up'. Once this has occurred however, the Ontario Act has a 'bargaining strength' exemption from the 'preventing recurrence' provisions of the statute. This exemption suggests that once the female comparators' job class reaches the same wage level as its male comparator' job class, unions could, through collective bargaining, start to restore the differentials. This is a major weakness of the Act.

**Gender Predominance**

Another key feature of Ontario's pay equity legislation is the use of the standard notion of gender predominance in pay equity. Throughout North America pay equity exercises, based primarily on job evaluation techniques, have involved establishing whether a 'job class' or 'job category' was male- or female-dominated. Some of the first pay equity exercises in the US in the early 1980s used quite a high standard for gender predominance, typically 90 per cent. Such a standard clearly captured the pay inequities caused by undervaluation in the heavily gender-segregated labour market, particularly in large state bureaucracies and institutions. If the job categories were wide enough, such as 'clerical support' and 'technical support', the exercise succeeded in covering a significant proportion of employees, and the wage differentials revealed were quite dramatic.

The Ontario Act stipulates gender predominance levels of 60 and 70 per cent. If women make up 60 per cent or more of the job class it is considered a 'female job class'; if men comprise 70 per cent or more it is considered a 'male job class'. (If a job class meets neither of these conditions, it is simply out of the exercise as either a female job class seeking a wage adjustment or as a male job class comparator.) The 60 per cent for women was thought an improvement in that it meant more women would be covered by the Act than if the cut-off was much higher. It was also hoped that the level of 70 per cent for male job classes would offer a broader range of male comparators and thus enable as many female job classes as possible to find an appropriate male comparator class. The problem with lowering the standard of gender predominance, as mentioned, is that it tends to reduce the differentials established and thus the amount of the wage adjustments.

Thus, in efforts to structure proactive pay equity legislation, care must be taken to think through the issue of gender predominance levels. Perhaps some type of flexibility would be best, so that arguments could be made for using different standards, depending on the gender structure of the workplace. It would seem that in all proactive schemes, and in many individual complaint-driven models, some type of gender predominance is necessary, in that wage differential between those doing 'men's' and 'women's' work is the very problem pay equity legislation is attempting to redress. However, it does ignore the position of women *within* male or female job categories who systematically earn lower wages than men. This is not an unusual pattern and indeed shows up as a by-product of many pay equity exercises. We will return to this topic shortly.

**Job Evaluation**

As mentioned, arguably the two strongest features of Ontario's Pay Equity Act are coverage of the private sector as well as the public, and the proactive nature of the scheme whereby the onus to demonstrate fair practices lies with employers. However, the two most serious weaknesses of the statute are: (1) its sole reliance on job evaluation methodology rather than allowing models of pay equity that involve analysis of data about the employer's current compensation structure; and (2) the so-called 'job-to-job' comparison process which requires each female job class to find a male job class with which to make the comparisons.

The Ontario Act does not actually use the term 'job evaluation', but rather 'job comparison'. However, the statute does set out the standard four factors that are universally used in job evaluation exercises: skill, effort, responsibility and working conditions. Indeed, almost all pay equity exercises under the Act have involved quite traditional job evaluation methodology. With few exceptions the tens of thousands of pay equity implementation exercises in Ontario have involved management consultants who typically employed elaborate, technical and often lengthy and costly processes.

Not only does the Act essentially mandate job evaluation, it allows each individual bargaining unit within a workplace to select a different job evaluation plan and then have each female 'job class' seek its own appropriate male comparator – the so-called 'job-to-job' approach. Given the structure of Ontario's industrial relations system, with its emphasis on decentralized bargaining, it is not unusual to have a dozen different trade unions within one workplace, all tending to represent primarily female or male workers, but typically not both in the same bargaining unit.[4] The result is incompatible measures of value which essentially prohibit many in female-dominated bargaining units from finding the appropriate male comparators needed to establish a wage differential. Also, the multiplication of job evaluation plans was costly, confusing and, in the end, largely ineffective. If proactive pay equity legislation is to rely on job evaluation, even if only optionally, then a great deal of effort must go into establishing levels of gender neutrality for any given technique, as well as ensuring that only one job evaluation methodology be used in each workplace.

It is not a goal of this chapter to present a critique of traditional job evaluation since a great deal has already been written on this topic (Blum, 1991; Feldberg, 1984; McCann, 1994). The point here is that undertaking a gender-neutral job evaluation properly is a costly process; this is one good reason why, during a time of restructuring and cost-cutting, in many settings such methods are strongly resisted. It is now critical that we investigate other options that could prove more fruitful in the present economic environment.

One option is to skip the evaluation process and move directly to the analysis of wage data. Actual wage data, when combined with other variables such as age, seniority, starting date and years of prior relevant experience, can often produce powerful evidence of an employer's inequitable pay practices. Sometimes the solutions to these problems could mean that wage costs to employers would not have to increase any more than during periods of 'normal' bargaining. 'Bottom-loaded' pay equity adjustment exercises could be phased in over a number of years to produce wage structures which are more equitable. There is also the very contentious issue of the attitudes of largely male-dominated unions to the idea that men's wages will be held back in some way while those doing 'women's' work receive a larger share of the wages in order to catch up.

### The Role of the 'Job Rate' in Pay Equity Schemes

Ontario's Pay Equity Act does not require the use of actual wage data in the implementation process. Basically, as is typical in many pay equity exercises in other jurisdictions, the 'wages' that are used to assess both wage differentials and potential wage adjustments are 'job rates' not average wages actually paid to those doing the job. It is very possible, and indeed not uncommon, for no one in the job class to be making the 'job rate'. The actual salaries of those in the job class can vary considerably for a variety of reasons such as seniority, merit, individual bargaining strength and, of course, sometimes for reasons such as favouritism.

In an implementation exercise, the job rate for the job class is established as the wage rate which those in the class achieve after they have learned the job and performed satisfactorily for a period of time. It is not the rate someone achieves when they perform in an exceptional manner, but the rate that most achieve in a set, standard period. Once the job rate is known and the job evaluation exercise is performed, establishing the value for a particular job class, the final step is a comparison between male and female job classes of equivalent value to calculate the differences in wage rates.[5] Once the differential is calculated each person in the female job class receives that adjustment, whether they are above or below the job rate.

The fixing of the job rate in proactive schemes is crucial, since this is the amount that establishes the differential between the job rates for equivalently valued male job classes for everyone in the female job class. Employers could establish the male job rate at a low level, even though most or all of the incumbents in a male job class earn above the job rate. If this is combined with fixing the job rate for a comparable female job class at a high level, which none or few of the incumbents in the class actually earn, the result could be a much lower level of wage adjustment. This could be avoided by using the average of actual wages paid in the job class for the job rate.

In the examination of an employer's wages system the data that are often more revealing when a comparison is made between female and male job classes are the averages of actual wages paid within the job class, not a theoretical job rate. Actual wages can be even more compelling if they are individual wages, or averages of wages for certain groups, presented in graphic form. For example, what proportion of women make wages that are in the top 25 per cent of wages paid by an organization? What about the bottom 25 per cent? The answers to such questions can start to paint a picture of the type of gender-based wage gap that exists within an organization, and suggest possible solutions involving a series of pay equity adjustments, rather than, for instance, 'across-the-board' wage settlements.

## USING DATA TO MAKE PAY EQUITY A UNION ISSUE

The role that trade unions have played in the pay equity arena is critical, and this will continue to be true whether pay equity legislation is introduced or not. A greatly contested issue among the unions is likely to be whether the goal is increased overall wages or redistribution. Bargaining units that have not made equal pay a negotiating demand are to some degree responsible for the perpetuation of unfair wages for women.

As many studies have demonstrated, male workers and their union leaders have resisted equal value initiatives. In many ways union leaders have to acknowledge their role, however passive, in discriminatory wage practices, if pay equity is to become a bargaining priority. To a great extent finding new ways to present equal value demands will be directed at unions as well as at employers and politicians.

One excellent example of the potential for getting union commitment to a pay equity agenda occurred in a large healthcare workers' union which represents over 10,000 healthcare workers employed in the provincial public sector (not Ontario). At the time, this province did not have pay equity legislation so some key women in the union leadership undertook a basic analysis of the wage structure of their membership. Most of the jobs were in maintenance, food preparation and non-professional healthcare support. The membership of the bargaining unit was 64 per cent female. Even the most rudimentary analysis of variables such as wages, gender and length of service exposed a serious gender-based wage gap within the organization.

Despite the fact that many jobs required a relatively low educational attainment – often 'some secondary school' – even this was not always adhered to because of the large number of immigrant workers who did not meet this requirement. When basic data were examined, they revealed that women tended to be hired in the bottom 20 per cent of the wage structure. Also, taking into account length of service, far more men than women were located in the top 20 per cent. It was also clear from the analysis that, given the nature of the work being done, the job categories tended to be highly segregated with women in the food preparation, cleaning and supportive care jobs while the men were heavily concentrated in 'maintenance' categories. Thus when job categories were analysed, using very simple statistical techniques, not only was the highly segregated nature of the workforce revealed, it was also found that the starting salary for every traditionally female job category was lower than for all the male job categories. The wage structure of this public sector employer, reinforcing what is now known about the undervaluation of 'women's work', was clearly obsolete and unfair.

The study done by the union was used initially to convince its own leadership and membership that the pay structure was patently unfair. Only then could the union develop a bargaining strategy aimed not only at their own government employer, but at the political arena as well. When confronted with understandable and compelling statistical analysis that demonstrated obvious inequities, male union leaders and members, as well as employers, found it difficult to deny that there was a problem.

In constructing a negotiating position that would begin to address the inequities, the union did not seek a wage settlement exclusively for the underpaid female job classes, but did deliver a modest 'across-the-board' wage increase. However, the vast bulk of the settlement went to the low-waged women within the bargaining unit. This was certainly a case in which the union itself admitted long-term compliance with unfair and outdated practices by failing to challenge the pay structure and by accepting differentials in starting salaries for women and men.

This example of healthcare workers demonstrates the usefulness and often the necessity of using gender predominance and job categories. A look at men's and women's individual wages revealed a gendered wage gap. To explain this, an exploration of job categories had to be undertaken. At this point a lengthy and expensive job evaluation technique could have been used; however, the focus on job descriptions and job requirements revealed that most women could easily have done the men's jobs, and vice versa. There was no need to engage in a debate about whether women making soup and sandwiches in the kitchen were as valuable as men removing the rubbish bins from the kitchen. This was clearly a case in which the move directly to data analysis made sense.

## WAGE DATA IN ONE JOB CATEGORY SETTING

Because of the gendered division of labour typically found in a sector like healthcare, pay equity schemes can reveal the problem of, and often the solutions to, unfair practices. The important role of assessing gender predominance of job classes is key to making a compelling argument about wages. The use of job categories, however, is not always possible. There are a growing number of workplaces where most of the men and women work in the same job category and yet legislated, proactive, pay equity remedies are not available to them. In most industrialized countries, including Canada, complaint-based 'employment standards' schemes, which involve claiming that someone is doing the same job and making more money, are available. This cannot be justified.

Employment standards legislation is not proactive and thus does not shift the onus to the employer to justify a particular compensation practice. Remedies that result from such cases are generally only applicable to the complainant. The standard weakness of these statutory schemes is the typically long list of exemptions, which can include merit bonuses and 'market mechanisms'. The lack of acceptance of systemic data and the shaping of a complaint only as an individual's problem render such schemes very weak indeed if the goal is to close a gendered wage gap in one workplace, let alone in an entire economy.

One example of the problem can be seen by looking at a large job class in which, for argument's sake, equal numbers of men and women do the same job. A good example would be a university or college. It is a well-known and documented fact that institutions of higher education through-out the industrialized world (and no doubt the developing world as well) have employed underpaid women academic staff for decades. This practice is closely related to the traditional resistance to hiring females in academia. Almost three decades of affirmative action on campuses in North America have resulted in many universities and colleges being far more integrated than in the past, and there are now some with equal numbers of men and women academics. Yet despite parity in numbers, there exist serious unexplained gendered wage gaps.

Obviously job evaluation techniques would not be helpful since everyone is doing the same job. Gender predominance could be somewhat revealing, not in a traditional pay equity sense of looking at job categories, but because it is often the case that in departments where there are significantly more women than average, wages tend to be lower. The most useful analysis, however, is to look at wages and gender. There is no doubt that a significant wage gap would be revealed. Pushing the analysis further to explain the disparity could involve introducing a number of factors. For example, is it because women have fewer years of teaching experience? Do they graduate later than men? Or do women tend to be hired at lower starting salaries? Do the data also show that despite women finishing their postgraduate training within the same time as men, it takes them longer to get their first full-time job?

Careful, straightforward assessment of data can go a long way to revealing serious unfair compensation problems. This is not to say that there is no place for sophisticated, multivariate data analysis techniques to demonstrate, for example, what women's salaries would be if, given the same academic profile, they were men at the same institution. However, a rudimentary look at wages, length of service, years of experience and gender can often sketch patterns of discriminatory pay.

CONCLUSION

We need legislation that will move us beyond the way we have engaged in pay equity if existing laws are not appropriate. We need legislation that would allow alternatives to standard job evaluation exercises. Given the centrality of wage data, employers could be compelled to release basic wage, gender and service data to employee representatives. Even without legislation, some unions may be able to negotiate access to the data necessary to undertake an analysis that could reveal long-term unfair pay practices. Besides being more compelling to both employers and employees alike (certainly when compared to often incomprehensible results from a traditional, albeit gender-neutral, job evaluation scheme), basic wage and personnel data can often reveal a profile of discrimination as well as suggest solutions. Not only can this process be fast and inexpensive, the solutions themselves can be straightforward – such as taking steps to close the wage gap. In this era of cost-cutting and downsizing, employer receptivity must be an issue in formulating strategies, without sacrificing the principles of equal pay.

The issue raised throughout this chapter, in the interests of making gains in this hostile climate, is whether the goal of pay equity should be redistribution rather than increased wages overall. This debate is important to resolve since it is crucial to whether employers, as well as politicians who must be lobbied for proactive legislative initiatives, can be convinced that the persistence of a gendered wage gap is intolerable. Finding solutions to unequal pay is especially urgent, with increasing numbers of women providing the bulk of family support either on their own or with unemployed or underemployed partners. New energy has to enter the pay equity arena. New ways to present the problem and to shape solutions must be found, but we cannot ignore the political and economic settings in which we find ourselves.

## NOTES

1. Canada's gender-based wage gap is approximately 30 per cent despite much pay equity legislation introduced across the country. In Ontario, which has a population of about seven million, and the most extensive pay equity legislation, the wage gap remains in the 30 per cent range.
2. The Ontario Pay Equity Act applies to all private sector employers with ten or more employees.
3. In Ontario there remains a separate law (the Employment Standards Act) which covers equal pay for equal work. This statute is complaint-driven.
4. Under Ontario labour law, bargaining units are certified using a standard called a 'community of interests'. If there is a group of employees for which a union is seeking designation by the Labour Board as the 'sole bargaining agent', the board will assess the nature of the work. If there is more than one

type of work being done, the Board will put the employees into separate bargaining units. Given the highly segmented nature of the labour market, most women will tend to be in one unit and the men in another.

5.    Another surprising weakness in the Ontario Act is the level of equity used. If there is more than one appropriate male job class that is of equal value to a female class, the male class used is that which offers the lowest wage adjustment.

## REFERENCES

Blum, L., *Between Feminism and Labour: the Significance of the Comparable Worth Movement.* Berkeley: University of California Press, 1991.

Feldberg, R.L., 'Comparable worth: towards theory and practice in the United States', *Signs* vol. 10 (1984) 311–28.

Figart, D.M. and Kahn, P., *Contesting the Market: Pay Equity and the Politics of Restructuring.* Detroit, Michigan: Wayne State University Press, 1997.

McCann, N., *Rights at Work: Pay Equity Reform and the Politics of Legal Mobilization.* Chicago: University Press, 1994.

# 10 Negative (Pay) Equity – an Analysis of Some (Side-) Effects of the Equal Pay Act
Sue Hastings

## INTRODUCTION

This chapter focuses on the UK Equal Pay Act 1970 and the Equal Value (Amendment) Regulations 1983. It demonstrates how particular features of the legislation have operated in the context of the increasingly deregulated labour market in the UK to the detriment of those whom the legislation should be assisting, that is, those experiencing unequal pay. It is argued that some developments in the field of pay and grading structures, which have tended to militate *against* the achievement of pay equity, have been facilitated, and even stimulated, by the detailed construction of the legislation. This has occurred even though the relevant features of the legislation are neither mentioned in, nor required by, the European provisions for equal pay contained in Article 119 of the Treaty of Rome and the 1975 Equal Pay Directive. Employers have exploited this situation, and trade unions and other organizations representing the interests of women employees have had great difficulty in countering these developments, although there are recent signs of more positive responses and some successes.

The arguments are based on the author's experience in assisting union officers and representatives in responding to labour market developments affecting their members. The sample of organizations is not, therefore, statistically sound, but does cover the private, privatized and public sectors, all of which have distinct characteristics in labour market terms. A range of industries and services from the motor industry through banking and finance to the utilities, local government and the National Health Service are included.

Three examples of the negative impact of the legislation are examined in detail. The first concerns 'separate collective bargaining' which, until its overthrow by the European Court of Justice (ECJ) in its decision in *Enderby* v *Frenchay Health Authority* ([1993] *Industrial Relations Law Reports* (IRLR) 591 ECJ), was used by employers as a 'genuine material

153

factor defence' and so encouraged employers to maintain indirectly discriminatory separate collective bargaining arrangements. The second concerns the job evaluation scheme's (JES) 'no reasonable grounds' defence against equal value claims, which has encouraged employers to adopt single JESs, many of which are arguably both inappropriate and discriminatory, but difficult to challenge. Some of these schemes have resulted in the implementation of broad-banded salary structures, which often involve the introduction of measures of performance or competence or similar barriers to the achievement of equal pay for previously lower-paid women, and which are also difficult to challenge for technical reasons. Finally, the 'same employment' provisions of the Equal Pay Act are analysed. These have tended to encourage greater devolution of organizational and collective bargaining structures, thus limiting the availability of comparators (men doing jobs that could provide the basis of an equal value claim) for many female applicants.

## THE 'SEPARATE COLLECTIVE BARGAINING ARRANGEMENTS' VERSION OF THE 'GENUINE MATERIAL FACTOR' (GMF) DEFENCE

### The European Context

European equality legislation, in particular the ECJ decisions in the *Bilka*, *Danfoss* and *Enderby* cases, allows for differences in pay between men and women, only where these are 'objectively justifiable'. For example, the *Danfoss* decision includes the following:

> The Court [the ECJ in the *Bilka* Decision] nevertheless held that the undertaking might establish that its pay practice was determined by objectively justified factors unrelated to any discrimination based on sex and that, if the undertaking succeeded, there was no infringement of Article 119 of the Treaty. Those considerations also apply in the case of a pay practice which gives special rewards for the adaptability of workers to variable work schedules and places of work. The employer may, therefore, justify payment for such adaptability by showing that it is of importance in the performance of the specific duties entrusted to the worker concerned.[1]

### The UK Context

The UK legislation is more complex and, from the applicant's perspective, more restrictive. It allows employers to argue that there is a 'genuine material factor', unrelated to the gender of the relevant jobholders, which provides a defence to claims for equal pay, even where the jobs are shown to be 'like work', 'work rated as equivalent' or 'equal value'. The legislation provides that:

> An equality clause shall not operate in relation to a variation between the woman's contract and the man's contract if the employer proves that the variation is genuinely due to a material factor which is not the difference of sex and that factor
>
> (a) in the case of [a 'like work' or 'work rated as equivalent' claim] must be a material difference between the woman's case and the man's: and
>
> (b) in the case of [an 'equal value' claim] may be such a material difference.[2]

The differences between the EU and UK legislation in respect of what might justify unequal pay have been exploited by lawyers and employers. Anecdotal evidence indicates that some lawyers are aware that they are using arguments that may be successful before the UK courts under UK legislation, but which would not succeed before the ECJ under European legislation.

A number of different GMF defences have been tried, but the one which proved most intractable, and may have influenced labour market and pay developments, is the 'separate collective bargaining arrangements' argument. This takes the form of arguing that the existence of separate and non-discriminatory collective bargaining arrangements for applicant and comparator job groups itself constitutes a GMF defence. In *Enderby*, for example, the respondents argued that the fact that the pay and other conditions of the applicant speech therapists was negotiated in a different Whitley Committee from that of the comparator clinical psychologists and hospital pharmacists (and that there was no evidence of discrimination in the minutes of the negotiating meetings of any of the relevant committees) was of itself a defence to the equal pay claims.

To anyone with any understanding of how labour markets in the UK operate it is immediately clear that this is a nonsensical argument and that historical separate collective bargaining arrangements are one cause of unequal pay, rather than a defence against it. However, this argument was accepted by the industrial tribunal and by subsequent appeal courts, until overturned by the ECJ in 1994.

## The Labour Market Consequences

The consequences of the 'separate collective bargaining arrangements' argument may not always be obvious, because it operates against the prevailing labour market trend for greater harmonization of pay and grading structures. However, there is some evidence that this line of defence may have deterred some employers from pursuing proposals for harmonization of terms and conditions of employment between different groups. This is certainly apparent in the National Health Service, where most health trusts have held back from trying to develop their own pay structures.

There have been other reasons for the lack of action by trusts, including opposing pressures from trade unions and lack of resources to lubricate change, but evidence from health service personnel conferences suggests that trust managers do see 'equal value' as a problem; and regard maintenance of the Whitley arrangements for centralized pay bargaining as 'protection', not to be discarded lightly.

The health service is a good example of the maintenance of separate collective bargaining arrangements operating against a movement towards equal pay for work of equal value. Figure 10.1 and some knowledge of the jobs reveal the inequalities in job value terms. The figure is based on 1993–4 salary and wage rates, the last year before the introduction of significant elements of local bargaining, but the relative positions shown are unchanged in most trusts. The top half of the Ancillary Staffs Council (ASC) structure covers jobs such as cooks, kitchen superintendents, domestic and dining-room supervisors, whose roles include responsibility for all or part of a support service and supervision of staff. On any system of assessment, such roles must be of at least equal value to many of the jobs in the lower grades of the Estates Officer structure, which cover maintenance workers and their supervisors.

Figure 10.1 also illustrates the basis of the speech therapists' claims for equal pay with hospital pharmacists and clinical psychologists, but suggests that similar claims could have been pursued by others from the professions allied to medicine, for instance, radiographers, physiotherapists or occupational therapists, or by some in the senior clinical nursing grades.

So, the 'separate collective bargaining arrangements' defence argued by the respondents in *Enderby* in 1987 has arguably delayed serious consideration of 'equal value' issues in the sector. It also appears to have deterred women in the NHS from taking equal pay cases or unions from supporting them. As the health service employs up to one million people, mainly women, the impact in this sector is significant.

The 'separate collective bargaining' defence has also arguably delayed until recently any reconsideration of pay structures in higher education, to the potential disadvantage in pay equity terms of many women employees. Again, those in the manual structure are especially disadvantaged in pay terms compared with comparable clerical and related administrative jobs

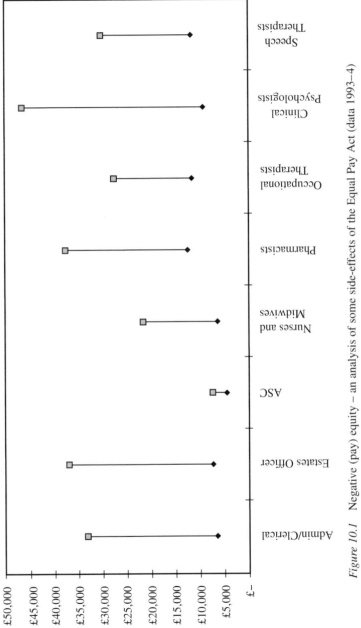

*Figure 10.1*   Negative (pay) equity – an analysis of some side-effects of the Equal Pay Act (data 1993–4)

on the one hand, and technical jobs on the other. And, on the basis of the overall demands of the jobs they do, women whose jobs are graded towards the top of the clerical and administrative structure are also likely to be disadvantaged relative to those in the academic and academic-related structures.

## The Response on Behalf of Applicants

This has been limited. Unions seem to have opted to await the outcome of the tortuous progress – seven years from the date of the originating applications – of the *Enderby* case through the appeal system to the ECJ decision. No doubt some claims raising the same issue were submitted during this period and stayed awaiting the final decision.

But what if there had been hundreds of claims addressing the 'separate collective bargaining arrangements' defence? Would the appeal process have lasted seven years then? What if a sympathetic tribunal had agreed to refer some cases subject to this defence argument to an independent expert and favourable decisions had been reached in the meantime on the 'equal value' question? Would such decisions have allowed negotiations to proceed on pay equity issues within the relevant sectors? Successfully settled claims in the electricity sector suggest that they would (see chapter 14).

THE JOB EVALUATION SCHEME DEFENCE

## The European Context

There is no specific mention of job evaluation in Article 119 of the Treaty of Rome or in the 1975 Equal Pay Directive.
Article 1 of the directive says:

> The principle of equal pay for men and women outlined in Article 119 of the Treaty [of Rome], hereinafter called 'principle of equal pay', means, for the same work or work to which equal value is attributed, the elimination of all discrimination on grounds of sex with regard to all aspects and conditions of remuneration.
>
> In particular, where a job classification system is used for determining pay, it must be based on the same criteria for both men and women and so drawn up as to exclude any discrimination on grounds of sex.[3]

The terms job evaluation and job classification are applied rather differently in the UK from other European countries, but it is nevertheless clear that there is no intention in the Equal Pay Directive for a job evaluation or classification system to be a bar to the pursuit of equal pay claims.

## The UK Context

However, job evaluation studies do feature as a barrier to further consideration of an 'equal value' claim by an industrial tribunal in the UK, under the 1983 Equal Value (Amendment) Regulations, which states that there are no grounds for ruling that a woman's work is of equal value if:

(a) that work and the work of the man in question have been given different values on a study such as is mentioned in s. 1(5) above [a job evaluation study]; and

(b) there are no reasonable grounds for determining that the valuation contained in the study was … made on a system which discriminates on grounds of sex.[4]

The assumption underlying the 'job evaluation study' defence is that jobs which have been analysed and evaluated under an acceptable job evaluation system have already been subject to an 'equal value' assessment, because they have been compared under headings such as 'effort, skill and decision'. This assumption ignores the reality that most job evaluation schemes in the UK have been designed, not to implement equal pay for work of equal value, but to reproduce the previous status quo and thus unequal pay. However, this appears still not to be clearly understood by industrial tribunals, which have seen job evaluation as good industrial relations practice. The result is that no applicant to date has mounted a successful challenge to an existing job evaluation scheme (some have evaded the barrier by showing that their jobs were not analysed or evaluated under the relevant scheme, but this is a different matter).

## The Labour Market Consequences

The unsurprising consequence of this is that job evaluation schemes have become very popular with employers concerned at the prospects of equal value claims by individuals or groups of women. Moreover, employers have assumed that the legal defence operates only if potential applicant and comparator jobs are covered by the same JES. This has led to organizations attempting to implement single schemes for all their employees (sometimes excluding the most senior managers). Two major developments have resulted from this. First, there is the introduction of new job evaluation schemes into areas which had previously had different bases for their grading structures, particularly public sector organizations and those with a high proportion of female employees: for example, the civil service, higher education, most of the privatized electricity and water companies, and retail and wholesale distribution. Secondly, we see the replacement of distinct job evaluation systems related to collective bargaining structures by single schemes, often 'cascading' downwards a scheme already in use for senior jobs in the organization, for example in the banking and finance sectors and in large manufacturing companies such as ICI. In many of these cases the introduction of job evaluation was associated with changes to relevant labour market and/or collective bargaining arrangements. Between them the above examples cover some millions of employees, so their impact is significant.

Ironically, in the early 1980s, before the implementation of the Equal Value (Amendment) Regulations, David Grayson of the Department of Employment Work Research Unit wrote a paper suggesting that job evaluation was not compatible with the trends then being observed towards greater flexibility of both jobs and individuals. Grayson thought that job evaluation would gradually wither away to be replaced by more flexibly based grading systems. Others shared his views. Yet the spread of job evaluation has not only continued since, but has increased.

The evidence suggests that the spread of single job evaluation systems would have been less extensive, had it not been for this feature of the equal pay legislation. Some managers admit this in private conversation. Some also admit that they follow fashions in labour management techniques, and that job evaluation is currently fashionable. There are few who resist the trend and argue that, as long as they construct new grading and pay structures on principles of equality, they do not need to use job evaluation techniques. The problem is that most of these 'fashionable' job evaluation schemes are introduced not to move towards equal pay for work of equal value, but to provide a legal defence against equal value claims. This can be observed in the way such job evaluation schemes are selected and implemented. Rarely are these exercises commenced on the premise suggested in the checklist on job evaluation produced by the Equal Opportunities Commission: that there should be no preconceived views on the resulting rank order. Nor is the first question on the checklist often either posed or answered:

Do the terms of reference [for the job evaluation exercise] recognise that avoiding sex bias will mean challenging existing relativities? (EOC, n.d.)

Other indicators of a scheme whose objective is a legal defence rather than a step towards equal pay for work of equal value include:

- the absence of training in the concepts and principles of equal value for all those actively involved in the exercise (a one-hour session with job analysts advising them not to refer to jobholders as 'he' or 'she' does not constitute such training);
- failure to include union, or employee, representatives, and women (with adequate training) in the choice of scheme;
- selection of a 'tried-and-tested' 'off-the-shelf' scheme, albeit one designed for the sector, rather than ensuring that the scheme is appropriate to the jobs in question;
- unwillingness to take into account the experience in the relatively small number of JE exercises undertaken on equal value principles, in the UK or elsewhere;
- a single job evaluation exercise to cover widely varying jobs without consideration of the implications.

The irony is that, even where the scheme is not genuinely implemented on equal value principles, the outcomes may still include the upgrading of some particularly undervalued female-dominated jobs relative to male-dominated jobs, simply as a result of applying a rational system and a consistent set of principles. A number of mechanisms have been devised to avoid the implications and costs of this. Green circling, or phased introduction of consequential pay increases, is one.

Another mechanism is the development of what are generally called 'broad-banded salary structures', which are consistent with trends towards organizational delayering and flatter hierarchies. They also have the advantage, from the employers' perspective, of at least delaying the payment of equal pay, and possibly of preventing it altogether by introducing barriers to progression within the salary range.

Such broad-banded salary structures following job evaluation exercises have been introduced into a significant number of organizations, including public sector organizations. These include the National Rivers Authority (before it became the Environment Agency) and the British Broadcasting Corporation. Some privatized firms, for example British Telecom and some of the utility companies, have also followed this path.

In a traditional incremental structure, those assimilated towards the bottom of a grade salary range move by annual instalments to the top, where they receive the same money as those assimilated towards the top. Normally this would be seen as acceptable by employees and their union representatives, even though it does not give equal pay in money terms immediately. Where the salary range is wide, this is potentially expensive for the organization in the medium term. So many employers operating broad-banded salary structures adopt alternative progression mechanisms, based on performance or competence or acquisition of qualifications, which mean that progression is no longer automatic. Such systems also have the advantage, from the employer's point of view, of allowing for changes to the criteria for progression over time.

From the employees' point of view, such systems result in the perpetuation of unequal pay. In some systems, for example where progression beyond the mid-point requires exceptional performance, equal pay may never be achieved by those with satisfactory or average performance assessments. So the system is used to thwart the attainment of equal pay, even where the jobs have been accepted as being of equal value through that job evaluation scheme.

**The Response on Behalf of Applicants**

Job evaluation undoubtedly causes great difficulties for union officials concerned about equal value. If an equal value claim is submitted and the organizational response is to propose a job evaluation exercise, it is difficult to refuse in order to avoid the expense of a legal case and the anomalies likely to result from an individual claim. But, once completed, the scheme may prevent any further claims. This imposes a great responsibility in relation to the quality of the scheme, over which union representatives will have probably only limited influence.

There have been few direct challenges to job evaluation schemes. In the *Dibro* case, the union decided not to appeal to the ECJ, partly because of fear of setting an unfortunate precedent.[5] A number of unions have considered challenges to the indirectly discriminatory effects of broad-banded salary structures. Some potential claims have not been pursued because the employer agreed to modify the progression system to meet some of the concerns. Other claims perhaps have appeared too complicated to get off the ground. However, it might be possible to pursue such claims more easily directly under Article 1 of the Equal Pay Directive, which refers to 'conditions of remuneration' (see above).

THE 'SAME EMPLOYMENT' CLAUSE

**The European Context**

There is no mention in the European primary legislation of the scope of equal pay provisions. The only elucidation appears to be that in a now quite old decision in the case of *Defrenne* when the ECJ held that:

> the principle of equal pay contained in Article 119 may be relied on before the national courts and ... these courts have a duty to ensure the protection of the rights which this provision vests in individuals, in particular as regards those types of discrimination arising directly from legislative provisions or collective labour agreements, as well as in cases in which men and women receive unequal pay for equal work which is carried out in the *same establishment or service*, whether private or public. (emphasis added)[6]

It may be surmised that the ECJ statement reflects the predominant pattern of collective bargaining in most other EU countries, which has been, and largely still is, at national industry or sector level, with only supplementary bargaining at company or workplace level.

## The UK Context

The UK provisions on the scope of the right to take an equal pay claim, enacted in 1970, are much narrower than those stated in *Defrenne*. They give the right to take an equal pay claim to a woman 'employed at an establishment in Great Britain' or where:

> two employers are to be treated as associated if one is a company of which the other (directly or indirectly) has control or both are companies of which a third person (directly or indirectly) has control, and men shall be treated as in the same employment with a woman if they are men employed by her employer or any associated employer at the same establishment or at establishments in Great Britain which include that one and at which common terms and conditions of employment are observed either generally or for employees of the relevant classes.[7]

The 'same employment' provision of the 1970 Equal Pay Act, it should be said, has not generally proved problematic for women who have taken equal pay claims, with the notable exception of cases against the British Coal Board, who contested whether employees could compare themselves with others at different sites and on different terms and conditions. The Board ultimately lost this argument.

Because of this case, it was thought that 'same employment' might prove an obstacle to some of the clerical applicants in the electricity sector, supported by the National Association of Local Government Officers (NALGO, now part of UNISON), who were comparing themselves with storekeepers and credit meter readers, some of whom worked at or from different bases or depots. However, the point was not contested by the electricity company respondents.

## The Labour Market Situation

The much more problematic area has been for thousands of women who believed, and whose unions believed, that they could not make equal pay claims when their work was contracted out or when their workgroups were split up, leaving them with little or no choice of male comparators in their new employing organization.

It is unlikely that the 'same employment' provision of the Equal Pay Act has been the cause of the trend towards decentralization of collective bargaining over the last two decades. Much greater forces, some of them political rather than economic, have been at work pushing the labour force in that direction. But this aspect of the legislation is consistent with what has been occurring.

## The Response on Behalf of Applicants

Until recently, the response has been limited. There has certainly been discussion of the issue in relation to the contracting out and competitive tendering processes that have occurred in most parts of the public sector. Chris McCrudden raised the possibility of a wider scope than 'same employment' for claims under European law in a paper published some years ago.[8] But unions have understandably preferred the TUPE route, once established via legal cases, to achieve some immediate protection for all employees subject to competitive tendering.[9]

However, recently the 'same employment' provision has been challenged by one applicant, Mrs Scullard, and her union, the National Association of Teachers in Further and Higher Education. Mrs Scullard was employed by the Southern Regional Council for Education and Training as the manager and director of its Further Education Euro Unit. She claimed equal pay for 'like work' with male comparators employed in similar posts in other regional further education Euro units, but was turned down by the Reading industrial tribunal on the grounds that she was not in the 'same employment' as they were (each unit being attached to a different regional advisory council).

Mrs Scullard appealed. Her barrister, Tess Gill, argued on her behalf that the 'same employment' provision of the UK legislation was not consistent with European legislation, as expounded by the ECJ in the *Defrenne* case. The Employment Appeal Tribunal accepted this argument.

It referred the case back to the industrial tribunal for examination of whether or not the units in question constitute the 'same service'. It suggested further investigation of the relationship between her employer and the Training and Education Directorate of the Department of Employment, and of whether common terms and conditions of employment were observed for the relevant class of employees, as well as taking into account the main source of funding ([1996] IRLR 344 EAT).

This decision has been appealed by the respondent and clearly has wide implications. How wide depends on how broadly industrial tribunals interpret 'same … service'. For example, are contracted-out catering jobs in the same service as non-contracted catering jobs in a health service trust? Are they in the same service as non-contracted ancillary jobs (for example, porters) in the same trust? Are they in the same service as non-contracted out patient care jobs in the same trust? Are they in the same service as non-contracted out catering jobs in a neighbouring trust? And so on.

## CONCLUSIONS – THE RESPONSES

Employers have exploited these features of the legislation to avoid the implications of pay equity. Sometimes this exploitation has been passive, in that no specific action needed to be taken to secure the advantages, for instance, of the 'same employment' provision. In other areas, employers have allowed some features of the legislation to influence their policies. This is most noticeable in relation to the introduction of single job evaluation schemes, but can be seen also in the retention of separate collective bargaining structures in some parts of the public sector, where otherwise this might not have been the case.

Those working on behalf of applicants have experienced considerable difficulties in responding to the combination of features of the equal pay legislation and labour market developments. The predominant response has often been to leave the issue either to the union which has revealed the obstacle or to the Equal Opportunities Commission. In spite of the best efforts of the Trades Union Congress to encourage a co-ordinated strategic response to issues with a legal dimension, including equal pay, such actions are rare. Indeed, I am conscious myself of having advised unions not to pursue claims raising legal issues which 'are nothing to do with' the central 'equal value' issue. I wonder on reflection whether this really has been always the right approach.

Recent concentration of union effort on strategic cases suggests a more optimistic future. The *Ratcliffe*[10] and the *Scullard* cases are good examples of strategies aimed at combating the effects of competitive tendering and decentralized bargaining. Careful exploration of possible 'same employment' cases, following *Scullard*, could extend protection to employees, men as well as women, adversely affected by current trends. A direct legal challenge to one of the unsatisfactory job evaluation schemes in the health service could have a reasonable chance of success, because the defects of traditional JESs are most apparent in relation to patient care jobs, and would have a much wider impact. Similarly, a strategic challenge to a broad-banded salary structure, possibly under European rather than UK legislation, might deter further negative equity steps in this area. Analysis of the relationship between particular features of the UK equal pay legislation and current labour market trends suggests that there is considerable scope for action on a number of fronts.

## NOTES

1. *Handels-og Kontorfunktionaererernes Forbund i Danmark* v *Dansk Arbejdsgiverforening* (acting for Danfoss) [1989] IRLR 532–7, especially para. 22. For discussion of the issues, see also *Equal Opportunities Review* No. 29 (January/February 1990) 41–4.

     The *Bilka* case dealt specifically with the exclusion of part-time employees from receiving benefits from an occupational pension scheme, but was held to apply to all pay practices (*Bilka-Kaufhaus GmbH* v *Weber von Hartz* [1986] IRLR 317 ECJ). See also *Equal Opportunities Review* No. 9 (September/October 1986) 29–31.

2. Equal Pay Act 1970, as amended, s. 1(3), reproduced in TUC section 2, 1991, pp. 57–8.

3. Directive 75/117/EEC, the Equal Pay Directive, reproduced in TUC, Section s, 1991, pp. 51–3.

4. Equal Pay Act, s. 2A(2), reproduced in TUC (1991) p. 60.

5. In *Dibro Ltd* v *Hoare*, the Employment Appeal Tribunal (EAT) held that an employer's job evaluation study is admissible in evidence at any time during the proceedings ([1990] IRLR 129 EAT). See also *Equal Opportunities Review* No. 31, May/June 1990, pp. 44–6, reproduced in TUC (1991) section 6, pp. 33–5.

6. ECJ: *Defrenne No. 2* [1976] ECR p. 455ff, especially p. 476, para. 40.

7. Equal Pay Act, 1970, s. 1(1) and s. 1(6)(c), reproduced in TUC (1991) section 2, pp. 57–8.

8. McCrudden, C. (1991). He quotes in this context Szyszcak (1987).

9. The Transfer of Undertakings (Protection of Employment) Regulations (TUPE) were passed in 1981 to comply with another European directive, the Acquired Rights Directive (77/187). The directive was intended to

ensure that workers transferring from one employer to another would have their existing terms and conditions protected, but the case law in this area has become exceedingly complex (see Cavalier, 1997).

10. In *Ratcliffe* v *North Yorkshire County Council* the applicants were employed by the local authority as catering assistants whose work had been assessed under a JES as equivalent to that of several manual jobs performed mainly by men. As a result of compulsory tendering, the women were sacked and re-employed at lower hourly rates. Their claim for equal pay with male workers still remunerated under the 1987 JES was upheld by the House of Lords ([1995] IRLR 439 HL).

## REFERENCES

Cavalier, S., *Transfer Rights: TUPE in Perspective*. London: Institute of Employment Rights, 1997.

Equal Opportunities Commission, *Good Equal Opportunities Practice in Analytical Job Evaluation, a Checklist*. Manchester: EOC, undated.

McCrudden, C., 'Between legality and reality: the implementation of equal pay for work of equal value in Britain', *International Review of Comparative Public Policy* vol. 3 (1991) 179–219.

Szyszczak, E., 'The Equal Pay Directive and UK law', in C. McCrudden, *Women, Employment and European Equality Law*. London: Eclipse, 1987.

Trades Union Congress, *Equal Value Manual*. London: TUC, 1991.

# 11 Independent Experts in Equal Pay

## Alan Arthurs

### INTRODUCTION

The British Equal Pay Act 1970 gives a woman the right to equal pay when she is employed in work which is the same or similar to that of a man in the same employment, or where her work has been rated as equivalent. However, in 1982 the British government was found by the European Court of Justice (ECJ) to be in breach of the 1976 EC Equal Pay Directive which provides that member states must give women the right to equal pay for work of equal value. The directive contains no definition of this concept and it is left to each country to decide how it is to be applied.

Britain responded with the 1983 Equal Pay (Amendment) Regulations, which give a woman the right to equal pay with a man when she is in the same employment and found to be employed on work which is of equal value 'in terms of the demands made on her' (Equal Pay Act 1970, as amended, section 1(2)(c)). Only individual women may bring a case and they must name the male comparator(s) whose work they believe to be of equal value to their own. Even when a woman wins a case there is no obligation on her employer to change the pay structure of which her job is a part. Furthermore, an employer can argue that the difference in pay is due not to sex discrimination but to a 'material factor'. Much legal argument in the past 15 years has concentrated on what is a valid material factor defence, particularly in what circumstances labour market conditions can be taken into account.

When a claim is submitted to an industrial tribunal it must normally engage an independent expert to report on whether or not the jobs of the female applicant and the male comparator(s) are equal in value. The tribunal may reject the report and must then appoint another independent expert. Grounds for rejection include that the expert has not complied with the legal procedure or that the conclusion could not reasonably have been reached. However, in most cases the report has been accepted. Hence the ability of a woman to achieve equal pay for work of equal value depends greatly on the decisions made by an independent expert on the values to be placed upon jobs.

This chapter provides a background to the debate about the role of independent experts in equal value cases. Their relationship to industrial tribunals, methods of investigation and evaluation and difficulties faced in evaluating jobs are discussed and the ways in which procedures might be improved considered. It is concluded that though fundamental changes in British equal pay law are needed, independent experts should continue to play a central role in those cases involving individual women seeking equal pay for work of equal value.

## WHO ARE THE INDEPENDENT EXPERTS?

The 1983 amendment to the Equal Pay Act gave responsibility for the selection of the independent experts to the Advisory, Conciliation and Arbitration Service (ACAS). Appointments are part-time for two years, with reappointments possible. An industrial tribunal contacts ACAS for a recommendation from the panel, but the expert is employed by and answerable to the tribunal which pays him or her for the time spent on a case.

The selection criteria are: the ability, integrity and experience to conduct an investigation in a manner which maintains the expert's independence and credibility; and the skills to deal with all the agents involved in the case[1] and to overcome any difficulties encountered, write a reasoned report and explain or defend it under cross-examination by barristers specializing in discrimination and equal pay law. The expert should be familiar with equal value and other sex discrimination legislation, the reasons for enactment and the underlying philosophy. Knowledge and experience of pay systems and in particular of job evaluation, preferably its introduction into an organization, are required, and an appreciation of the strengths and weaknesses of different approaches to job evaluation.

The original panel of 15 was broadly representative of employers and employees: seven were managers or acted for employers, or had at some point in their careers, and seven had been trade union representatives or officers at some time. Only four were women, but by 1998 a gender balance had been achieved and now half of the 12 experts are women. Only five of the original 15 remain: the majority on the panel are now self-employed consultants and the rest are academics.

## INDEPENDENT EXPERTS AND TRIBUNALS

The expert receives from the tribunal: the Order requiring a report; the Requirement giving details of the question on which the report is required;

the Originating Application(s) from the person(s) claiming equal pay; and the Notice of Appearance from the respondent, giving the grounds on which the application is opposed. The expert will not necessarily be told what has led to his or her appointment; details of the tribunal hearing might not be forwarded, but are sometimes made available by one of the parties.

The question put to the expert is normally 'whether or not the work of the applicant is of equal value to the work performed by the comparator(s) in terms of the demands made upon them'. The expert is enjoined to act fairly at all times and take no account of sex.

The expert must consider all relevant information and representations and prepare a summary of these for the parties, so that they can comment on it. The final report must contain the summary and a brief account of any representations the parties have made, the expert's conclusion and the reasons for it.

Within these requirements the expert is free to conduct the investigation and write his or her report in whatever way he or she wishes. However, all experts have attended induction courses and other meetings organized by ACAS, receiving advice on developments in the law, tribunal procedures and approaches to conducting an investigation. These meetings also enable experts to discuss methods. As a consequence of this and of tribunal judgments there has been some convergence in approach, but the experts still remain independent of both the parties and each other and therefore some differences remain. Typical steps in the process are shown in Figure 11.1.

If the report concludes that the job of the applicant is not equal to that of the comparator(s) the woman may withdraw the case, particularly if she does not have strong financial and legal support. If the report favours the woman's claim the employer has an incentive to seek a settlement. In well over half of the cases in which experts have reported the case has been settled or withdrawn without a further full tribunal hearing (Equal Opportunities Review (EOR) No. 76, November/December 1997, p. 19).

Unresolved cases go forward to a resumed tribunal hearing, where either party may argue that the report should not be accepted because the expert did not act fairly or did not follow the required procedure; or has produced a report which was wrong in its facts or missed out important facts; or has reached an unreasonable conclusion. If the tribunal considers the report to be unsatisfactory for one of these reasons, it may reject it and commission a fresh one. This has happened only about five times in the 15 years since the regulations were introduced.

Before it accepts or rejects the report the tribunal, or either party, normally requires the attendance of the independent expert at a reconvened hearing

1. Tribunal selects IE via ACAS
2. Requirement and other papers sent to IE
3. IE contacts parties' representatives
4. IE carries out interviews and observation. Seeks other information
5. Parties send information and representations
6. IE clarifies and seeks to resolve points of difference
7. Summary of Information and Representations sent to parties
8. Further representations from parties
9. IE clarifies and seeks to resolve differences between parties
10. IE writes brief account of further representations
11. IE brings together and analyses all information
12. IE devises method to compare jobs
13. IE makes valuations and draws conclusions
14. IE sends report to tribunal
15. If case not settled or withdrawn at this stage a further tribunal hearing is scheduled
16. IE normally cross-examined at resumed tribunal hearing
17. Tribunal accepts or rejects report or asks for further information

*Figure 11.1*    Stages in the independent expert's (IE) investigation
*Note*: Not all these stages will always be in sequence. In order to save time the independent expert may pursue some of the stages simultaneously.

for cross-examination by lawyers. A battle may ensue as the parties may call expert witnesses who may also be cross-examined. The independent expert is not legally represented and cannot question the parties' experts.

The independent expert's report has no greater weight in law than evidence from the parties (*Tennants Textiles Colours Ltd* v *Todd* [1989] Industrial Relations Law Reports (IRLR) 3 N. Ireland Court of Appeal) and the credence given to the report depends upon the extent to which inaccuracies, misinterpretation and methodological weaknesses have been avoided. In practice, however, the independent expert has two important advantages. First, he or she is disinterested; and second, he or she normally appears to spend longer than other experts on observing the jobs and, to that extent, can be seen to 'know' them better.

## EVALUATING THE WORK

There are three stages in the process of assessing the relative values of the jobs: (1) the content of each job is established; (2) a method for analysing and comparing the demands of each is devised; and (3) the value of each job is compared and a conclusion reached as to whether the applicant(s)' and comparator(s)' jobs are of equal value.

## Job Content

The content of the jobs to be assessed is pieced together from interviews, documents and observation. Not only the applicant(s) and comparator(s), but normally also their supervisors will be interviewed. The expert may also interview line managers, personnel managers, union representatives and officers, other employees carrying out the same work, expert advisers to the parties and legal representatives. Written representations from the parties may include formal job descriptions. To establish how a job relates to other jobs the expert may examine contiguous jobs and ask for an organization chart.

Most independent experts believe it important, where feasible, to observe the jobs concerned, or a sample where there are a number of very similar jobs. Where the timespan of the work is short this is not difficult, but in jobs where major variations occur over a period of weeks, months or even years (for example, building a ship) only limited observation is possible.

Invariably there are differing perceptions as to what a particular job involves and the demands made upon the jobholder. Employers may say that certain tasks carried out or responsibilities assumed by employees are 'not part of the job description'. However, if the expert becomes convinced that an employee does work in a certain way, then that is part of the job to be assessed. The question of whether the person is supposed to work in that way is outside the expert's remit.

Only the 'demands made by the job' must be considered, and the expert must seek to distinguish between these demands and the overall contribution of the individual worker. Thus she or he is not concerned with the relative competence of the applicant and comparators, nor with how they work. Such matters may, however, be relevant if an employer seeks to establish a 'material difference' between jobs at the tribunal hearing.

Draft job descriptions prepared by the expert from the evidence collected are normally checked with the parties, and further interviews or observations may be made to resolve points of contention before final descriptions are written. In *Evesham* v *North Hertfordshire Health Authority and Secretary of State for Health* the tribunal was critical of the expert's reliance on the descriptions provided by the parties, stating that it 'is essential that a job description of the jobs being compared should be drawn up from the outset by the independent expert, with the agreement of the jobholders as far as possible' (quoted in EOR No. 76, 1997, p. 28).

**Method of Analysis**

The legislation provides that the work of the applicant and comparator be compared 'in terms of the demands made .... for instance, under such headings as effort, skill and decision' (Equal Pay Act, as amended, section 1(2)(c)). This rules out two other possible ways of assessing relative values, namely comparing market values (what is actually paid in the market) and comparing the marginal productivity of the two jobs (McCrudden, 1983). Implicit in the legislation is that job evaluation-type techniques should be used and the headings suggested imply that an analytical approach is needed.

However, assessing equal value is different in important respects from conventional job evaluation. First, the Act does not use the term 'job evaluation' to describe the duties of independent experts and it has been suggested that this may be in order to allow the assessment of equal value to be conducted in a less formal and more limited manner than is the case with a fullscale job evaluation study (McCrudden, 1983). To some extent some of the early experts' reports reflected this view, but informality is impossible to maintain when reports are subject to detailed scrutiny and cross-examination. Second, job evaluation is normally designed to accord where possible with the labour market. Equal value assessments must ignore the market. Third, in job evaluation an employer may make allowances for traditional differentials which may enshrine past discrimination. Equal value assessments must take no account of existing pay relationships.

Finally, there is the question of acceptability. This is an important test of a job evaluation scheme, since its introduction is normally in order to replace relative pay rates which have lost credibility with employees and managers. To be successful a new structure must gain the acceptance, or at least the acquiescence, of the great majority of employees to whom it applies. The scheme will have to take account of the bargaining strength of the employees involved, otherwise it will be challenged and its credibility damaged. It is when a pay structure acceptable to all parties has not been agreed and conciliation has failed that an equal value case may be instituted.

The independent expert must find the jobs to be equal or not equal; it is not his or her task to seek a compromise. Without the constraints imposed by the need to take account of the market or traditional differentials the expert may find an assessment method acceptable to the parties, but the overriding considerations are the rights of the parties and freedom from sex bias.

How do experts devise a method of comparing and valuing jobs? Little advice is available. *Judging Equal Value*, published soon after the legislation came into operation, contains the most substantial discussion of how, in practice, a method free of sex bias may be constructed (Equal Opportunities Commission (EOC), 1984). This publication, the subsequent experience of independent experts and the judgments of tribunals can be used to outline some guiding principles:

- job evaluation methods used before the 1984 legislation cannot be relied upon, since they may contain implicit sex bias;
- all aspects of the jobs must be incorporated in the factors to be used in the comparison;
- the factors and sub-factors chosen should be clearly identified, defined and comprehensible;
- factors and sub-factors should have definitions which are free from double-counting and do not identify the same demand under more than one heading;
- unjustifiable weight should not be given to aspects of the work which predominate in a job, or features which are an important part of a job underplayed;
- value must be assessed strictly in terms of the demands made on the worker by the job. It must not include the value of the work to the employer nor existing pay structures.

These principles should help to focus the independent expert's mind. The problem remains, however, of what factors are chosen to be compared. There are several possibilities and it is likely that experts use one or more of the following in varying degrees of emphasis: first, the criteria in the Act of 'effort, skill and decision'; second, the expert's experience of job evaluation schemes, perhaps modified to take into account the particular features of the jobs in the case; and third, the parties' own suggestions, built on and modified as the expert thinks appropriate.

Ensuring the absence of any sex bias in both the choice of factors and the weightings given to them is crucial. Certain kinds of work such as caring, dexterity and human relations are widely seen as 'women's work' while work such as heavy lifting, responsibility for machinery and unpleasant working conditions is seen as 'men's work'. The expert must be aware of these beliefs and make sure that undue weight is not given to 'male' factors in evaluating jobs. *Judging Equal Value* (EOC, 1984) lists factors which are said respectively to favour 'male' jobs, favour 'female' jobs and be neutral. Should the expert make sure with arithmetical precision that the factors chosen are equally balanced between those which normally favour women and those which normally favour men? And how reliable are these assertions about factors favouring either men or women?

*Judging Equal Value* does not say how the lists were constructed, so their validity is uncertain.

Another assumption of which the expert must be aware and if necessary take into account is that some tasks undertaken by women are regarded conventionally as unskilled or less skilled, not because they have been dispassionately examined but because it is women who carry them out.

## Comparing the Jobs

Having determined the content of the jobs and devised a method for comparing them the expert must then carry out the comparison. This can be done most convincingly if the assessment criteria are set out fully, for example, the skills and knowledge required, using overall definitions of skills and of different kinds of skills and knowledge. The expert can then explain why, on each criterion, she or he has rated the jobs relative to each other.

When the comparison is between a single applicant and single comparator relative values may be assessed without resorting to numerical scoring. However, where there are several applicants perhaps carrying out different but closely related jobs and several different comparators numerical scoring systems may be needed.

Having compared the jobs the expert must then conclude whether or not they are of equal value. This may appear obvious, but there are differences of approach. An early issue was whether, if the woman's job was found to be of greater value than the man's, this provides the basis for a claim of equal value. This has now been settled by the ECJ and the expert can work on the assumption that a higher valuation qualifies a woman for equal pay (*Murphy* v *Bord Telecom Eireann* [1988] IRLR 267 ECJ).

The second more contentious issue is whether 'equal' means 'exactly equal'. If, for example, a numerical scoring system shows that the woman's job score is almost identical to the man's (say 56 to 57) should the expert conclude that for all practical purposes they are of equal value? Tribunals have differed and so have experts, but it is unlikely that the higher courts will find equality where an applicant scores less than a comparator, however insignificant the difference.

## DOES THE SYSTEM WORK?

Independent experts have been subject to criticism for technical incompetence, inconsistency, delays in producing reports and for being part of a process which is unduly complex, long, costly and unpredictable. Equal pay law has been characterized as a 'paradise for lawyers but hell for women' (EOC, 1990).

## Technical Competence?

The most trenchant criticism claimed that some of the experts adopted practices and procedures that would be unacceptable in a normal job evaluation exercise and that they appeared to have a limited knowledge of job analysis techniques (Beddoe, 1986). However, the use of 'normal job evaluation' as the standard by which to judge the reports cannot be accepted. As argued above, assessing equal value is not the same as job evaluation.

In addition, this criticism was based on a very small sample of cases involving only a few of the independent experts and was written at a time when they were developing a wholly new process for which there were no existing models either in the UK or abroad. The criticism was not part of a balanced overall assessment but drew mainly on material produced for the purpose of challenging experts' reports. Only a handful of the reports have been rejected.

## Consistency?

A study of 24 reports (Plumer, 1992) concluded that there was 'remarkably little consistency between experts' and that judgments seemed to depend mainly on experts' choices of the methods of analysis. The study concluded that 'until a more consistent method can be produced, Industrial Tribunals will need to be aware of the influence that choices of methods of assessment can have on the evaluation of jobs' (ibid., p. 4). It warned industrial tribunals to make appropriate allowances when reaching their decisions, but it was not made clear how this was to be done.

The EOC has suggested prescribing in detail the evaluation process to be followed by independent experts, either in regulations or a code of practice (EOC, 1998). However, any move towards a standard method of job evaluation would capture a particular set of values and assumptions around which a consensus would be unlikely. It would not ensure greater justice.

## Delays?

The tribunal rules which envisaged that reports would be received within 42 days have been found totally unrealistic – the average is 11 months – and the widespread concern at the time taken is understandable. Delays have been ascribed to 'inefficiency or lack of expertise and training and to lack of effective judicial control of the timetable' (Justice, 1987, p. 39).

One solution proposed is to have full-time as well as part-time experts (EOC, 1990). Undoubtedly full-time experts would generally be able to produce reports more quickly and build up expertise and experience faster. However, if mainly full-timers were employed the accumulated expertise of the current panel would be largely lost, since very few are in a position to become full timers. The low fees would not attract people with adequate experience to work full time (Bowey, 1988). A further disadvantage of full-time experts would be that a very small group of specialists would develop, involved only in equal pay cases and therefore potentially out of touch with other issues. Assessing equal value cannot be treated simply as a narrow technical specialism and those carrying it out must be seen to be in contact with, and reflecting, wider community values.

Moreover, the reliance on part-time experts is not the main explanation for delays, since a range of other factors are more significant:

- the legal procedures (see Figure 11.1);
- lines of communication between the expert and the parties and between the parties take time to become established and may change as the investigation proceeds;
- it can be in the interests of the respondent to delay the investigation;
- applicants' jobs change or disappear before or during the investigation;
- comparators' jobs change or disappear before or during the investigation;
- comparators do not want to cooperate, or they may change jobs or employers during the investigation.

Furthermore, most cases do not reach the expert for several months and in some cases years after the application to the tribunal. After the report has been submitted cases may be held up because of administrative delays or communication failures or because barristers are busy elsewhere. Appeals, interlocutory hearings, judicial reviews, and so on can keep the ball in the air for years.

Judicial timetables are now mandatory and these may reduce delays, but cases vary so much in their complexity and idiosyncrasies that the quality of some investigations would be damaged unless the timetables were applied sensitively.


RESOLVING EQUAL VALUE DISPUTES

Despite the criticisms, the 1983 legislation has clearly helped to achieve change: many cases have been settled after the law has been invoked or threatened; nearly two thirds of the cases referred to an independent expert and subsequently decided by a tribunal have found in favour of the female applicant (Equal Opportunities Review no. 76, November/December 1997, p. 19). Since the legislation came into force in 1984 women's hourly rates of pay have risen from 74 to 79 per cent of men's rates. Not all of this narrowing of the gap can be explained by the direct or indirect effect of the legislation, but it is clear that a substantial number of major employers have implemented new pay structures more favourable to women as a result of this law.

Further progress will depend on more effective legislation. A strong case has been made for a radical change which would shift the focus from individual to collective remedies. The EOC has proposed that employers should be placed under a statutory duty to review their pay systems and structures in order to identify areas of potential and actual pay inequality between men and women that cannot be objectively justified (EOC, 1998). Employers would then be required to publish the results of their reviews to their employees and outline a programme for dealing with any pay inequalities identified. A more collective focus would require industrial tribunals to go beyond providing remedies for individual equal pay grievances and enable them to make changes to a collective agreement or pay structure consistent with the findings in an individual case.

Governments through the 1980s and most of the 1990s were wholly unsympathetic to this approach and it is far from clear that the Labour government will accept any of these proposals. Even without changes in the law some public sector employers are nevertheless introducing or discussing new, comprehensive pay structures in response to difficulties and anomalies caused by their losing individual equal pay cases. However, while in the National Health Service a long-running claim by speech therapists has started to bring victories for some of the women concerned the employers have continued to fight each individual case. This is despite the legal costs they have incurred since 1986, when the women first made their claim to a tribunal and is because of the enormous costs of a full settlement, estimated by one of the unions at 70 million pounds. Not only would this be likely to give substantial pay increases for many speech therapists, but other female-dominated occupations in the health service, such as physiotherapists, midwives and occupational therapists can be expected to claim that their work is also undervalued. Even if the government were to be sympathetic to claims that many female-dominated jobs in the health service and other parts of the public sector are undervalued, it is unlikely that any new money injected will come anywhere near to meeting the costs of full implementation of equal pay.

Even if Britain does move towards legally imposed changes in pay structures an adequate procedure and effective remedies for individual equal pay claims will still be needed. Changes have been made to the original legal procedures with a view to reducing costs and delays, but no significant improvement has yet been achieved. Further changes suggested by the EOC for consideration include: hearing the question of equal value before the often tortuous legal arguments involved in an employer's defence; time limiting hearings; restricting the use of experts by the parties; and provisions for group or representative hearings.


## A FUTURE FOR INDEPENDENT EXPERTS?

The report *Industrial Tribunals* (Justice, 1987) proposed that independent experts be dispensed with and the money saved go to the EOC to enable it to pay the costs of an expert for a party whom it had decided to support. The report suggested that this would solve the problem of unequal representation of applicants and respondents, but this would of course do nothing for the applicant who does not receive EOC support.

The law was changed in 1996 to allow tribunals to dispense with independent experts, but precisely how a tribunal would then choose between the conflicting parties' evidence is not clear. It would surely take more time and involve more witnesses, therefore costing more money than would be saved by not calling on an independent expert. Confronted by conflicting views of a job an independent expert can often resolve them by observation. Is it suggested that a tribunal should observe the work, even when there are multiple applicants and comparators? So far no tribunal has taken up the 1996 'opportunity': assessment of equal value by an independent expert has proved to be a cost-effective means of resolving many cases.

The concern over the time taken to produce reports has drawn attention away from the fact that the majority of cases are settled or withdrawn whilst the expert is conducting investigations or after the report has been produced. This has saved the time and expense of employers, applicants, lawyers and tribunal staff. This is not by chance: some experts feed back information to the parties during the course of the investigation and this often concentrates people's minds not just on the facts but also on the strength or weakness of their case. Any procedure which cuts out the independent expert would in many cases impose further costs on the parties and on the tribunal and lead to less rather than more justice.

The legislation on equal pay has been particularly widely criticized for its emphasis on individual complaints rather than on excising sex discrimination from whole pay structures, and a shift towards collective remedies and the changing of whole pay structures is clearly needed.

However, independent experts should continue to play a role in providing remedies for individual women seeking equal pay for work of equal value.

NOTE

1.    Employers, employees, trade union representatives and officials, lawyers and experts representing each party as well as the Equal Opportunities Commission and tribunal staff.

REFERENCES

Beddoe, R., 'Independent experts?', *Equal Opportunities Review* no. 6 (March/April 1986).
Bowey, A., *Evaluation of the Role of the Independent Experts in Equal Value Cases.* Manchester: Equal Opportunities Commission, 1988.
Department of Employment, *Resolving Employment Rights Disputes: Options for Reform.* London: Department of Employment, 1994.
Equal Opportunities Commission, *Judging Equal Value.* Manchester: EOC, 1984.
Equal Opportunities Commission, *Equal Pay for Men and Women: Strengthening the Acts.* Manchester: EOC, 1990.
Equal Opportunities Commission, *Equality in the 21st Century – a New Approach.* Manchester: EOC, 1998.
Equal Opportunities Review, 'Independent expert's report has limited status', *Equal Opportunities Review* no. 23 (January/February 1989) 39–40.
Equal Opportunities Review, 'Equal value update', *Equal Opportunities Review* no. 76 (November/December 1997) 18–32.
Industrial Relations Law Reports, *Murphy* v *Bord Telecom Eireann* [1988] IRLR 267 ECJ.
Industrial Relations Law Reports, *Tennants Textiles Colours Ltd* v *Todd* [1989] IRLR 3 N. Ireland Court of Appeal.
Justice, *Industrial Tribunals.* London: Justice, 1987.
McCrudden, C., 'Equal pay for work of equal value: the Equal Pay (Amendment) Regulations 1983', *Industrial Law Journal* 11 (December 1983) 197–219.
Plumer, A.-M., 'Equal value judgements: objective assessment or lottery?' *Warwick Papers in Industrial Relations* no. 40, 1992.
Trade Union Research Unit, 'Independent experts and their reports', *Technical Note* no. 103, 1988.

# Part IV
# The Strategic Use of
# Equal Pay Law

# 12 Public Sector Reforms in a Changing Economic and Political Climate: Lessons from Michigan

Peggy Kahn and Deborah Figart

## INTRODUCTION

The trajectory of pay equity reform for workers employed by the State of Michigan illuminates the project of public sector pay equity in the United States as a whole.[1] Pay equity policy in the US has been concentrated in the public sector, especially in state civil services. In the absence of federal law prohibiting unequal pay for work of equal value, the private sector has been unwilling to raise wages through pay equity adjustments. More densely unionized than workers in the private sector, women in the public sector have been able to make alliances with feminists in the state bureaucracies and legislatures to win wage reforms (Evans and Nelson, 1989). In addition, state managers, traditionally reliant on elaborate personnel systems employing job evaluation, have been relatively receptive to comparable worth arguments and techniques (Johnston, 1994).

During the 1980s, therefore, while the Reagan administration blocked pay equity developments in national law and policy, over 20 states and several localities adopted some form of pay equity for their employees. As in Michigan, these efforts often involved whole-workforce studies and systemic pay reform. Although states relied on job evaluation systems uncleansed of gender bias and failed to correct the full wage gap revealed by comparable worth studies (Steinberg, 1990; 1989; Acker, 1989), these adjustments amounted to about $383 million between 1979 and 1989 (Hartmann and Aaronson, 1994; National Committee on Pay Equity, 1989).

In fact, the pay equity movement expanded in the US as a whole in the mid-1980s, a contradictory moment for progress in women's pay. On the one hand, women's expanding labour force participation, the women's movement and the development of equal opportunities programmes created a powerful impetus for women to claim their right to fair pay, while a few highly visible court cases amplified the possibilities for

183

comparable worth reform (McCann, 1994). On the other hand, pay equity hit the policy agenda in the context of a new politics of deregulation, tax revolts, and general neoliberal anti-state sentiment. The politics of the 1980s and 1990s embodied a response to global economic restructuring which in much of the midwestern US took the form of rapid deindustrialization combined with an expansion of a service sector bifurcated between 'good' and 'bad' jobs (Blank, 1990). Business and its conservative allies argued that reduction of taxes and deregulation of labour were central to competitiveness. As a state which has suffered serious recession, deindustrialization and a powerful anti-tax revolt, Michigan illuminates the dilemmas involved in pursuing pay equity reform in new economic and political times.

## THE POLITICAL ECONOMY OF MICHIGAN IN THE 1980s AND 1990s

The pay equity movement emerged in Michigan as the postwar boom was giving way to a deep recession. This coincided with the longer-term decline of automobile manufacturing in the state: between 1950 and the late 1980s the US auto industry, concentrated in Michigan, lost more than half its world market and much of its domestic market share. In general, auto employers responded by attacking labour costs, not only by demanding concessions over wages and work practices but also by relocating manufacturing capacity to lower-waged economies both in the US South and overseas. Automobile and other manufacturing workers, mainly male, experienced immense losses in employment and considerable deterioration in their terms and conditions of work. Other workers dependent upon the auto industry or auto workers' wages also suffered.

Michigan's severe cyclical recession ended in the 1980s but the long-term economic restructuring continued, bringing an expanded service sector with lower average wages and less unionization than in manufacturing (Michigan Department of Commerce, 1991). By the 1980s a densely unionized public service sector had become an important concentration of women's employment. While women public sector workers continued to be segregated vertically and horizontally into lower-paying 'women's jobs', they enjoyed better terms and conditions than many women employed in private services. With new competitive pressures the use of women's cheap and flexible labour became an important cost reduction strategy in the private sector, with women disproportionately occupying the increasing percentage of low-paid, insecure, contingent jobs (Callaghan and Hartmann, 1991). The feminized public sector also became a target of cost reduction. A high percentage of women lived in poverty while a small proportion worked in professional and managerial jobs, and the pay gap between men and women was thus greater than the US average (Institute for Women's Policy Research, 1996; Sarri et al., 1987).

In the early l980s, in an attempt to stem the tide of job losses, increasing economic insecurity and deunionization in Michigan, male-dominated manufacturing unions supported Democrats for both the governorship and the legislature. In 1982 a Democrat, James Blanchard, was elected governor and the Democrats also won majorities in both the Michigan House of Representatives and the Senate. The 1988 elections returned Blanchard, along with a Republican Senate and a House with a narrow Democratic majority. Yet the Democrats, positioning themselves as both pro-business and pro-labour, did little to restore manufacturing jobs. Organized labour and its Democratic allies focused upon managing the consequences of industrial job loss for its largely male membership, paying little attention to the emerging problems of women workers. Responding in particular to their small-business allies, Republicans kept up a decade-long effort to improve the business climate by decreasing the costs of employing labour and producing goods through a strategy of deregulation. Within mainstream political discourse it was almost impossible to promote the interests and needs of workers as opposed to corporations. The latter were represented as job creators and goods producers, embodying the public interest. A dramatic anti-tax revolt occurred early in Blanchard's first term as governor. This was partly a local Republican strategy, which through a recall petition and election[2] changed the party balance in the state Senate. The tax revolt was also a manifestation of more general anti-government sentiment. The Michigan tax revolt explicitly articulated the view that state taxation was responsible for Michigan's economic decline, and focused on the proposal that overpaid public sector workers should accept the sort of wage cuts that auto workers had conceded. Blanchard responded to these forces by trying to lower taxes and began to talk about increasing efficiency by cutting the number of public employees.

John Engler, a conservative Republican who had been majority leader in the state Senate, won a narrow electoral majority in the gubernatorial election of 1990 and was re-elected in 1994 as the legislature also shifted towards Republican majorities. From the beginning of his tenure Engler asserted the importance of tax cuts as the key to business prosperity and individual freedom. His militant budget-cutting stance was combined with an ideological commitment to decrease the size and functions of the state. His administration abolished whole departments, reorganized offices and undertook a broad-ranging privatization initiative. Defence of state workers had never been a priority for the Blanchard Democrats, but reduction in the state workforce became a major priority for Engler. In his first two years, the number of civil servants declined by about 6,000, or nearly 10 per cent. Their wages and benefits were frozen and annual wage increases were reduced.

Although pay equity reform had inched forward during the Blanchard administrations without support from the governor, it made no progress under the Engler administration which was strongly committed to reducing labour costs in the state, resolutely opposed to modifying the sway of the market and entirely silent on issues of gender. The pay equity movement faced not only labour cost reduction strategies, but also the more conservative politics of the 1980s and 1990s which viewed the state as an institution to be reduced, rather than as a vehicle for ameliorating broader social and economic problems or as an employer which might serve as a positive model. Nevertheless pay equity advocates, located mainly in state government itself, succeeded in putting pay equity on the agenda for civil service workers. The new politics of the 1980s, however, continued to limit the progress of pay equity through policy decision and implementation phases.

## THE CIVIL SERVICE COMMISSION DETERMINES REFORM

With the Democratic Party and organized labour focusing on the decline of private manufacturing, the impetus for putting pay equity on the policy agenda in Michigan came from a small number of determined advocates within state government. They were integrated into a national network of women's policy advocates and were familiar with the longstanding problems within the civil service classification and pay system. In other states the legislature used its authority to pass laws mandating pay equity within the state civil service (Acker, 1989; Evans and Nelson, 1989; Remick, 1986). In Michigan regulation of state employment is reserved to, and ultimately determined by, the Civil Service Commission, a part-time body appointed by the governor and supported and guided administratively by the Department of Civil Service. Its composition reflects a balance between the two main political parties.

Between 1980 and 1981 the Office of Women and Work, an extremely small division within the Department of Labour, produced three reports critical of gender bias in the civil service. The findings of the reports, the most important of which was a 1980 study by the consultants Arthur Young, Inc. (1981), converged around the theme that Michigan's job evaluation system and pay practices embodied gender discrimination.[3] In 1981 Karon Black, a state employee, supported by the Michigan State Employee Association (MSEA), at the time the largest labour union in state employment, lodged a complaint of sex discrimination with the Michigan Civil Rights Commission and federal Equal Employment Opportunity Commission on behalf of all female employees in the classified service.[4] The MSEA, using evidence from the Arthur Young study, demanded that the Civil Service Commission and Department act immediately to correct discrimination in classification and pay. The Commission responded that the issues surrounding comparable worth were unclear and the economic climate not conducive to action.

Finally, in response to legal pressure, the Arthur Young study and the changing national political environment for pay equity, the Commission set up a Comparable Worth Task Force (CWTF) in June 1983 to make authoritative recommendations regarding pay equity. Deliberately intended to distance the 'neutral' and 'legitimate' state from the advocacy-oriented Office of Women and Work, the newly appointed task force was a 'blue ribbon' committee of 11 people, including private and public sector executives, state Women's Commission members, elected representatives and labour unionists. It was dominated by its chair, a former automobile company executive and business activist. Several of the corporate representatives managed large numbers of workers in predominantly female jobs, yet civil service unions were purposely excluded on the grounds that they had a direct interest in the outcome of discussions.[5] Overall, the labour and feminist representation was weak.

The CWTF issued its findings, recommendations and supporting documentation in June 1985 (Michigan CWTF, 1985). A weak and contradictory document, the report acknowledged that the state civil service was characterized by gender-based wage disparities that ought to be reduced but advocated affirmative action for eliminating women's low pay. The task force distanced itself from the concept of comparable worth, and reiterated the validity of pay setting based on the market and budgetary constraints. While not endorsing a pay-for-points policy, the report did concede that pay should take into account the value of work, as determined by gender-neutral job evaluation.

The report instructed the Department of Civil Service to establish a less gender-biased job evaluation system. It endorsed non-discriminatory job evaluation for all civil service classes based upon factors of skill, effort and responsibility; and recommended that within four years the civil service reduce the 11 gender-segregated service groups that formed the basis for job evaluation under the Michigan Benchmark Evaluation System (MBES) to five non-gender dominated groups.

The report suggested, in no particular order of priority, that collective bargaining, prevailing labour market comparisons and coordinated pay setting should all remain important and legitimate determinants of pay, but recommended special pay adjustments for female-dominated classes, defined as those which were 70 per cent or more female. It recommended that the State Employer[6] develop a salary line composed of the average wages of all classes. The female-dominated classes below the average line should receive special adjustments consisting of a substantial percentage of the gap between their current wage and base line. Making pay adjustments across 11 gender-segregated service groups in advance of job re-evaluation was clearly problematic, as there was no sound basis for constructing a cross-group pay-for-points line.

Several of the policy recommendations clearly limited the positive consequences for women in predominantly female job classifications in the state. First, the CWTF accepted gendered market wages as appropriate in setting pay, and stated that budgetary constraints might be a reason not to adjust the pay of female-dominated classes quickly or fully. Second, the report recommended the use of a pay line comprised of male and female classes and based upon a tainted, outdated job classification system against which to measure the pay in predominantly female jobs. The CWTF's definition of predominantly female jobs as those that were at least 70 per cent female precluded some predominantly female jobs from receiving adjustments. It made clear that longer-term job re-evaluation and reclassification need not dictate further wage adjustments. The task force recommended multiple rather than single job evaluation, a recommendation many feminists saw as a defeat.

## IMPLEMENTING REFORM IN MICHIGAN

Between 1985 and 1986 management came to the bargaining table prepared to grant special pay equity increases as recommended by the CWTF. The United Auto Workers' (UAW) lawsuit (the continuation of the original Karon Black complaint) created additional pressure for negotiated increases. The Department of Civil Service, working with the Office of State Employer, improvised a pay line and estimated the average gender-based wage gap at $0.80 per hour. This figure evolved into a target for labour negotiators. By 1987 the largest unions, the UAW, the American Federation of State, County, and Municipal Employees (AFSCME) and the Service Employees International Union (SEIU) had negotiated adjustments of about $0.40 per hour. In 1987 the state refused to award the remaining identified discrepancy, and the civil service unions began to deploy new strategies. Between 1987 and 1989 unions targeted occupations perceived as historically underpaid whether or not they were 70 per cent female. In addition the UAW, as it awaited the outcome of a broader reclassification exercise, negotiated an additional $2 million pay equity fund for one-off lump sum wage awards, to distribute according to internally agreed priorities.

In the reclassification exercise, the Equitable Classification Plan (ECP) developed and implemented by the state of Michigan between 1986 and 1996, the process was separated from the issue of pay awards. This meant that reclassification was more insulated from broader economic pressures here than in other states. The Department of Civil Service was sensitive to issues of gender bias as it constructed factors and factor weights inhouse, breaking with its own past practices and the practices of leading job evaluation consultancies like Hay Associates.

However, the ECP divided workers into groups and employed group-specific evaluation. These groups were constituted not on the basis of occupational classifications, which tended to be gender-segregated, but on the basis of education and supervisory responsibility. Group one, the largest, comprised 38,000 workers without university degrees and in non-supervisory positions. Non-supervisory business and administrative, human services, scientific and engineering and professional occupations normally requiring a bachelor's (university) degree comprised group two. Supervisors comprised group three.

The state decided to use ten weighted factors (without sub-factors) for groups one and two: knowledge and skill, judgement, responsibility for financial and material resources, responsibility for the well-being of others, responsibility for information, responsibility for communications and public relations, physical effort, mental and visual effort, work environment and work hazards. In general, these tended to make visible the skills, responsibilities and demands traditionally associated with women's jobs which are minimized in other job evaluation systems. However, the maintenance of separate groups for evaluation meant that it was impossible to compare women's jobs with those of their hierarchical superiors, and the job groupings imported formal education and hierarchical position into the evaluation as 'hidden factors'.

As the new ECP for the first large group of employees reached completion in 1990 the civil service unions, primarily the UAW, used the result to re-estimate the differential between pay in female-dominated occupations and average wages. In addition they continued to pressure the state to target the remaining $0.40 of the previously measured disparity. However the Office of State Employer, now appointed by conservative Republican

Governor John Engler, refused to use unbiased job classification to evaluate wages and denied there had ever been a commitment to close the earlier identified disparity completely. The reclassification never provided a basis for pay adjustments, and the state is not legally required to use it as such. While the Michigan Civil Service declined to use the ECP to adjust pay or even to assess whether pay practices remained discriminatory, our regression analysis shows that there continues to be a significant negative correlation between female composition of job class and pay (Figart and Kahn, 1997). Thus, although Michigan spent between $19 and $25 million on pay equity wage adjustments between 1985 and 1990, the effect of adjustments on the female/male wage ratio was minimal, maintaining the ratio just above the national average for state civil servants and the US workforce as a whole. By 1991 even general wage increases had become problematic, and layoffs of state workers had accelerated, reducing pay equity's importance to unions and their members.

## CONCLUSIONS: LESSONS FROM MICHIGAN'S STATE GOVERNMENT REFORM

Others who have studied and written about state reform in the United States have demonstrated that many apparently technical issues – the construction of job evaluation systems, the definition of predominantly female jobs, the construction of a pay line for wage adjustments and the extent of actual wage reforms after disparities have been identified – are actually political, decisively shaping outcomes for women workers (Sorensen, 1994; Steinberg, 1990; 1991; 1992; Acker, 1989). The Michigan case illustrates less the problem of the gender-biased construction of job evaluation systems than the problem of translating the findings of comparable worth studies into actual pay increases for women workers. While feminist arguments about job evaluation have by now entered standard best personnel practice, actual wage gains for state employees have become more problematic in the current political and economic climate.

However, the long-running reform in the State of Michigan and the lack of significant wage reform in any US state in the 1990s also suggest that meaningful pay equity reform is unlikely to continue in state government as long as state government is seen as harbouring overpaid workers who drain resources from the private sector. These difficulties, however, create an opportunity for pay equity advocates to rethink their strategies. State workers have always comprised a small percentage of the total workforce in the state, and have traditionally had relatively secure and well-paid jobs.

It is now clear that to be successful and to reach the lowest paid working women, pay equity strategies need to become more informal and decentralized and extend beyond the state sector. This depends on invoking powerful social arguments rather than relying on simply technical and economistic ones.

There has always been a steady, only partly documented, stream of attempts to pursue pay equity on a smaller scale outside the larger state jurisdictions in the United States: in cities and towns, hospitals, schools, county social service departments, universities, newspaper offices and manufacturing plants. There have also been less aggregated reforms that fall short of whole workforce re-evaluation and efforts to recognize the value of predominantly female jobs which have not been identified as 'pay equity' campaigns. Unions, including Michigan's state employee unions, have negotiated flat rate increases for the lowest paid workers, often disproportionately in traditionally female jobs, since across-the-board percentage wage increases accentuate the gap between low and highly paid workers. These small-scale efforts are critical in addressing the undervaluation of women's work.[7] Pay equity needs to enter the everyday bargaining agenda of unions in all workplaces, and it may be most effective if it does so in a more limited and less technically complex manner.

The argument for diffusion of pay equity outward and downward presupposes, however, an organizational infrastructure outside the public sector that can help carry such efforts forward. One of the reasons pay equity reform became focused in the US public sector was that women were more highly unionized there. There is a well-developed discussion in North America about how to organize feminized service sector jobs, particularly in view of the growing fragmentation, flexibilization, and polarization of the labour market (Cobble, 1994; Fudge, 1993), and labour organizers have begun to put low-paid women and minorities at the centre of their efforts. Because pay equity brings women's concerns into unions (Blum, 1991; Fudge and McDermott, 1991) its broad approach should become a part of these organizing strategies.

Occupationally based national networks supportive of local initiatives might also carry pay equity forward. Childcare workers in the US often work for small employers outside the public sector, and their labour has historically been devalued. While seldom unionized, they have a strong occupational identity and are involved in local and national campaigns to improve their pay. Because equitable pay would improve the quality of staff and thus increase children's welfare, such workers could join forces with childcare advocates to argue for pay equity on social welfare grounds. In addition, the pay equity movement needs to be linked to anti-poverty and welfare rights struggles. Recent welfare policy changes in the US are based on the spurious assumption that a movement from welfare to the labour market will move women and children out of poverty. Yet women in female-dominated occupations find it difficult to support families. The percentage earning less than the official poverty level for a family of three ranges from 15 per cent in administrative support to 54 per cent in the category of 'other services' (Lapidus and Figart, 1994). Case studies in the United States and United Kingdom suggest that pay equity reforms, especially those targeted to the lowest paid or most undervalued grades, contribute to the alleviation of household poverty (Kahn and Meehan, 1992; Acker, 1989). In addition, because it targets low-waged workers, many of whom work in female-dominated jobs, raising the minimum wage on a regular basis would go a long way towards improving the economic status of working women and reducing the gender-based pay differential (Figart and Lapidus, 1995).

Efforts to create a fair and living wage for workers in predominantly female jobs and occupations remain critical in the 1990s and beyond. The positive potential for the pay equity movement lies in broadening the approach, in terms of both location and strategic content. New, decentralized, more creative approaches in a broadbased pay equity movement can further women's efforts to contest the gendered labour markets central to economic restructuring.

NOTES

1.    We use the term 'pay equity' here to refer to rectification of the relatively
      low wages paid for predominantly female jobs. Pay equity reform has tradi-
      tionally used the technique of 'comparable worth' (equivalent to 'equal
      value' in Britain), using job evaluation to assign points to predominantly
      male and predominantly female jobs. Pay is equalized for similar point
      totals in male and female jobs within organizations.
2.    A recall procedure enables voters to remove an elected official from office
      before his or her term has expired. The required number of valid signatures
      (usually 25 per cent of those voting at the previous election) triggers a new
      election.
3.    In the US public sector comparable worth initiatives have tended to be sys-
      temic, looking at the whole workforce rather than focusing on a few female
      job classes and their comparators. The Arthur Young study was a whole
      workforce study which used two different job evaluation plans to evaluate
      209 job classes. It showed that the existing job evaluation and pay systems

were discriminatory. Pay rates for male-dominated classes were higher than would be predicted from job evaluation and lower than predicted for female-dominated job classes.

4.  This was a class action suit. After the United Auto Workers (UAW) won the right to represent state workers, it continued the claim as a major federal court case. In 1985 individually named plaintiffs and the union alleged that the results of the comparable worth study conducted by Arthur Young were evidence that the state had violated Title VII of the 1964 Civil Rights Act by paying employees in predominantly female jobs less than similarly valued employees in predominantly male jobs. The case was dismissed on the grounds that there was insufficient evidence of intentional discrimination. This decision was upheld by a US Court of Appeals in 1989. In the 1980s it became increasingly difficult to prevail on the basis of arguments about disparate impact rather than intentional disparate treatment (Gregory, 1992; McCann, 1994).

5.  Business in the state actively opposed pay equity even within state government. When in 1988 a group of feminist unionists and others tried unsuccessfully to amend the state's civil rights statute to include the requirement that work of equal value be equally paid in the private and public sectors, business again mobilized to defeat the amendments.

6.  An office attached to the Governor's office with responsibility for collective bargaining as approved by the Commission.

7.  For example, a contract between one branch of the UAW, Local 2110, representing clerical workers and Columbia University corrected internal inequities between clerical workers and maintenance and security guards based on job comparisons (National Committee on Pay Equity, *Newsnotes*, Fall 1995). This is more a tactical suggestion than a principled argument that large-scale pay equity objectives should be abandoned. However, smaller-scale pay equity projects may mobilize women workers more effectively than large state government reform projects, which tend to be controlled by state managers. The idea of exploring smallscale, class-to-class pay equity does strike a slightly different note from British critics of existing equal value law, who wish to collectivize and extend the very individualized procedures of the Equal Value Regulations (see for examples Jarman (1994), Gregory (1992)). On a job re-evaluation campaign not explicitly identified as pay equity, see Sacks (1988). She describes how data terminal operators at Duke University Medical Center, mostly African-American women, succeeded in getting their work re-evaluated without job evaluation technology. Flat-rate wage increase strategies resemble British and Irish 'low pay campaigns', though in the US they are less driven by ideas of equality and solidarity.

## REFERENCES

Acker, J., *Doing Comparable Worth: Gender, Class and Pay Equity*. Philadelphia: Temple University Press, 1989.

Blank, R.M., 'Are part-time jobs bad jobs?', in G. Burtless (ed.), *A Future of Lousy Jobs? The Changing Structure of US Wages*. Washington, DC: The Brookings Institution, 1990.

Blum, L., *Between Feminism and Labour: the Significance of the Comparable Worth Movement*. Berkeley: University of California Press, 1991.

Callaghan, P. and Hartmann, H., *Contingent Work: a Chart Book on Part-time and Temporary Employment*. Washington, DC: Economic Policy Institute, 1991.

Cobble, D.S., 'Postindustrial unionism possible', in S. Friedman, R.W. Hurd, R.O. Oswald and R.L. Seeber (eds), *Restoring the Promise of American Labor Law*. Ithaca, New York: ILR Press, 1994.

Evans, S. and Nelson, B., *Wage Justice: Comparable Worth and the Paradox of Technocratic Reform*. Chicago: University of Chicago Press, 1989.

Figart, D.M. and Kahn, P., *Contesting the Market: Pay Equity and the Politics of Economic Restructuring*. Detroit: Wayne State University Press, 1997.

Figart, D.M. and Lapidus, J., 'A gender analysis of labour market policies for the working poor in the US', *Feminist Economics* 1(3) (Fall 1995).

Fudge, J., 'The gendered dimension of labour law: why women need inclusive unionism and broader-based bargaining', in P. McDermott and L. Bresleen (eds), *Women Challenging Unions*. Toronto: University of Toronto Press, 1993.

Fudge, J. and McDermott, P. (eds), *Just Wages: a Feminist Assessment of Pay Equity*. Toronto: University of Toronto Press, 1991.

Gregory, J., 'Equal value/comparable worth: national statute and case law in Britain and the USA', in P. Kahn and E. Meehan (eds), *Equal Value/Comparable Worth in the UK and USA*. London: Macmillan; and New York: St. Martin's Press, 1992.

Hartmann, H, and Aaronson S., 'Pay equity and women's wage increases: success in the States, a model for the nation', *Duke Journal of Gender Law and Policy* (1) 69–87 (1994).

Institute for Women's Policy Research (IWPR), *The Status of Women in the State of Michigan*. Washington, DC: IWPR, 1996.

Jarman, J., 'Which way forward? assessing the current proposals to amend the British Equal Pay Act', *Work, Employment, and Society* vol. 8, no. 2 (1994) 243–54.

Johnston, P., *Success While Others Fail: Social Movement Unionism and the Public Workplace*. Ithaca, NY: ILR Press, 1994.

Kahn, P. and Meehan, E. (eds), *Equal Value/Comparable Worth in the UK and USA*. London: Macmillan, 1992.

Lapidus, J. and Figart, D.M., 'Comparable worth as an anti-poverty strategy: evidence from the March 1992 CPS', *Review of Radical Political Economics* 26 (3 September 1994) 1–10.

McCann, M., *Rights at Work: Pay Equity Reform and the Politics of Legal Mobilization*. Chicago: University of Chicago Press, 1994.

Michigan Comparable Worth Task Force (CWTF), *The Report of the Comparable Worth Task Force to the Michigan Civil Service Commission*. Lansing, June 1985.

Michigan Department of Commerce, *The Michigan Economy, 1979–1990*. Lansing, 1991.

National Committee on Pay Equity (NCPE), *Pay Equity Activity in the Public Sector, 1979–1989*. Washington, DC: NCPE, 1989.

National Committee on Pay Equity (NCPE), *Newsnotes*. Various dates.

Remick, H., 'The case of comparable in Washington State', *Policy Studies Review* 5 (1986) 838–48.

Sacks, K.B., *Caring by the Hour: Women, Work and Organizing at Duke Medical Center.* Urbana and Chicago: University of Illinois Press, 1988.

Sarri, R., Butts, J., Morrow, P., Russell, C. and Zinn, D., *Women in Michigan: a Statistical Portrait.* Lansing and Ann Arbor: Michigan Women's Commission, Michigan Equal Employment Opportunity Council, and University of Michigan Institute for Social Research, September 1987.

Sorensen, E., *Comparable Worth: Is it a Worthy Policy?* Princeton: Princeton University Press, 1994.

Steinberg, R., *Mainstreaming Comparable Worth: Reforming Wage Discrimination to Palatable Pay Equity.* Unpublished manuscript, 1989.

Steinberg, R., 'Social construction of skill: gender, power and comparable worth', *Work and Occupations* (17) (1990) 449–82.

Steinberg, R., 'Job evaluation and managerial control: the politics of technique and the techniques of politics', in J. Fudge and P. McDermott (eds), *Just Wages: a Feminist Assessment of Pay Equity.* Toronto: University of Toronto Press, 1991.

Steinberg, R., 'Gendered instructions: cultural lag and gender bias in the Hay system of job evaluation', *Work and Occupations* (19) (1992) 387–432.

Young, A., *A Comparable Worth Study of the State of Michigan Job Classifications.* Detroit: Arthur Young and Company, 1981.

# 13 Strategic Litigation in Pursuit of Pay Equality

Robin Allen, QC and Gay Moon

This chapter focuses on the case of *Regina* v *Secretary of State for Employment, ex parte Seymour-Smith.*[1] This case concerns the period of employment needed to qualify for protection from unfair dismissal, which was increased from one year to two by a Variation Order in 1985.[2] Two women who were affected by the increase in this period have brought a case arguing that proportionately more women than men were affected, that women are more likely than men to have interrupted careers due to family responsibilities, and that therefore the Order is indirectly discriminatory and contrary to European law.

The case has taken a very long time. It began in 1991, was heard in a Divisional Court in 1994 and the Court of Appeal in 1995. The following year it was heard in the House of Lords which made an Order on 13 March 1997 referring the case to the European Court of Justice (ECJ). At the time of writing [October 1998] the ECJ have not given judgment. When they do, the case will have to be referred back to the House of Lords and perhaps then to lower courts.

The authors act for the two women applicants, Gay Moon as solicitor and Robin Allen, QC as leading counsel. In this chapter we describe the experience of initiating the case and the conduct of the litigation, examining the difficulties encountered and the gains which have been made. A large campaign has been built around the case. Although the case has not yet been determined it very much looks as though the campaign to repeal the two year rule has been successful. Accordingly we believe that there is much to be learned from this case about the strategic use of litigation in pursuit of pay equality.

The case has broken new ground in a number of ways. It relied on detailed national statistical evidence to demonstrate the difference between men and women's career patterns and the unequal treatment of women and men by the Variation Order. There were no precedents for this kind of case and therefore both the legal and forensic approach had to be developed from scratch. Cooperation between the legal team and academics was crucial to the gathering and presenting of the evidence.

The original nature of the legal argument meant that the Legal Aid Board was at first unwilling to recognize that there was a valid case. Indeed, the initial application to the High Court for leave to challenge the order was made without legal aid which was obtained only on the third attempt, following an application for judicial review of earlier refusals.[3]

## HOW THE CASE STARTED

The case arose out of Gay Moon's work at Camden Law Centre in London where she advised women on employment issues. One of the most frequent questions raised by clients of the Law Centre in 1991 and even now is: '*Can my employer change the terms and conditions of my work?*' In advising such employees the crucial question is: '*How long have you been in employment?*' The answer to that question determines the nature of the advice that is given.

Although as a matter of contract law the employer cannot change terms and conditions without the employee's consent, the employee has been in a very weak position if s/he has worked for under two years. Since 1985 if such consent is withheld, the employee will not be able to present a complaint to an Industrial Tribunal of unfair dismissal should the employer dismiss the employee. On the other hand, if the employee has over two years employment, s/he may refuse any unreasonable changes to his/her contract. If the employer tries to force the changes on the employee s/he may well be able to present a complaint of unfair dismissal.

Thus in the late 1980s and early 1990s we came to see this issue of the two-year qualifying period as a barrier of fundamental importance for women. We felt that it was probable that more women than men were adversely affected by this provision as we believed that because of family responsibilities women were likely to have shorter average periods of continuous employment.[4] This seemed to reflect the experience of work in the law centre. However we did not have any evidence and without any evidence we could do little.

The Department of Employment[5] were contacted for advice as to where statistics in relation to the national picture might be found. They referred to information published from time to time in the *Employment Gazette*, which analysed length of employment by sex. This went some way towards confirming our impression, but the figures were not sufficiently defined to found a case.

A labour market statistician, Professor Peter Elias of Warwick University, was approached with more refined questions in order to reduce any distortions. He produced statistics from the *Labour Force Survey* which showed the differential as expected. Women *were* affected more than men by this two-year rule. Armed with that knowledge we had the basic evidence needed for a case.

Several women were identified as adversely affected by the Order, but not all wished to take up litigation over their dismissals and in one case an employer settled after the case had begun. Two women are continuing to pursue their challenge and remain determined in spite of the considerable strain imposed by the protracted nature of the case.

## THE TEST FOR INDIRECT DISCRIMINATION

The next question was how to apply the law to the evidence. Indirect discrimination, although well recognized, is not precisely defined in European law.[6] However section 1 of the UK Sex Discrimination Act 1975 does provide a precise definition:

> A person discriminates against a woman ... if ... he applies to her a requirement or condition which he applies or would apply equally to a man but
>
> i) which is such that the proportion of women who *can comply* with it is considerably smaller than the proportion of men who *can comply* with it, and
> ii) which he cannot show to be justifiable irrespective of the sex of the person to whom it is applied, and
> iii) which is to her detriment because she *cannot comply* with it.

One of the major problems was how the impact of the Variation Order on men and women should be compared. The test for adverse impact in the Sex Discrimination Act compares only those who 'can comply', thus it compares the effect of the impugned requirement or condition on the *advantaged* group: see i. Intuitively this seemed wrong; after all it was the disadvantaged women who needed a remedy: see iii. However, under European law, we felt that this should not be a problem because the Equal Treatment Directive EC/207/76 (ETD) provides in Article 2(1) that *there shall be no discrimination whatsoever*. This statement reflects the general principle of equal treatment under European law. As an approach it directs consideration to a comparison of the *disadvantage* suffered by men and women.

Comparing the proportions of women and men who 'can comply' can suggest a very different conclusion from a comparison between the proportions of women and men who 'cannot comply'. The importance of this point can be demonstrated by considering a hypothetical example. Take a requirement that is easy to comply with: say a requirement for a job to have a particular skill, which 98 per cent of men and 96 per cent of women could comply with. Comparing the proportion of 'can comply's' the statistics do not look widely significant; however, if you look at the 'cannot comply's' there are 2 per cent of men who cannot comply and 4 per cent of women who cannot comply. One figure is double the other. From the point of view of the disadvantaged group the requirement hits the female group twice as hard as the male group.

Moreover, the question of the right legal approach had a particular significance for this case because we found that the disparity between the percentage of women and men who could comply with the two-year rule was much more obvious when we looked at the differences between the proportion of disadvantaged women and disadvantaged men (see Table 13.1), although a clearer difference is shown in Table 13.2 which includes figures for all employees, including those working less than 16 hours per week.[7]

It seemed to us that we needed a test that did not give a different result according to whether the advantaged or disadvantaged groups were considered but that simply tested for uneven impact or the extent of the deviation from the principle of equal treatment. We asked the advice of statisticians and they advised us to compare the actual figures with what might be predicted on the basis of no discriminatory effect.

So first we considered how many men and women (allowing for the different numbers of men and women in the workforce) would be expected to be in the advantaged and disadvantaged groups if the two-year rule did

*Table 13.1*     Percentages of workforce working 16 or more hours per week qualified for protection from unfair dismissal

| Year | Unqualified % Males with less than 2 years | Unqualified % Females with less than 2 years | Qualified % Males with 2 years or more | Qualified % Females with 2 years or more |
|------|------|------|------|------|
| 1985 | 22.6 | 31.0 | 77.4 | 68.9 |
| 1986 | 22.9 | 31.6 | 77.2 | 68.4 |
| 1987 | 24.7 | 32.9 | 75.3 | 67.1 |
| 1988 | 26.6 | 34.5 | 73.4 | 65.6 |
| 1989 | 28.0 | 36.2 | 72.0 | 63.8 |
| 1990 | 27.6 | 35.8 | 72.5 | 64.1 |
| 1991 | 25.5 | 32.6 | 74.5 | 67.4 |

*Source*: Labour Force Survey.

*Table 13.2*   Percentages of workforce working 8 or more hours per week
qualified for protection from unfair dismissal

| Year | Unqualified % Males with less than 2 years | Unqualified % Females with less than 2 years | Qualified % Males with less than 2 years | Qualified % Females with less than 2 years |
|---|---|---|---|---|
| 1985 | 22.7 | 32.5 | 77.3 | 67.5 |
| 1986 | 23.1 | 33.7 | 76.9 | 66.3 |
| 1987 | 25.2 | 35.2 | 74.8 | 64.8 |
| 1988 | 27.3 | 36.6 | 72.6 | 63.4 |
| 1989 | 28.8 | 38.4 | 71.2 | 61.7 |
| 1990 | 28.3 | 38.0 | 71.7 | 62.0 |
| 1991 | 26.4 | 35.1 | 73.7 | 65.0 |
| 1992 | 22.9 | 30.2 | 77.1 | 69.9 |
| 1993 | 22.4 | 28.3 | 77.6 | 71.7 |
| 1994 | 24.2 | 28.9 | 75.8 | 71.1 |
| 1995 | 26.7 | 30.8 | 73.3 | 69.2 |
| 1996 | 28.7 | 31.8 | 71.3 | 68.2 |
| Average 1985 to 1996 | 25.56 | 33.29 | 74.44 | 66.73 |
| Average over last 5 years | 24.98 | 30 | 75.02 | 70.02 |

*Source*: Labour Force Survey.

not have a different impact on men and women. We then compared what this hypothesis of nil effect predicted with the actual figures of who could comply and who could not comply. This showed the difference between the expected result, if there were no discrimination, and the actual result. Using this method of analysing the statistics we showed that there was a pattern of discrimination against women which was consistent over time.

In 1985 when the order was introduced, there were 370,000 fewer women in the 'can comply' category than would be expected if the rule had an equal impact on men and women. This figure amounted to 5 per cent of the total female working population at the time.[8] Additionally, we relied on academic studies which have shown that the average job tenure of women is shorter than that of men (Elias and White, 1991).

However proving adverse impact in this way was not enough by itself because the government argued that it was legally justified in imposing the qualifying period, claiming that keeping employees unprotected from unfair dismissal for two years helped to create jobs. At the time the accepted legal test for justification, following the *Rinner-Kühn* judgment, was that the requirements are 'appropriate, suitable, and requisite' for a particular policy.[9] We agreed that job creation is an appropriate aim of social policy, but did not accept that the two-year time limit is 'suitable' or 'requisite' for achieving that aim.

The government relied on a number of papers from the Department of Employment to justify its position, including a research paper by the Director of the Policy Studies Institute, Bill Daniel, investigating employers' motives for creating new jobs (Daniel and Stilgoe, 1978). Written before the two-year rule was introduced it certainly did not establish that this was a priority for employers who were found to be much more concerned about tax levels and national insurance and health and safety regulations. Other research papers showed that employment protection law was a long way down any list of concerns and indeed few employers even knew what was the correct qualifying period. Later the government produced a further tranche of papers but these mainly concerned the national position in an international perspective, including Organization for Economic Cooperation and Development reports, and none directly addressed the qualifying period. Although the government attempted to use Bill Daniel's paper to build its case, he, together with Peter Elias and Professor Linda Dickens of Warwick University, assisted us in preparing our evidence, reviewing the material produced by the Treasury Solicitor and refuting the assertions made to back up the government's claimed justification.

## THE COURT HEARINGS

The case went first to the Divisional Court in 1994. It rejected some of the arguments advanced by the government and accepted others advanced by the women, and held that the two-year qualifying period was not objectively justified. The Court did not, however, find for the two women because, although it accepted that over a long period there had been a disparity in the extent to which men and women were protected from unfair dismissal, it was not persuaded that the difference in its impact on men and women was sufficient to amount to discrimination under European law. It did not accept our approach to the statistics.

Because the women lost at that stage, the political significance of the fact that the Divisional Court condemned the policy after looking at it at such length went largely unnoticed at the time.

The applicants and the Secretary of State both appealed, and a year later the Court of Appeal reversed the judgment of the Divisional Court.

The Court held that it was not bound by the Sex Discrimination Act definition of indirect discrimination. It concluded that under European Law it could and should look at both the advantaged and disadvantaged groups both as proportions and as numbers. It held that the differential impact of the 1985 Order was significant, stating that it was impressed by the 'persistency and consistency' of the figures[10] from 1986 to 1991 (see Table 13.1). The Court avoided saying anything about the figures after 1991 when the gap had narrowed although a significant gap remained. It also agreed with the Divisional Court in rejecting the government's justification, making a very strong finding:

> We have found nothing in the evidence either factual or opinion which obliges or enables us to infer that the increase in the qualification period has led to an increase in employment opportunities.[11]

However, while the Court of Appeal was clear that the two women had suffered unlawful discrimination contrary to EC law, it merely declared that our clients had been deprived of their rights under the ETD. This declaration did not take them very far, since it did not mean that an industrial tribunal had to hear their case: it merely provided one of the necessary conditions for an action to claim damages against the state.[12]

We had also relied on Article 119 of the EC Treaty of Rome which guarantees equal pay for equal work, as well as the ETD which is concerned with working conditions, to claim that this was an issue of pay inequality. The nub of our argument is that Article 119 applies to protection from unfair dismissal because the remedies for such an unfair dismissal are by way of compensation based on lost wages. However we failed at that stage to persuade the Court that Article 119[13] applied to protection from unfair dismissal.

In 1996 the women took the case to the House of Lords, seeking the right to take their claim to an industrial tribunal although they had worked for less than two years. However, they faced a renewed challenge in the House of Lords in relation to the justification argument. Although the government had been unable to produce evidence to support its argument in the Divisional Court and the Court of Appeal, there were by now some signs of a backlash from member states faced with difficulties in establishing justification in indirect discrimination cases. This was beginning to be reflected in European law. The decisions of the ECJ in *Nolte* v. *Landesversicherungsanstalt Hannover* and *Megner and Scheffel* v. *Innungskrankenkasse Vorderpfalz*[14] appear to suggest that the state can justify indirectly discriminatory legislative proposals merely by claiming a belief that a policy will achieve a social purpose. These cases suggest that the courts need not require evidence of actual effect and that governments have a wide margin of discretion in relation to justification of discriminatory legislation.

One of our main tasks in the House of Lords was, therefore, to try to differentiate our case from *Nolte* and *Megner*, which are concerned with social security issues. The main thrust of our submissions to the House of Lords and the ECJ is that protection at work, unlike social security benefits, is not concerned with the fiscal regime. The latter arguably has a particular complexity over and above the difficulties attached to the labour market.[15]

The House of Lords has denied the two women a right to rely on the ETD to seek a remedy against their employers,[16] but so far has not said that they cannot rely on Article 119. It determined that this point should be referred to the European Court of Justice. The complete set of questions referred to the ECJ are:

1. Does an award of compensation for the breach of the right not to be unfairly dismissed under national legislation such as the Employment Protection (Consolidation) Act 1978 constitute 'pay' within the meaning of Article 119 of the Treaty of Rome?

2. If the answer to question 1 is 'yes' do the conditions determining whether a worker has the right not to be unfairly dismissed fall within the scope of Article 119 or of the ETD?

3. What is the legal test for establishing whether a measure adopted by a member state has such a degree of disparate effect as between men and women as to amount to indirect discrimination for the purposes of Article 119 unless shown to be based upon objectively justified factors other than sex?

4. When must this test be applied to a measure adopted by a member state? In particular at which of the following points in time, or at what other point in time, must it be applied to the measure: when (a) the measure is adopted; (b) the measure is brought into force; (c) the employee is dismissed?

5. What are the legal conditions for establishing the objective justification, for the purposes of indirect discrimination under Article 119, of a measure adopted by a member state in pursuance of its social policy? In particular what material need the member state adduce in support of its grounds for justification?

These questions raise some of the most basic issues in indirect sex discrimination. Since the case started, the idea of 'mainstreaming' women's issues has become a central tenet of EU and member state policy-making.[17] First introduced at the United Nations World Conference on Women in Beijing in 1995, 'mainstreaming' in the EU means incorporating the dimension of equal opportunities for men and women during the elaboration, application and monitoring of all the policy measures of the EU and its member states. These questions provide the ECJ with an opportunity to underline the importance of mainstreaming by making consideration of gender impact a necessary stage in the development of governmental policy.

## THE IMPACT OF THE CASE

Although the case has not yet been resolved, it has already had a major impact. The press response to the victory in the Appeal Court was sensational. It was front page news in *The Times* and innumerable articles were written about it. In spite of the weight of evidence produced to demonstrate the contrary, many newspapers suggested that the judgment would have a devastating effect on job creation.[18] The blanket coverage after the Appeal Court hearing was in marked contrast to the lack of interest shown by the press in the judgment of the Divisional Court the previous year, when the judgment had been not dissimilar.

The case also represented a major shift in the role of the courts. The UK, unlike many European states, has no constitutional court to review the wider legitimacy of legislation, a situation which has been frequently commented upon by the courts. With Parliament dominated by men, laws have been enacted from a predominantly male perspective, reflecting an agenda set and debated by men. Many laws have therefore seemed unreasonable to women, but they have had no recourse to the law on the grounds of 'unreasonableness'. In a recent case[19] the House of Lords said that in the absence of some exceptional circumstance, such as bad faith or improper motive on the part of the Secretary of State, it was inappropriate for the courts to intervene on the ground of 'unreasonableness' in a decision in respect of public administration which had been a matter for the political judgment of the Secretary of State and the House of Commons.

It was, therefore, all the more significant that in 1994 the Divisional Court[20] spent several days during our case considering the legality of a specific government policy in the context of European law since the challenge was not about bad faith or improper motive. The review under the *Rinner-Kühn* test in European law was on the question of whether the policy was justified on broader grounds. This required the Court to look at detailed evidence from labour market economists, sociologists and civil servants and to assess their expert opinions. Judges are not social policy-makers by training, and this was therefore novel territory for them.

No court has yet definitively stated quite how to approach the statistical evidence in this area. In the light of both the tradition of English law and the subsequent press criticism, it is remarkable that the courts were prepared to carry out such a review of the justification of a government policy.

The reference has already had an effect on the way that employers treat their workforce. It is now widely accepted that, pending the outcome of the litigation, employers must take care to ensure procedural and substantive fairness if they dismiss employees with less than two years' service.[21] Even more importantly the new Labour government has now[22] given a firm commitment to repeal the two-year rule and replace it with a one-year rule, arguing that with a reduced period employees would be less inhibited about changing jobs and thereby losing their protection, which should help to promote a more flexible labour market; and more employers would see the case for introducing good employment practices, which should encourage a more committed and productive workforce. So many women and men already have reason to be grateful to these two women for sticking with this case over so many years. If the European Court of Justice back our approach to the test for indirect discrimination, this case will become the essential legal point of reference.

The case has been based on a partnership between women determined to fight for their rights, lawyers and academics. We are grateful to the academics who gave their time to help us build the argument as this would have been impossible without their input. Our experience has shown that strategic litigation faces enormous obstacles but that the solidarity of such a partnership greatly increases the prospects of success.

## NOTES

1. The judgment of the Court of Appeal is reported in [1995] Industrial Court Reports (ICR) 1989 and that of the House of Lords in [1997] ICR 371.
2. The general right of an employee not be unfairly dismissed, conferred by section 54(1) of the Employment Protection (Consolidation) Act 1978, does not apply to a dismissal where the employee has not been continuously employed for the minimum period specified in section 64(1)(a) of the Act. The government order increasing the qualifying period of employment from one to two years was the Unfair Dismissal (Variation of Qualifying Period) Order 1985. These provisions have now been re-enacted in sections 94 and 108(1) of the Employment Rights Act 1996 respectively.
3. The Equal Opportunities Commission was already involved in expensive litigation in a related case concerning the exclusion of part-time workers

from protection under the Employment Protection Act (*R* v *Secretary of State ex parte The Equal Opportunities Commission* [1995] 1 Appeal Court (AC) 1) (see Introduction, p. 8). It was, therefore, unable to assist with this case.

4. The European Court of Justice have recently considered the effect of stereotypical assumptions that a woman will want to have more career breaks than a man: see *Marschall* v. *Nordrhein-Westfalen* [1997] All ER (EC) 865 at p. 884 e–f para. 29.

5. Even though they were to become the Respondent Department to the litigation they seemed the obvious place to start in seeking information on any statistical differences in the labour market as between the two genders.

6. The most general statement of the principle of non-discrimination in EC law is that 'comparable situations are not to be treated differently and that different situations are not to be treated alike unless such treatment is objectively justified' (*Kingdom of Spain* v *Council of the European Communities* (case 203/86 [1988] European Court Reports (ECR) 4563 para. 25).

7. The *Labour Force Survey* does not give good statistics for those who work less than eight hours per week since such employment is regarded as marginal.

8. The figure approximates to the total female working population of Ireland, and is more than the population of Luxembourg.

9. *Rinner-Kühn* v *FWW Spezial-Gebaeudereinigung GmbH & Co KG* case 171/88 [1989] ECR 2743.

10. The figures the Court referred to excluded those employees who worked for less than 16 hours per week. Since this case started the House of Lords has outlawed discrimination against such part-timers in *R* v *Secretary of State ex parte The Equal Opportunities Commission* [1995] 1 AC 1 (see note 3).

11. See [1995] ICR 889 at p. 955.

12. The condition is necessary but not sufficient (joined cases C 46 and 48/93 *Brasserie du Pecheur SA* v *Germany* and *R* v *Secretary of State for Transport ex parte Factortame Ltd* [1996] 1 Common Market Law Reports (CMLR 889).

13. The original application relied solely on the ETD but following the decision of the House of Lords in *R* v *Secretary of State ex parte The Equal Opportunities Commission* [1995] 1 AC 1, the Court of Appeal allowed an amendment to rely upon Article 119.

14. [1996] IRLR 225 and 236.

15. It has subsequently come to light that the provisions in question in *Nolte* and *Megner* had already been approved in the German constitutional court. This is not apparent from the official reports but may be discerned from the report the Judge-Rapporteur lodged in the Registry of the ECJ. The prior approval of the German constitutional court may have been a persuasive or even decisive factor in those cases. Moreover in both cases the German government made powerful arguments that the rules were justified because of the dangers of encouraging the black economy outside the fiscal regime.

16. However a careful reading of its judgment shows that the House of Lords did not rule out employees' applications for judicial review of statutory provisions on the grounds that they are contrary to the Equal Treatment Directive or indeed any other provision of EU law.

17.  See Article 2 of the Council of Ministers' Decision of 22 December 1995 on an EC medium-term action programme on equal opportunities for men and women (1996 to 2000) (95/593/EC) (*Fourth Medium Term Action Programme on Equal Opportunities Policy*) OJ no. L335, 30/12/1995 pp. 37–43. Also see, the discussion on mainstreaming in chapter 2.

18.  A typical example of the more extravagant criticism of the judgment was an article in *The Times* on 3 August 1995 by Warwick Lightfoot (a former Special Adviser to the Secretary of State for Employment and to the Chancellor of the Exchequer). This argued, with no reference to the evidence before the Court, that 'this week's decision will damage employment prospects ... for women'.

19.  *R v Secretary of State for the Environment ex parte Nottinghamshire County Council* [1986] AC 240.

20.  The Divisional Court was the first court to hear the women's application. Its judgment, like that of the Court of Appeal, is reported in [1995] ICR 889.

21.  The President of the Industrial Tribunals (England and Wales) has directed ([1998] IRLR 351) that cases of unfair dismissal brought by persons with less than two years service should be stayed pending the outcome of this litigation, following guidance given by the Employment Appeal Tribunal in *Davidson v. City Electrical Factors Ltd.* ([1998] ICR 443).

22.  See the Government White Paper 'Fairness at Work' Command 3968 at paragraph 3.9.

## REFERENCES

Daniel, W. and Stilgoe, E, *Impact of the Employment Protection Laws*. London: Policy Studies Institute, 1978.

Elias, P. and White M., *Recruitment in Local Labour Markets*, Department of Employment Research Paper no. 86. London: Department of Employment, 1991.

European Court Reports (ECR), *Rinner-Kühn v FWW Spezial-Gebaeudereinigung GmbH & Co KG* case 171/88 [1989] ECR 2743.

Industrial Relations Law Reports (IRLR), *Nolte v Landesversicherungsanstalt Hannover* case C-317/93 [1996] IRLR 214 and *Megner and Scheffel v Innungskrankenkasse Vorderpfalz* case C-444/93 [1996] IRLR 225 ECJ.

# 14 Union Strategies in Pursuit of Pay Equity: the Role of UNISON

Virginia Branney and Marisa Howes, with Ariane Hegewisch

INTRODUCTION

Industrial tribunals in the UK have heard more equal value cases than all the other European Union (EU) member states put together. This is due in no small part to the work of trade unions, many of whom began a systematic review during the 1980s of the ways in which European and UK equal pay legislation could be used in support of their women members. There was a growing recognition that the UK has one of the largest pay gaps between average male and female earnings in the EU. After more than 20 years of equal pay legislation, women working full-time still earn only 80 per cent of the average hourly earnings of men working full-time. When average weekly earnings are considered, the gender pay gap widens to 72 per cent, due to differences in working hours. These averages also hide wider disparities. Between 1975 and 1996, there was virtually no narrowing of the hourly pay gap between part-time women workers and full-time men workers, with part-time workers' pay remaining at just 58 per cent of men's full-time hourly earnings. Thus *prima facie* evidence for gender discrimination in payment systems was high. The Conservative government in power from 1979 to 1997 pursued a policy of deregulation, with the explicit aim of reducing the power of trade unions to negotiate on behalf of employees. European legislation remained one of the few potentially powerful options to challenge labour market inequality and improve pay and conditions, particularly for the predominantly female lower-paid workforce.

UNISON is the largest trade union in the UK, representing 1.3 million workers in the public services and utilities.[1] Seventy per cent of the members are women and about 40 per cent of them work part-time. Women in the public services are among the lowest paid and most under-valued workers in the United Kingdom. In all the areas where UNISON organizes – local government, healthcare, higher education, transport, the gas, electricity and water industries – women are concentrated in low-paid jobs and on low grades. It is not surprising, then, that since its formation, UNISON has made the achievement of pay equity one of its core aims. Its equal pay policy, however, should not be seen in isolation. It is indivisible from other policies to achieve fair treatment at work, such as tackling low pay, campaigning for the introduction of a minimum wage at an acceptable level and for the abolition of the policy of compulsory competitive tendering and seeking to improve part-time workers' rights.

Policies aimed directly at challenging low and unequal pay fit into a broader framework of providing access to training and education and increasing women's awareness of the value of their own jobs and broadening their career options. The increasing prominence of fair and equal pay policies is also a reflection of changes in the values, organization and power structures of the union, ensuring that the demands and requirements of lower-paid employees, particularly part-time workers, receive greater priority within UNISON's bargaining agenda. UNISON's equal pay strategy involves a combination of collective bargaining, legal action, campaigning and lobbying for legislative change, a policy which can be summed up in the call to 'educate, negotiate, litigate'. Litigation is seen as a strategy of last resort, once all the avenues for negotiation are exhausted. Given the complexity of UK equal pay legislation and the fact that it does not include the possibility of class action, a strategy primarily focused on supporting individual cases would be very limited in its impact. Also, equal pay cases are highly resource intensive, not least in terms of the emotional staying power required from individual applicants.

UNISON's strategy is proving successful, not just for the individual women concerned, but also in clarifying the application of equal pay legislation in the UK. A number of high-profile cases illustrate the successes.

## RECENT SUCCESSES IN PURSUING EQUAL PAY CLAIMS

### Market Forces Tainted by Sex Discrimination

In the North Yorkshire region, UNISON took a case on behalf of members employed in the school meals services through to the House of Lords, the highest court in the UK.[2] The case, lodged in 1992, was finally settled in 1995 when the House of Lords ruled in favour of the claimants. The claim challenged a decision by the employer to cut the pay of school meals workers in order to prepare a more competitive bid in the compulsory tendering process for school catering services; management were afraid that private contractors, paying lower wages, would be able to undercut the in-house bid. Significantly, the wages of the workforce in the male-dominated manual services had not been reduced during the preparation of the Council's in-house tender proposals. The employer argued that this was due to the different labour market conditions applying to the services; private sector pay for such services as cleaning and catering, typically done by women, was generally lower than the rates enshrined in the collective agreements applying to the local government sector, whereas in the case of jobs typically done by male manual workers, private sector pay tended to be at least as high, if not higher.

The claim was based on the fact that the women had been graded as equal in value to the jobs performed mainly by men under the Local Authority Manual Workers Job Evaluation Scheme; this was the first major review of pay and grading systems in the wake of the 1983 Equal Pay Amendment (see Hastings, 1992). The Council's in-house bid won in the tendering process, leading to a situation where the women were re-employed, receiving less than their entitlement under the job evaluation scheme. When the employers refused to reinstate pay parity, UNI-SON lodged equal pay cases on behalf of the 1,300 women affected. The employers argued that the inequality in pay was justifiable because market forces constituted a genuine material factor causing the difference in pay. The House of Lords ruled against the employers, holding that market forces did not constitute a defence in this case because the labour market in which they were operating was itself tainted by sex discrimination.

This victory for UNISON resulted in some £2 million back pay for the women involved and the regrading of their posts. It also established the legal precedent that where the labour market is tainted with sex discrimination, 'market forces' will not constitute a genuine material factor defence to differences in pay. The case was far-reaching in its implications, both as a challenge to employers who sought to justify unequal pay in terms of market forces and as an attack on the policy of compulsory competitive tendering. It did however create a potential dilemma by apparently making it more difficult for local authorities, through their Direct Service Organizations (DSOs) to continue to provide services 'in-house' in the face of competitive bids from private contractors paying low wages. UNISON therefore compiled a briefing for local union negotiators in the local government sector, outlining the implications of the Ratcliffe decision (see Box 14.1).

*Box 14.1*   Common Questions and Answers on Ratcliffe

**Question:** Has the union applied the Ratcliffe judgment successfully in other cases?
**Answer:** Yes, for example in Cheshire County Council, settled with UNISON in a 'Ratcliffe' case concerning cleaners.

Branches and regions are asked to notify the Service Group of any successes through negotiation and/or industrial tribunals.

**Question:** Won't Direct Service Organizations (DSOs) be uncompetitive as a result of Ratcliffe?
**Answer:** No, firstly, the Ratcliffe case predates the wide application of the Transfer of Undertakings regulations (TUPE). Secondly, as the Association of Direct Labour Organisations (ADLO) has advised, "the assumption that the DSO could only compete with the private sector on the basis of massively reduced labour costs is not borne out by the evidence of tendering. DSOs have been able to achieve improved productivity, efficiency savings and economies of scale, reductions in overheads and direct costs in order to compete for school meals contracts without undermining the National Joint Council (NJC) rates and terms and conditions." This would also apply to other contracts in which women workers predominate. And, overall, manual services such as education catering are making large surpluses.

Nevertheless, local negotiators should be alert for cuts which might be made elsewhere, e.g. in additional payments, which employers may not consider Ratcliffe-related.

If a DSO did run into financial problems, the Department of the Environment (DoE) has been reported as stating that legal action is "most unlikely" to be taken against a DSO which failed to meet its statutory financial requirements in the current and/or previous financial year, as a result of charging back arrears of pay and interest arising from the Ratcliffe judgment. However, the DoE also advises that re-tendering is the proper cause of action if the Ratcliffe decision causes DSOs to fail. Of course this is highly unlikely.

**Question:** What if individual employees agreed to cuts in their individual contracts of employment in the tendering process?
**Answer:** The legal advice is that any agreement to such cuts by individual members would probably preclude them from bringing a Ratcliffe-type claim. If members are forced to agree cuts under duress, then it is important that they lodge written objections with management. Even where there is no agreement (whether forced or otherwise) by members, it is still important that they lodge written formal objections to the cuts in their terms and conditions so that the employer is precluded from arguing that there was any form of consent to the changes.

Union policy is to oppose making such cuts. Local negotiators should note that under the law individual members may have the right to challenge pay cuts when these have been agreed.

*Box 14.1*    Continued

**Question:**    Would the Ratcliffe judgment cover temporary workers in similar circumstances?

**Answer:**    Yes, temporary workers are covered by the Equal Pay Act.

**Question:**    Doesn't Ratcliffe only apply to manual workers?

**Answer:**    No, because Ratcliffe is a landmark case in equal pay law, the principles will apply to other local government workers and indeed employees in other services.

*Source*:  Extract from 'Equal Pay and the Ratcliffe case: The implications for local government' – A UNISON Briefing.

## Clerical and Administrative Workers in the Electricity Supply Industry

UNISON succeeded in achieving equal pay for thousands of clerical workers in the electricity supply industry, using its strategy of submitting individual equal pay claims at the same time as negotiating equal pay in salary structures as part of the move from national to company bargaining (see also Gilbert and Secker, 1995).

Job segregation in the electricity industry meant that between 70 and 80 per cent of clerical staff were women, and between 90 and 100 per cent of industrial staff were men. The two groups of staff were covered by different bargaining agreements. After the 1983 Equal Value Amendment was passed, the union submitted a national claim for a grading structure which reflected equal value principles. In contrast to local government, where employers actively supported a reassessment of their pay structures using equal value principles, year after year the employers in the electricity supply industry, at that time still part of the public sector, rejected the claim and challenged the union to seek legal remedies if they believed they had a case.

The final rejection of the equal value pay claim coincided with privatization of the industry. The union lodged individual cases in 1990 and 1991 against each company on behalf of clerical workers comparing themselves with industrial workers. This strategy finally produced a positive reaction from the industry. Some of the companies requested immediate adjournment because they were committed to introducing equal value in the move to company bargaining. Others still refused to negotiate, but once they found themselves caught up in lengthy legal procedures, most agreed to settle. The UNISON strategy has proved successful in achieving equal pay with comparable industrial staff for some 20,000 clerical staff and in winning a total of over £100,000 in back pay for individual applicants.

### Ancillary Workers in the Health Service

In December 1996 a settlement was finally reached of equal pay cases brought by UNISON on behalf of women domestic assistants in Northern Ireland. The first claims were lodged in 1985 by five domestic assistants employed at Belfast's Royal Victoria Hospital on grade one of the pay scale. They claimed that their work was of equal value to the work of male porters and groundsmen employed on grade four in the same hospital (see also Sutton, 1992). Eleven years later, the number of claims lodged had risen to over 900 and the Health Board eventually agreed a settlement. This came after widespread criticism that, given the legitimacy of the claim, the legal costs arising from the employer's refusal to enter into negotiations amount to the illegitimate squandering of public funds. UNISON estimates that the total cost of the settlement could be over £1 million, and provides for: equal pay for the original five applicants, backdated to two years before their claims were lodged, together with interest; a range of *ex-gratia* payments or pro-rata back-pay for the other applicants; a settlement for ancillary staff who had not lodged claims, including ex-staff and staff who had transferred to private contract firms.

## EQUALITY THROUGH NEGOTIATION

### Bonus Payments and Inequality

In January 1997, a joint claim by UNISON and the General, Municipal and Boilermakers Union (GMB) achieved a settlement of an equal pay claim for over 1,500 school meals workers employed by the former Cleveland County Council in the Northern region. These women, most of whom work part-time, claimed equal pay with male workers including ground maintenance staff. Although they were on the same basic rate of pay, their male comparators regularly received a 40 per cent productivity bonus. The unions argued that the women's exclusion from the bonus payments was discriminatory. The four unitary councils which now cover the former Cleveland Council area agreed to settle the claim before it went to tribunal. The settlement, worth £4 million, not only provides compensation of between £600 and £5,400 for the individual women concerned, but also includes a commitment by the employers to work with the unions to develop pay systems free from sex discrimination.

**Harmonizing Terms and Conditions**

In 1997, UNISON, together with the GMB and the Transport and General Workers Union (TGWU), negotiated a new national agreement for 1.5 million local government workers. It harmonizes the terms and conditions of manual and white-collar workers, and firmly enshrines the principles of equal pay in the agreement. Prior to the agreement, workers in non-manual government jobs had shorter working hours and better terms and conditions in several areas; it was also common to have different pay and grading structures for people in manual and non-manual jobs. The agreement introduced a £4 per hour minimum wage, which will particularly benefit part-time workers; a single pay spine for all; a new grading structure, to be negotiated locally, based on equal pay legislation and the EOC Code of Practice on equal pay; harmonization of the working week at 37 hours, involving a reduction in working hours from 39 hours for manual workers but ensuring part-time workers also benefit through increased hourly rates of pay; equal access to increments, holiday and sick pay, unsocial hours payments and paid leave for training for men and women, full-time and part-time workers; equal treatment for temporary workers. The agreement makes explicit the requirement on employers to ensure that pay and grading of jobs is fair and non-discriminatory and complies with equal pay legislation and associated codes of practice.

**A New Job Evaluation Scheme for Local Authority Employees**

The unions and employers have jointly designed a new job evaluation scheme to help achieve fair and non-discriminatory grading. The scheme was developed by a joint employer–union technical working group with assistance from specialists in the field of job evaluation and equal pay. Advice was also sought from the Equal Opportunities Commission and the Commission for Racial Equality. The new scheme has been developed specifically for local government and so covers a wide range of jobs. It is unique in that it is not based on any existing UK scheme, and emphasizes the centrality of equal treatment and the requirement to ensure that both process and outcome conform to equal pay and other anti-discrimination legislation. Guidance accompanying the scheme, compiled jointly by the unions and the employers, also emphasizes the importance of training in equality awareness for everyone involved in operating the scheme. In the view of UNISON, in these key respects the scheme is in advance of any other in the UK. It incorporates factors such as emotional demands, caring and interpersonal communication skills which have been undervalued in the past and should result in some female-dominated jobs, such as nursery nurses and home care assistants, moving up the grading structure.

Unfortunately, although the job evaluation scheme forms part of the new agreement, the unions were unable to persuade the employers to make it mandatory for all local authorities to use this scheme, and they will be able to adopt other schemes if they wish. However, UNISON has made it clear that local employers will face legal challenges if they use alternative methods of grading which do not meet the requirements of the national agreement in terms of equal pay, fairness and non-discrimination. The agreement does not cover bonus schemes, which are negotiated at local level. However, following the Cleveland settlement, the agreement provided for the setting up of a working party to examine the operation of bonus schemes with particular reference to equal pay. Guidance has been produced to ensure that future bonus schemes, and other incentive measures, are based on equal treatment. UNISON, together with the employers, has also prepared training materials for local negotiators to assist them in implementing the agreement and ensuring equal pay principles are adhered to. This includes detailed guidance on the implementation of the agreement and the use of the job evaluation scheme and training courses for negotiators. Joint training materials on the new scheme have also been prepared jointly with the national employers' organization.

## GENERALIZING EQUAL PAY VICTORIES

During the last two decades, the service sector from which UNISON derives its membership has become increasingly decentralized. Employers continue to negotiate with unions at national level, but individual local authorities, hospitals or National Health Service trusts are able to break away from the national collective agreements and can conclude their own local agreements. The compulsory tendering procedures have meant that an increasing range of issues about work organization, pay and conditions are dealt with at local level, whether in addition to the national agreement or substituting for it. This means that the role of local and regional negotiators is becoming increasingly important. As a consequence, a key element in the union strategy on equal pay involves training for negotiators at local, regional and national level. UNISON is developing a package of training materials which include a basic introduction to the concepts of equal pay and equal value, negotiating for equal pay, job evaluation and the use of equal pay legislation and the EOC Code of Practice on

Equal Pay. Along with these training packages, UNISON produces detailed guidance on these issues.

UNISON's strategy on equal pay is paying dividends. Employers are now more willing to negotiate to achieve equal pay, rather than risk costly court cases. Success has been aided by the introduction of the European Union and the EOC Codes of Practice on Equal Pay and the new European Union framework agreement on part-time workers. However, we also know that having achieved equal pay for some of our members we will need to be vigilant in maintaining pay equity and preventing pay drift to the detriment of women workers.

## NOTES

1.  UNISON was founded in 1993 as the result of the merger of three public sector unions: the National Association of Local Government Officers (NALGO), representing mainly non-manual workers in local government and the utilities; the National Union of Public Employees (NUPE), representing mainly manual workers in local government and the health services, and the Confederation of Health Service Employees (COHSE), representing mainly professional workers in the health services.
2.  *Ratcliffe and others* v *North Yorkshire County Council* [1995] Industrial Relations Law Reports 439.

## REFERENCES

Equal Opportunities Commission *Code of Practice on Equal Pay.* Manchester: EOC, 1997.

Gilbert, K. and Secker, J., 'Generating equality? Equal pay, decentralisation and the electricity supply industry', *British Journal of Industrial Relations*, vol. 33(2), 1995, pp. 191–207.

Hastings, S. 'Equal value in the local authorities sector in Great Britain', in P. Kahn and E. Meehan (eds) *Equal Value/Comparable Worth in the UK and the USA.* Basingstoke: Macmillan, 1992.

Sutton, K. 'Fighting for equal value: health workers in Northern Ireland', in P. Kahn and E. Meehan (eds) *Equal Value/Comparable Worth in the UK and the USA.* Basingstoke: Macmillan, 1992.

UNISON *Equal Pay and the Ratcliffe Case: the Implications for Local Government*, A UNISON Briefing from the Local Government Service Group, 1996.

# Index